SAGE was founded in 1965 by Sara Miller McCune to support the dissemination of usable knowledge by publishing innovative and high-quality research and teaching content. Today, we publish over 900 journals, including those of more than 400 learned societies, more than 800 new books per year, and a growing range of library products including archives, data, case studies, reports, and video. SAGE remains majority-owned by our founder, and after Sara's lifetime will become owned by a charitable trust that secures our continued independence.

Los Angeles | London | New Delhi | Singapore | Washington DC | Melbourne

REVISITING THE
POLITICAL THOUGHT
OF
ANCIENT INDIA

REVISITING THE POLITICAL THOUGHT OF ANCIENT INDIA

Pre-Kautilyan Arthashastra Tradition

ASHOK S. CHOUSALKAR

Los Angeles | London | New Delhi
Singapore | Washington DC | Melbourne

Copyright © Ashok S. Chousalkar, 2018

All rights reserved. No part of this book may be reproduced or utilised in any form or by any means, electronic or mechanical, including photocopying, recording, or by any information storage or retrieval system, without permission in writing from the publisher.

First published in 2018 by

SAGE Publications India Pvt Ltd
B1/I-1 Mohan Cooperative Industrial Area
Mathura Road, New Delhi 110 044, India
www.sagepub.in

SAGE Publications Inc
2455 Teller Road
Thousand Oaks, California 91320, USA

SAGE Publications Ltd
1 Oliver's Yard, 55 City Road
London EC1Y 1SP, United Kingdom

SAGE Publications Asia-Pacific Pte Ltd
3 Church Street
#10-04 Samsung Hub
Singapore 049483

Published by Vivek Mehra for SAGE Publications India Pvt Ltd, typeset in 10.5/13 pts Sabon by Zaza Eunice, Hosur, Tamil Nadu, India and printed at Chaman Enterprises, New Delhi.

Library of Congress Cataloging-in-Publication Data

Name: Chousalkar, Ashok S., author.
Title: Revisiting the political thought of ancient India: pre-Kautilyan
  Arthashastra tradition/Ashok S. Chousalkar.
Description: New Delhi: SAGE Publications India Pvt Ltd, 2018. | Includes
  bibliographical references and index.
Identifiers: LCCN 2018023935 | ISBN 9789352807680 (print: hb) | ISBN
  9789352807697 (e-pub 2.0) | ISBN 9789352807703 (e-book)
Subjects: LCSH: Political science—India—History. | Political
  science—Philosophy. | India—Politics and government—To 997.
Classification: LCC JA84.I4 C57 2018 | DDC 320.0934—dc23 LC record available at https://lccn.loc.gov/2018023935

ISBN: 978-93-528-0768-0 (HB)

SAGE Team: Rajesh Dey, Vandana Gupta and Anupama Krishnan

To my parents
Mrs Triveni and Mr Shivajirao Chousalkar
for their constant encouragement

Thank you for choosing a SAGE product!
If you have any comment, observation or feedback,
I would like to personally hear from you.

Please write to me at **contactceo@sagepub.in**

Vivek Mehra, Managing Director and CEO, SAGE India.

Bulk Sales

SAGE India offers special discounts
for purchase of books in bulk.
We also make available special imprints
and excerpts from our books on demand.

For orders and enquiries, write to us at

Marketing Department
SAGE Publications India Pvt Ltd
B1/I-1, Mohan Cooperative Industrial Area
Mathura Road, Post Bag 7
New Delhi 110044, India

E-mail us at **marketing@sagepub.in**

Get to know more about SAGE

Be invited to SAGE events, get on our mailing list.
Write today to **marketing@sagepub.in**

This book is also available as an e-book.

Contents

	Preface	ix
1.	Introduction	1
2.	The Royal Priests and the Black Magic of the Atharva Veda	14
3.	The Origin of State and Early Political Speculation in Ancient India	29
4.	The Origin of Arthashastra Tradition	43
5.	The *Lokayata* Philosophy and the Early Arthashastra Tradition	59
6.	The Arthashastra Teachers	76
7.	Political Thought of Early Arthashastra Thinkers	92
8.	Vijnyan Bala and *Apaddharma*	135
9.	Ethics and Politics in the Arthashastra Tradition	153
10.	Supremacy of Politics	167
	Annexure: Methodology of Kautilya's Arthashastra	173
	Bibliography	185
	Index	196
	About the Author	201

Preface

Kautilya, in the Arthashastra, stated that the book on the science of politics had been prepared by consulting many treatises on the science composed by earlier teachers. He had cited views of these teachers as well as schools. But, unfortunately, these treatises are not available today. Views of these teachers are cited by other ancient texts as well. These texts formed the core of political thought in ancient India. As rightly pointed out by N. Palmer, apart from the dominant tradition of western political thought, ancient Indian political thought is the second important political tradition.

In this book, we aim to revisit political thought in ancient India with the help of the account of political thought of early Arthashastra tradition, because in the later period, political thought in ancient India was dominated by *Dharmashastra* tradition. As against conservatism of the *Dharmashastra* tradition, the pre-Kautilyan Arthashastra presented a radical alternative which was influenced by the *Lokayata* philosophy. The tradition believed in rationalism and freedom of individual will. It opposed the performance of costly sacrifices and asked kings to develop agriculture, trade and cattle breeding. It also held that only with the help of human efforts, life on the earth could be improved.

I am thankful to my daughter Rita for taking keen interest in the publication of this book. This book is developed out of the major research project granted to me by the UGC, for which I am thankful to them. I am also thankful to Professor N. J. Pawar, the Vice-Chancellor of Shivaji University, for providing me necessary facilities. I thank the librarians of the Shivaji University Library,

Kolhapur; University of Mumbai Library; and the Library of Bhandarkar Oriental Research Institute, Pune, for their assistance. I am also thankful to Mr Pandurang Bhoye, Dr Nilkanth Lokhande, Mr Kishor Khilare, Mr Nagnath Chobe, Dr Suryakant Gaikwad and Mr Sachin Bhosale for their help.

I thank SAGE for agreeing to publish this book.

1

Introduction

Ancient Indian political thought is one of the important traditions of political thought, and barring the dominant Western political thought, it is the most creative and developed political thought. It originated in the 5th century BC, and the last book on it was written by Mr Malhar Ramrao Chitnis in 1810.[1] The basic principles, theories and concepts of ancient Indian political thought were developed by the Arthashastra thinkers who flourished before the establishment of the Mauryan empire. Kautilya's Arthashastra is the best specimen of the Arthashastra tradition. Kautilya wrote, 'This single (treatise on the) science of politics has been prepared mostly by bringing together the teachings of as many treatises on the science of politics as have been composed by ancient teachers for the acquisition and protection of the earth'.[2] Unfortunately, the treatises that were available to Kautilya at the time of the composition of Arthashastra are now lost forever. However, Kautilya names some of the Arthashastra thinkers who composed their own works on the science of politics. The *Shantiparva* of the Mahabharata also quotes the views of these thinkers.[3]

[1] Malhar Ramrao Chitnis was a biographer and historian of the Marathas. He wrote *Rajniti* in Marathi, which is divided into seven chapters. Please see Sarkar, *The Positive Background*, 600–608. It was largely based on Sanskrit Nitishastras.

[2] *The* Arthashastra, 1.1.1.

[3] In both the texts, there are references to ideas of Manu, Ushanasa, Brihaspati and Bharadvaja.

The science of politics originated in ancient India during the pre-Mauryan period. It had been subsequently developed by the Vedic, Buddhist and Jaina traditions. The purpose of this research is to study the origin of science of politics in India as well as to discuss the nature of political thought of pre-Kautilyan Arthashastra tradition.

In ancient India, the science of politics was called *Dandaniti* or science of using rod for punishment. Arthashastra is the other famous name given to it. Apart from these names, it was called *Kshatravidya*, *Rajshastra-Rajaniti*, *Nitishastra* and *Nitisara*. Of these names, *Kshatravidya*, *Dandaniti* and Arthashastra were more ancient names, and the word *niti* became more prominent after the 1st century AD, as all the subsequent works on polity written by Kamandaka, Somadeva Suri, Chandeshvara and Shukra used the word *niti* instead of Arthashastra.

The Arthashastra was a comprehensive science which dealt with different aspects of policies of the state. While defining Arthashastra, Kautilya wrote, 'The source of livelihood of men is wealth, in other words, the earth inhabited by men. The science which is the means of the attainment and protection of the earth is science of politics'.[4] According to Dr Ghoshal, the Arthashastra was a comprehensive science, of which *Dandaniti* was only the branch.[5] In view of Dr A. S. Altekar, *Dandaniti* deals with the totality of social, economic and political relationships and indicates how they are properly organized and integrated with one another. All relationships, says Ushanasa, are rooted in *Dandaniti*.[6] A number of Arthashastra schools and teachers existed before Kautilya. He mentions four schools of Arthashastra, namely, that of Manu, Ushanasa, Brihaspati and Parashara. He also provided insight into the views of thinkers such as Vishalaksha, Bharadvaja, Vatavyadhi and Kaunapadanta. The Shantiparva named seven teachers as originators of *rajshastra*

---

[4] The Arthashastra, 15-1-1-2.
[5] Ghoshal, *A History of Indian*, 84.
[6] Altekar, *The State and Government*, 3.

or the science of politics. These teachers were Manu, Brihaspati, Ushanas, Vishalaksha, Bharadvaja, Mahendra and Gaurishiras.[7] In addition, the Buddhist-Pali literature mentions a teacher like Potthapada.[8] Kautilya, the Mahabharata, the Ramayana, the *Manusmriti*, the *Kamandakiya Nitisara*, the *Mudra Rakshasa*, the *Dashkumar Charitam* and *Buddha Charita* also mentioned these thinkers. Thus, there is an agreement among the scholars that there existed a number of Arthashastra thinkers in ancient India during the pre-Mauryan period. Many of these thinkers had composed their books on politics, and Kautilya and especially the Mahabharata quoted the *gatha*s or verses and discourses from these books. However, unfortunately, except the Arthashastra of Kautilya, all these works have now disappeared. Hence, progressive and vibrant discipline of political science had not been developed during the later half of the first millennium of the Christian era. Even the Arthashastra was not available earlier, and its manuscript was discovered in Kerala only in 1907.

In the 6th century BC, India underwent a tremendous intellectual ferment as new religious and philosophical ideas were expounded by different thinkers. Of these thinkers, Gautam Buddha and Mahavir Vardhamana developed their own religions which exercised great influence on subsequent history. Along with Buddha, Mahavira and Makhali Gosala, other heterodox philosophies were expounded. *Lokayata* philosophy was one of the most prominent schools of philosophy. It believed in direct evidence of senses and rejected the authority of the Vedas and held the validity of reason. It being an important school of philosophy, Kautilya included it as one of the philosophies along with *Samkhya* and *Yoga*.[9] The Buddhist literature also mentions *Lokayata* philosophy, and *Lokayatavidya* is identified with Arthashastra or science of politics.[10] Brihaspati was considered

[7] Mahabharata, 12.58-1-3.
[8] Rajwade, C. V. *Digha Nikaya*, vol. I, 2002.
[9] Arthashastra, 1.2.10.
[10] *Lokayata Vidya* is considered one of the disciplines and in the Brahmajal Sutra of the *Digha Nikaya* (vol. I), it is considered a low science.

the originator of the *Lokayata* philosophy, and he was also recognized as one of the originators of political science. The Mahabharata referred to his ideas as 'Barhaspatya Niti'.[11] Thus, it seems that there was a close relationship between *Lokayata* philosophers and Arthashastra teachers.

The science of politics in India was developed by three sets of people. The first set included the wandering teachers of political science, who were called *parivrajaka*s. The second set was composed of ministers of the kings and the third set included royal priests or the *purohita*s of the kings. It is pertinent to mention here that both Shukra and Brihaspati were the priests of demons and gods, and they are often saluted as originators of the science. Some of the wandering teachers or *parivrajaka*s were revolutionary thinkers who were interested in the secular affairs of the state. Ministers and priests were conversant with the affairs of the state. Hence, Kautilya divided the teachers into two categories: the teachers who had expertise in theoretical matters and those who possessed the practical knowledge.[12]

The ideas of pre-Kautilyan political thinkers have not been properly studied and discussed. One of the principal causes of this neglect was the non-availability of sources as all the books on politics, except that of Kautilya, were lost. Their ideas are found quoted in different books on political science. It is necessary to bring together these ideas and make an attempt to prepare an integrated version of political ideas of pre-Kautilyan political thinkers.

The sources for the study of the Arthashastra tradition are meagre, which is one of the reasons for neglect of its study. Even today, we could gather some information about it with great difficulty.

It is our contention that one set of originators of the Arthashastra tradition were royal priests. During the Vedic and

---

According to C. V. Rajwade, *Lokayata Vidya* means Arthashastra (Rajwade, *Digha Nikaya*, 29). The same is referred to on pages 103 and 151.

[11] The Mahabharata, 3.33.
[12] The Mahabharata, 1.5-8.

post-Vedic periods, the royal priests played an important role in the politics of Vedic society. It was believed that the priests knew certain magical formulae and had expertise in performance of different sacrifices and incantations. Performance of sacrifices, according to the Vedic prescription, was considered important to secure the worldly good. The priests were experts in the *Atharva Veda*, and there were the *Atharvan* and *Angirasa* traditions. The Brahmans of the *Bhrigu* and the *Angirasa gotras* were considered experts in these practices. Since Shukra and Brihaspati, the originators of the Arthashastra, belonged to the *Bhrigu* and *Angirasa gotras*, we have to gather information about this from the *Rig Veda*, the *Atharva Veda*, different *Brahmanas*, the *Aranyakas* and the principal *Upanishads*. We could gather some information from the *Dharmasutras* as well.

The second source of the study is the early Buddhist literature, which was written in Pali. The Arthashastra or the *Lokayata* teachers were wanderers who delivered their discourses in the *kutuhalshalas*,[13] which were maintained by the rich *grihapatis*. They were the *parivrajakas*, and some of them like Potthapada were interested in the political affairs. Ministers such as Katyayana, Deergha, Charayana, Ghotakamukha and Vassakara were exponents of the new politics and had contributed to the development of science. We obtain important information about the identification between the Arthashastra and the *Lokayata* traditions from the *Kutadanta Sutta* of the *Digha Nikaya*. Some of the *Jatakas* also mention the Arthashastra ideology.

The Arthashastra is one of the most important sources, as Kautilya has said that the Arthashastra had been composed with the help of treatises written on the subject. Hence, he refers to four schools of the tradition: Manu, Shukra, Brihaspati and Parashara. He also refers to political ideas of Vishalaksha, Bharadvaja, Vatavyadhi, Kaunapadanta, Pishuna, Bahudaniputra, Pishuna

---

[13] During the 5th and 6th centuries, *kutuhalshalas* in the cities were raised in the gardens and parks. These *kutuhalshalas* were maintained by the king or rich *grihapatis*. These halls were used by wandering teachers to deliver their discourses on religion and politics (Thapar, 1996, 154).

Putra and Ambhi. In several places, he quotes *acharya*s or teachers of political science. However, views expressed in the name of the *acharya*s do not represent the pre-Kautilyan ideas, as it seems that in many places, the artificial nature of its presentation makes it clear that they might be drafted by Kautilya himself to put the matter in proper perspective.[14]

The great Indian epic—the Mahabharata is also an important source of science as it contains considerable Arthashastra material. The Shantiparva, 12th book of the epic, contains two sections—the Rajdharmanushasan Parva and the Apaddharma Parva—that discuss different aspects of political science. It throws light on the origin of Arthashastra. The Mahabharata quotes the views of Manu, Brihaspati, Shukra and other thinkers. The most important thing about the epic is that there are five lengthy dialogues of ancient origin, and of them, three discourses are delivered by Brihaspati—one in the Aranyaka Parva and two in the Shantiparva. In addition, there are two discourses: first delivered by Kanika to Dhritarashtra in the Adi Parva and second by Kaninka Bharadvaja to the Sauvira king Shatruntapa. They are delivered by the same person and are similar in a number of ways.[15] The Apaddharma Parva of the Shantiparva contains a number of pre-Kautilyan political ideas as it advances extremely intelligent ideas about political realism and rationalism. In

---

[14] There is a difference of opinion about the exact meaning of *acharya*s or teachers. In the text, Kautilya used the word 'Acharyah' in plural. Dr R. Shamashastri contended that 'Acharyah' means the teacher of Kautilya, as he has referred to the names of other earlier teachers. However, Dr P. V. Kane contended that 'Acharayas' means all earlier teachers of political science (Kane, 'The Meaning of Acharyah', 206–13).

[15] There are two discourses of Bharadvaja in the Mahabharata. The first discourse is found in the AdiParva and the second discourse is included in the Shanti. There are a number of identical verses in both the texts, though with a different emphasis. Dr V. S. Sukhtankar, the editor of the critical edition of the epic, decided to drop the AdiParva discourse and retained the Shantiparva discourse. Although, normally, we have followed the critical edition, in this case we are making exception because Kanika's discourse is a part of ancient Indian political tradition and the redactors of the great epic had saved this important discourse.

Chapters 130, 136, 137 and 140, the ideas of Arthashastra are elaborately discussed. The Mahabharata also contains some interesting ideas about the philosophy of *Lokayata* because its thinkers considered the *Lokayata* philosophers their principal adversaries.

The Ramayana contains some quotations from the Arthashastra of Manu. The most important chapter in the Ramayana is the discourse delivered by minister Jabala to the Prince Ram. Jabala was an Arthashastra teacher who had close ideological links with *Lokayata* philosophy. In this epic also, there is considerable Arthashastra material but it seems that it was written in the Christian era.

Apart from these major sources, some minor sources include the *Nitisara* of Kamandaka, the *Barhaspatya Sutra* and the *Shukra Nitisara*. We obtain useful information from the *Pancha Tantra*, the *Katha Sarit Sagar* of Somdev and the Jatakas. Similarly, the *Kamasutra* of Vatsyayana, the *Mudra Rakshasa*, the *Dashkumar Charitam*, *the Naishadhiya* of Sri Harsha and the *Rajdharma* section of the major *smriti*s such as *Manusmriti*, *Yajnyavalkya Smriti*, and other *smriti*s are also important as they contain some useful information about the pre-Kautilyan Arthashastra tradition.

We have some information about *Lokayata* philosophy from the *Sarva Darshan Sangraha*, Vishnu *Purana*, the *Naishadhiya Charitam*, the *Ashtadhyai* of Panini and different Jain and Buddhist sources. Thus, the literary sources of the science of politics are limited, and we have to piece together necessary information to prepare coherent account of the pre-Kautilyan Arthashastra tradition.

As far as the chronology of these sources is concerned, the Arthashastra of Kautilya was the most ancient source that was written in the 4th century BC. The Mahabharata, and especially the Shantiparva, was written in the 1st century AD. The Ramayana and the Smriti literature were written in the 2nd or the 3rd century AD. Thus, the sources available to us are not contemporary to the early Arthashastra tradition. However, the Mahabharata always referred to these ideas as 'ancient legends' because they represented the ancient ideas of pre-Kautilyan period.

The political ideas of the pre-Kautilyan Arthashastra tradition were described by the scholars who wrote the history of ancient Indian political thought. Dr D. R. Bhandarkar, in his lectures on the ancient history of India delivered under the Carmichael Lectures, examined the nature of pre-Kautilyan political thought. He provided some information about the individual teachers of the science. He was of the opinion that the works on Arthashastra prior to Kautilya were written in verse and Kautilya cited these verses from these sources.[16]

According to K. P. Jayaswal, the Arthashastra tradition originated in the 7th century BC, and views of scholars such as Shukra and Brihaspati were quoted by the later writers as it seems that the works of these authorities were available to them.[17] B. K. Sarkar discussed the nature of pre-Kautilyan political ideas which are referred to in the Buddhist literature.[18] Professors B. A. Saletore and A. S. Altekar also discussed the nature of political ideas of the Arthashastra tradition.

Professors U. N. Ghoshal and R. P. Kangle dedicated chapters in their books on pre-Kautilyan Arthashastra tradition. In his book *A History of Indian Political Ideas*, Professor Ghoshal discussed the conditions that were responsible for emergence of the Arthashastra in the 5th century BC. In the chapter on the works of Kautilya's predecessors, Ghoshal pointed out that the works of earlier authors were known and studied down to the medieval times, and it was proved by a considerable body of literature.[19] He has provided definition, scope and method of Arthashastra. He held that the masters followed the methods of observation, analysis and deduction in respect of phenomenon of political life. While concluding his discussion, he wrote:

[16] Bhandarkar, *The Carmichael Lectures*, 97, 102.
[17] Jayaswal, *The Hindu Polity*, 10–11.
[18] Sarkar, *Positive Background*, 149–150.
[19] Ghoshal, *A History of Indian*, 81.

To the early Arthashastra thinkers belongs the credit of separating politics from theology and raising it to the dignity of independent science. With them came a rich store of new material in the shape of categories and concepts belonging to the foundations of the science of government.[20]

He further held that 'the early Arthashastra masters, in accordance with their avowed objective of ensuring the acquisition and preservation of the state, were led to sacrifice moral principles for political end'.[21] Ghoshal took the help of the material from the Arthashastra of Kautilya and citations of their ideas found in the Mahabharata. According to him, the dialogues in the great epic, which are introduced as 'ancient legends', are in reality the expositions of the later writers more or less on the lines of the earlier Arthashastra masters. Ghoshal provided one of the most systematic discussions on the topic.

In the third volume of his work on the Kautilya's Arthashastra, Professor R. P. Kangle has discussed the nature of political ideas of predecessors of Kautilya. He had provided some information about Shukra, Brihaspati, Bharadvaja and Kaunapadanta. According to him, the opinions of the teachers of the *shastra* were not artificially prepared by Kautilya to present the pros and cons of a question. He held that in some cases, the views attributed to the teachers had been thought of by Kautilya himself. Opinions of the earlier teachers were schematically arranged by the author for the convenience of the readers.[22] While concluding the discussion, he wrote:

> Nevertheless, one can hardly suppose that their contents stem from Kautilya himself, implying that he was an expert in all these technical studies. He probably derived the material for these chapters from manuals of these various subjects, which were supposedly written before the days of Kautilya and have not come down to us.[23]

[20] Ibid., 102.
[21] Ibid., 105.
[22] Kangle, *The Kautilya* Arthashastra, 51–52.
[23] Ibid., 54–55.

Professor P. V. Kane, in an article on *Rajashastra*s of Ushanasa, Brihaspati, Bharadvaja and Vishalaksha, stated that the *Rajashastra* of Brihaspati was a work in mixed prose and verse like the Arthashastra of Kautilya. It embraced all the topics that fall to be treated under the *rajdharma,* and it was the most popular work on *rajdharma* in the times of the Mahabharata and several centuries thereafter. Similar works on political science were written by Ushanas and Bharadvaja.[24]

Wilhelm, a great German Indologist, sought to study the political ideas and biographical details of pre-Kautilyan Arthashastra thinkers. He tried to investigate all the passages that were found in the Sanskrit, Pali and Prakrit literature. He also drew attention to the fact that the opinions of the earlier teachers were expressed in a uniform style. He also revealed the stylistic peculiarities in the various opinions expressed there. According to Professor Kangle, Wilhelm's discussion on the topic is in-depth.[25] This study was published in 1960.

Professor A. D. Pant has written a long introduction to the second edition of Professor Beni Prasad's book *Theory of Government in Ancient India.* He has discussed the meaning of term *kshatravidya,* which is found in the Buddhist literature and the Upanishads. It was condemned by the Buddhists as knowledge of low type, and the exponents of this science were involved in relentless pursuit of self-interest.[26] He has also discussed the material and intellectual milieu of the period which gave birth to the Arthashastra tradition. He pointed out that the Brahmana *parivrajaka*s were interested in studying social and political problems as well as philosophical questions. In the Buddhist literature, the names of Arthashastra teachers such as Ghotak Mukha, Bharadavaja and Parashara were mentioned.[27]

---

[24] Kane, 'The Rajshastras of Brihaspati', 79; Kane, 'The Meaning of Acharyah'.
[25] Kangle, *The Kautilya* Arthashastra, 48.
[26] Pant, *Introduction to Beniprasad's Theory*, 19.
[27] Ibid., 38.

B. C. Law studied references to the wandering teachers in the Buddhist literature. He concludes, 'Examining carefully the import of all these passages, we may perhaps go so far as to maintain that these wanderers were the sophistic predecessors of Chanakya to whom tradition ascribes the authorship of Arthashastra'.[28] He has also discussed the account of wandering teachers of political science in his book *Gleanings from History of India*.

Professor D. D. Kosambi, in an article on 'The Line of Arthashastra teachers', first published in 1979, described the biographical details of the Arthashastra teachers such as Katyayana, Deergha, Charayana, Ghotamkha, Bharadvaja, Kinjalka, Pishuna and Pishuna Putra. He also discussed close internal relationship between the Arthashastra and the Mahabharata. He contended that the material in the Arthashastra was older than that of the Shantiparva because the Shantiparva did not refer to the problem of state-owned *Sita* lands of the Arthashastra, because at that time, this problem had been already settled. According to him, Chanakya drew from many sources. He was also a student of the *Itihasa* Veda.[29]

Professor R. P. Kangle wrote a couple of articles on the individual Arthashastra teachers. The first article was on 'Manu and Kautilya'. He viewed the author of *Manusmriti* different from the Arthashastra teacher Manu, whose views are quoted by Kautilya and the Shantiparva.[30] He also wrote an article on relationship between the Arthashastra teacher Bharadvaja and Kautilya. He had discussed the ideas of Bharadvaja as found in the Arthashastra and the Shantiparva. His ideas were extreme but Professor Kangle pointed out, 'the echoes of teaching of Bharadvaja are to be found in all works dealing with the shastra, it is not Bharadvaja alone who can be called unscrupulous, though he perhaps represents an extreme example of that tendency'.[31]

[28] Quoted in Pant, *Introduction to Beniprasad's Theory*, 32.
[29] Kosambi, *Combined Methods in Indology*, 260–68.
[30] Kangle, 'Manu and Kautilya'.
[31] Kangle, 'Bharadvaja: An Ancient Indian', 20–21.

Dr Walter Ruben, in one of his research articles, describes the nature of political ideas of minister Jabala in the Ramayana.[32] Research articles by Dr B. H. Kapadiya and Dr Ashok Chousalkar throw light on political ideas of the early Arthashastra thinkers.[33]

The survey of the literature shows that some work has been carried out on the predecessors of Kautilya, particularly by Wilhelm, who has done a detailed study on these thinkers. However, the production of a systematic and coherent account of the political philosophy of the early Arthashastra tradition remains to be done. The Buddhist or the Brahmanical criticism of these thinkers was misplaced and negative as these thinkers put forward progressive alternatives before the society and pleaded for the development of agriculture, trade and cattle rearing.

In this book, an attempt has been made to study the emergence of political ideas in the 5th century BC along with the growth of the state system in the form of *Janapada* states and with reference to the advent of new social and intellectual forces. The book tries to analyse epistemological and ethical position of *Lokayata* philosophy as well as Arthashastra politics. It seeks, through historical perspective, to show how the Arthashastra provided progressive alternative to the society. Thus, the book is a revisit to political thought in ancient India with the help of political thought of pre-Kautilyan Arthashastra tradition.

Bibliography

Altekar, A. S. *The State and Government in Ancient India*. Delhi: Motilal Banarsidass, 1975.

Bhandarkar, D. R. *The Carmichael Lectures on Ancient History of India*. Calcutta: University of Calcutta, 1918.

Chousalkar, Ashok. 'Development and Political Thought of Early Arthashastra Teachers'. *Journal of University of Bombay* 46 (1976–77): 31–44.

---

[32] Ruben, 'The Minister Jabali', 446–66.
[33] Chousalkar, 'Development and Political Thought', 31–44; Kapadia, 'Predecessors of Kautilya', 355–58.

Ghoshal, U. N. *A History of Indian Political Ideas*. Bombay: Oxford University Press, 1966.
Jayaswal, K. P. *The Hindu Polity*. 3rd ed. Bangalore: Bangalore Press, 1955.
Kane, P. V. 'The Rajshastras of Brihaspati, Ushanas, Bharadvaja and Vishalaksha'. *Journal of University of Bombay* (New Series) 2 (1942): 73.
———. 'The Meaning of Acharyah'. *Annals of Bhandarkar Oriental Research Institute* 23 (1943): 206–13.
Kangle, R. P. 'Manu and Kautilya'. *Indian Antiquary* (New series) 2 (1964): 48–54.
———. *The Kautilya* Arthashastra: *A Critical Study*. Vol. III. Bombay: University of Bombay, 1965.
———. 'Bharadvaja: An Ancient Indian Teacher of Political Science'. *The Bharatiya Vidya* 20–21 (1960–61): 20–21.
Kapadia, B. H. 'Predecessors of Kautilya'. *Journal of Indian History* 39 (1961): 355–58.
Kosambi, D. D. *Combined Methods in Indology and Other Essays*. Delhi: Oxford University Press, 2007.
Pant, A. D. *Introduction to Beniprasad's Theory of Government in Ancient India*. 2nd ed. Allahabad: Central Book Depot, 1968.
Rajwade, C. V. *Digha Nikaya*. Vol. I, 29 (in Marathi). Aurangabad: International Centre for Buddhist Studies, 1999.
Ruben, Walter. 'The Minister Jabali in Valmiki's Ramayana: The Portrait of an Indian Materialist'. *Indian Studies: Past and Present* 4 (October–December 1964): 444–66.
Saletore, B. A. *Ancient Indian Political Thought and Institutions*. Bombay: Asia Publishing House, 1971.
Sarkar, B. K. *Positive Background of Hindu Sociology*. Delhi: Motilal Banarsidass, 1985.
Wilhem, F. *Politische Polemiker in staatslehrhuch de Kautalya* [Political polemics in the text on statecraft of Kautilya. Wiesbaden, 1960.

2

The Royal Priests and the Black Magic of the Atharva Veda

The Arthashastra, or the science of politics in India, was composed by three sets of people: the royal priests, the ministers of kings and the wandering teachers or ascetics. Kautilya saluted two priests—Shukra and Brihaspati—as the originators of science of politics, who were the priests of demons and gods, respectively. Shukra belonged to *Bhrigu gotra,* and Brihaspati belonged to *Angirasa gotra.*

In the Vedic literature, especially in the Rig Veda, the Atharva Veda, different Brahmanas and the Upanishads, there is discussion on politics as well as the role of the royal priests in it. During that time, the Vedic society was largely a pastoral society, and in many cases kingship was a normal form of government. Kingdoms had not yet assumed the territorial form; hence, they were essentially chief ships.

In the Vedic period, the major occupation of the people was cattle rearing, and the society was divided between tribes (*jana*s) and clans. In the Vedic society, some sections of society were considered antithetical to the Vedic Aryans. They were called *Panis, Dasyus, Keakatas* and *Ibhyas.* There was tremendous hostility between Indra and these communities. The word *jana* occurs 234 times in the

Rig Veda, which meant people or a band of tribe. The term *Vish* is also used. The society moved from the pastoral to the agricultural stage of development. Due to the influence of the pastoral economy, the cow occupied an important position. The Vedic society was divided into four major classes, namely, Brahmans, Rajanyas or Kshatriyas, Vish and the Shudras. These classes emerged when tribal society disintegrated and class society was formed. That was a period when agriculture was introduced and land became an important part of their lives. Roving tribes along with their animals got settled on land. Of these four classes, Brahmans and Rajanyas were considered important, and the two lower classes—Vish and Shudra—were exploited.

The Vedic polity consisted of three important components: the king, his royal priests and other kingmakers or *rajkartaraha*s, the two tribal assemblies *Sabha* or *Samiti* (*Vidatha* also) and the *Jana* or people. These three components constituted kingdom. In the Vedic polity, the priest played an important role. The Rig Veda refers to both Shukra and Brihaspati as the priests of the *asura*s and the gods. It also informs us that Ushanasa-kavi was appointed as the priest of Manu.[1] He was admired for his intellectual capacity and intelligence.[2] There are many hymns in the Rig Veda which exhort Indra—the king of gods—to defeat the *asura*s.

During this period, the king was a tribal chief—king of the *Jana* which consisted of many clans. Hence, the king was called *janeshvara*. He had to perform his duties with the help of two tribal assemblies—*Sabha* and *Samiti*—and on the advice of the priest.[3] The priest played a crucial role, because he had command over Vedic rituals and expertise in performance of various sacrifices. It was believed that the performance of the sacrifices was necessary to achieve earthly goods.

---

[1] The Rig Veda, 8.23.16.
[2] Ibid., 9.8.73.
[3] Sharma, *Aspects of Political Ideas*, 186–87.

There was gradual development of kingship during this period. In the first phase of development, king was the chief of the tribe chosen by consensus and he ruled with the help of *Sabha* and *Samiti*. *Sabha* was a body of selected people, and *Samiti* was the general assembly of the people. The king was assisted by his priest, who knew rituals as well as magical formulae to ensure security of the people during adverse natural conditions. In the second stage of development, though kingdom secured some territorial toehold, still it was tribal in character. Due to increasing material needs of the tribe, several tribes or tribal bands came together. Some outsiders were also allowed to settle. A rudimentary form of government was organized. The priest organized a consecration ceremony to bestow the authority on the king. In this ceremony, several 'king makers' or the *rajkartarahas* took part. Who were these kingmakers? They were village headman, tax collector, distributor of the shares, messenger, carpenter, chamberlain, the *suta* (bard and charioteer), the queen of the king and several artisans. Thus, the original clan-based kingdom was now based on a more diversified class of people.

In the post-Vedic period, a large number of *janapada*s emerged. The *janapada* was a meeting place of several tribes. Agriculture became the dominant mode of production, and labour was divided. The Kshatriyas and Brahmans emerged as ruling classes and Vaishyas and Shudras were reduced to subordinate position. The advent of iron increased the power of chiefs to bring more land under cultivation, which brought more wealth and provided the material base to the *janapada* state. The king ruled over the *janapada* by bringing together diverse populations.

Originally, only three Vedas (*Trayi*) were recognized as the Vedas, but subsequently the fourth Veda, the Atharva Veda, was added to it. This Veda consisted of the rituals and prayers that were considered necessary for the material progress and social well-being. The Veda was closer to the *Angirasas*: the Brahmans of *Angirasa gotra*. According to Max Muller, the Atharva Veda consisted of both *Atharvan* and *Angirasa* matters, the first referred to the auspicious practices of the Veda and the second to the practices which consisted of 'yatu' and 'Abhichara'. The first part laid stress upon medicine and the second on magic, which was called terrible or 'ghora'. This is the double character of the Atharva Veda.[4] It is said that the interests of the king and his sovereignty were obviously dependent upon magical rites performed by the priest. In all the periods, the safety of the king and the prosperity of his subjects depended on the skills of his *purohita* in magic.[5]

Two schools of priests that existed were the *Angirasas* and the *Bhrigus*. The first were specialized in the 'Abhichara' or magical part of the rituals and the *Bhrigus* excelled in the *Atharvan* part of it. Brihaspati, the royal priest of gods, belonged to the family of *Angirasa*, and Shukra, who was the royal priest of the *asuras*, was the scion of the *Bhrigu* family. Both the priests used their special skills to secure victory for their masters in the war of attrition that took place between them. The *Atharvan* rites, hymns and prayers were benevolent in general; therefore, they were well regarded. Hymns or the charms were designed to establish harmony in the family and village life. It sought reconciliation of enemies.[6] The *Atharvan* priest performed for the king inestimable service, including causing injury and overthrow of the enemy. Therefore, as a rule, the royal priest was an expert in the *Atharvan* rites.[7] The priests protected everything through the charms. They performed different sacrifices for the king so that he could secure the things that he desired. The king was dependent on his capacity to use the magical formulae. These rites were called 'Brahman Parimara'. The king derived from it his own safety and ascendancy over his hostile enemies and prosperity of his people. The dreadful 'Abhicharas' or incantations were used to kill the hostile enemies of the king. These activities were the part of *Rajkarmani* section of the Atharva Veda.

---

[4] Muller, *The Shatapatha Brahmana*, Vol. 42, 22.24.
[5] Ibid., 47.
[6] Ibid., 33.
[7] Ibid., 46.

The priest performed different sacrifices to bring glory to the king. He performed three sacrifices—*Rajasuya*, *Vajpeya* and *Ashvamedha*—to consecrate him as the sovereign king. Because of the first sacrifice, one could be anointed the king. The *Shatapatha Brahmana* says that by offering *Rajasuya*, one could become the king and by offering *Vajpeya*, one could become the emperor.[8] The third sacrifice, *Vajpeya*, was the sacrifice of the horse, in which 'king makers' played an important role. This sacrifice was performed to bring glory, wealth and sovereignty to the king. It became popular in later periods. It is said that by performing this sacrifice, the king secured strength, eminence, support and excellence.[9] The fourth important sacrifice, which had a political connotation, was 'Sautramani' sacrifice. This sacrifice was performed to restore the exiled king to his kingship. The priest evoked the help of different gods and prayed, 'The opponent would call thee! Indra, Agni and all the gods had kept prosperity with thy people'.[10] It was prayed that king's men and strangers who opposed him would drive away, and he would be restored to his office. This sacrifice was devised to cure Indra of overindulgence in *Soma*. When the priests chanted their songs and applied the 'Sautramani' to his restoration, it was hoped, Indra would restore friendly relations with his people.[11] According to Professor B. A. Saletore, the Srinjayas expelled their king Dushta-Kritu from their kingdom. They also expelled the sage Rivottaras Patava Chakra Sthapati along with him. Sthapati performed 'Sautramani' sacrifice for Dushta Kritu and reinstated him to the throne of the 'Srinjayas'.[12] During the interval, the Srinjayas were without the king.

Thus, the priest who performed different sacrifices and rituals would ensure both 'Abhyudaya' or prosperity and progress of the king and annihilation of his enemies through various 'Abhichara' practices. In the 'Abhyudaya' aspect of the Atharva Veda, prayers

[8] Ibid., Part II, I.I. 13.
[9] Ibid., Part II, Vol. 43–45.
[10] The Atharva Veda, V. 5 112.
[11] Ibid., 327.
[12] Saletore, *Ancient Indian Political*, 132.

were used to secure harmony and reconciliation among the people. Hence, in the Atharva Veda, it is prayed: 'Unity of hearts and unity of minds, freedom from hatred, do I procure for you'.[13] There is a prayer for securing influence in the assembly. The king prayed: 'May *Sabha* and *Samiti*: two daughters of Prajapati concurrently aid me, May he with whom I shall meet co-operate with me. May I, Ye Fathers, speak agreeably to those assembled'.[14] In the tenth book of the Atharva Veda, there is a beautiful hymn of goddess Earth. It praised the earth for all its benevolence to the human beings, who benefited from it in many ways and unfolded themselves. The gods overcame the *asura*s and procured all sorts of cattle, horses and fowls, good fortune and glory for men. The earth is praised for bountiful natural gifts bestowed on men. It said, 'In the villages and in the wilderness, in the assembly halls that are upon the earth; in the gatherings and in the meetings may we hold forth agreeably to thee'.[15] There are charms to secure harmony and allay discord against strife and bloodshed. Also, charms were used to procure influence in the assembly and to bring about submission to one's own will.[16]

The Atharva Veda also had a section which taught how to use the charms against enemies.[17] These charms included the use of various medicinal plants against the enemies and pronouncing imprecations against them, thwarting their work. Prayers were used for the destruction of the enemies; Because of the effect of the charms, the enemy would float down like a ship cut loose from the moorings.[18] The art of sorcery was further developed in the Brahman period as certain sacrifices were performed to annihilate the enemy kings. The *Aupanishadic* section in the Arthashastra of Kautilya is the example of the survival of the tradition.[19]

[13] The Atharva Veda, II, III, 30, 134.
[14] Ibid., VII 12 I. 138.
[15] Max, *Hymns of the Atharva Veda*, Vol. 41, 206.
[16] Ibid., 134–38
[17] Ibid., 64–93.
[18] The Atharva Veda, 91.
[19] The Arthashastra, Chapter 14.

Due to their expertise in both *Atharvan* and *Angirasa* aspects of the rituals, royal priests enjoyed a very important position during the Vedic period. Support of the priests was necessary, and the Bharata king Sudas won the famous battle of ten kings with the support of his priest Vashishtha. Gradually, the influence of the priests grew. Hence, the Brahmana says, 'Verily, the gods did not eat the food offered by the king who is without *purohita*. Hence, a king who wants to perform sacrifice should appoint a priest'.[20] It further says that 'the priest constantly protects and surrounds the king as the ocean surrounds the earth'. The kingdom of such a king is undisturbed. *Purohita* is a guardian of his realm. Apart from this, 'the priest performed various sacrifices for the king to secure him vigour, strength and success'.[21]

The king wanted the priests to use black magic or incantations to defeat and kill his enemies. They also performed sacrifices to obtain prosperity. The *Shatapatha Brahmana* informs us that the sacrifice was performed by kings and Rajanyas to secure the royal dignity and prosperity. Suplan Sarngaya performed it for the Srinjayas and won prosperity.[22]

The *purohita* was considered a shepherd of the kingdom, and the subjects of such a king were obedient and loyal. The *purohita* could employ the *Atharvan* charm to deprive enemies of their strength.[23] He should be well versed with the *Atharvan* practices and an expert in administration of sacrifices. He could use these measures to destroy enemies. There was a ritual in the *Aitareya Brahmana*[24] that ensured destruction of the ring of enemies of the king, if it was precisely executed. This ritual was called 'Brahmana Parimara'. The Aitareya is a Rig Vedic Brahmana, and the ritual was called 'Brahman Parimarath'. One who knew this charm could use it to annihilate his enemy.

[20] Muller, *The Shatapatha Brahmana*, Vol. I, Introduction, XIV.
[21] Ibid., XV.
[22] Ibid., I, 371–77.
[23] The Atharva Veda, 93.
[24] *Aitereya Brahmana*, 8.28.

The ritual is called 'Dying round the holy power'. He who knows this charm round him the rivals that vie with and hate him, die. Dr Zimmer explains this ritual and writes:

> He who blows here (i.e. the wind all pervading ever moving microcosm, the vital break (*Pran* of all Universe) is holy power (Brahman) that (Brahman) is secret of life essence of everything. who knows thus participates in that vital principle's relentless strength, and in his own restricted sphere can enact its overwhelming role Round him, (who blows here) die these five deities, the lightening, the rain, the moon, the sun, the fire. The lightening after lightening enters into rain (vanishes into rain, disappears, dissolves, and dies in the rain), it is concealed, and the men do not perceive it. In the first phase of the ritual, all natural forces such as wind, rain, moon, sun, fire were organized, deployed and controlled to direct them against the enemy. The curse of death was then pronounced for the last time.[25]

According to Professor Zimmer, the second phase of controlling the reverse process began. From the wind was born the fire, the fire from sun, the sun from the moon, from the moon rain was born, and all these energies were directed against the enemy so that the curse became effective. He held that the effectiveness of the charm was guaranteed by its origin and success. The priest Maitrayana Kausharva proclaimed this 'dying round the holy power' for king Sutvan Kairishi Bhargayana. As a result, five kings died round him. King Sutvan attained greatness. He became maharaja, reducing all other kings to his vassalage or forced allegiance.[26] For the effectiveness of this ritual, the king had to follow the vow. Zimmer pointed out that he should not sit down before the foe. If he thought that he was standing, he should stand as well. He should not lie down before his enemy. The result of these painstaking observances was 'even if his enemy had head of stone, swiftly he lays him low'.[27] To ensure the success of this dreadful ritual, the king would have to be alert. If king was to

---

[25] Zimmer, *Philosophies of India*.
[26] Ibid., 72–73.
[27] Ibid., 73.

cast his spells at the distant enemy with any hope of success, he should quickly mutter his curses at precisely the same correct instance. If he succeeded in his efforts, he would get rid of a ring of kings and become a paramount ruler.[28]

In the *Shatapatha Brahmana*, there is a mention of use of wooden sword by the priest who held that it consisted power of *vajra* and sharp-edged wind and it would kill the enemy[29] Gods used the same ritual to defeat *asura*s. After completing the ritual, the priest, using his sword as a thunderbolt, pronounced, 'I fling thee as a thunderbolt for so and so and as a thus thunderbolt the wooden sword accordingly strikes down the enemy'.[30] There is a mention of Brihaspati *Angirasa* as the priest of gods.[31] Also, the sacrifice in the same Brahmana was mentioned, through which gods appropriated summer, rain, seasons and deprived their enemies of the same.[32] Gods defeated the *asura*s with the sacrifices and made their conquest long standing by firmly establishing it.[33]

Professor V. V. Mirashi pointed out that, 'the priest could use the *Atharvan Abhichara* to kill his enemies. In the *Rajatarangini*, Kalhan tells us that prince Tarapida killed his brother Chardrapid through the secret practice of magical formula.[34] Therefore, the priest was called 'Rashtra gopa', the protector of the kingdom by the *Aitareya Brahmana*.[35] Thus, there was a close relation between the Atharva Veda, the royal priests and their ability to perform sacrifices to secure victories over their enemies. Due to its close relations with the Atharva Veda, the Arthashastra is called the Upaveda of the Atharva Veda.

In the Indian tradition, initially only first three Vedas or 'trayi' were recognized. Subsequently, the Atharva Veda was added to

[28] Ibid., 73–74.
[29] Muller, *The Shatapatha Brahmana*, Vol. I, 52–53.
[30] Ibid., 66.
[31] Ibid.
[32] Ibid., 146–48.
[33] Ibid., 151.
[34] Mirashi, *Bhavabhuti*, 330.
[35] *Aitereya Brahmana*, 8.50

it as the fourth Veda. *Itihasa* or history was considered the fifth Veda, though it did not receive the recognition that four Vedas got. *Itihasa* was also called *Purana, Akhyan* and *Gatha*. In the *Itihasa* or history, past stories, legends and histories and six classes of the Vedanga are included. This knowledge of history was considered supplementary to the study of the Atharva Veda. In the Upanishads also, there is mention of *Itihasa Purana*. The Brihadaranyaka Upanishad says that *Itihasa* means the story of Urvashi and Pururava,[36] and the *Chhandogya Upanishad* says that *Itihasa* is the fifth Veda.[37] According to the Gopatha Brahmana,[38] *Itihasa* is one of the five Vedas, which is an Upaveda of the Atharva Veda. According to Sayana, '*Itihasa*' means cosmological myths or accounts, and the *Purana* means stories of the olden times, that is, those of Urvashi and Pururava.[39] It is said that the study of *Itihasa Purana* fulfilled all the material desires of man.[40]

There was a close relationship between the fourth and the fifth Vedas. In fact, Kautilya, in his Arthashastra, divided the Vedas in two sections: *Trayi* or three Vedas was the first and the Atharva Veda and the *Itihasa* Puranas the second. According to him, the Sama Veda, Rig Veda and Yajur Veda were called *Trayi* and the Atharva Veda and *Itihasa Purana* were the Vedas.[41] He defined '*Itihasa*' to consist of Puranas, legends, stories of the past, fables, *Dharmashastra* and the Arthashastra.[42] Thus, according to Kautilya, *Itihasa* consists of Arthashastra. Explaining the meaning of these two terms, Professor D. K. Bedekar held that *Itihasa* stood for the stories and legends of the past which had mythological content, and it did not mean history in the modern sense of the term. The Puranas stood for the stories of the past;

---

[36] The Brihadaranyaka Upanishad, 2.4.10.
[37] Ibid., 7.6.12.
[38] *The Gopatha Brahmana*, I.10.
[39] Muller, *The Shatapatha Brahmana*, Part III, 98.
[40] Ibid., 101.
[41] The Arthashastra, 1.3.1.2.
[42] Ibid., 1.5; 13–14.

hence, they came closer to the modern concept of history. From that point of view, both the epics are not histories.[43]

The *Itihasa* Puranas had a close relation with the sacrifices, because at the time of sacrifices, the *Suta* bards, who were trained in the *Itihasa Purana* tradition, used to recite the Puranas to the people during recess. At that time, the performance of the sacrifices was a long-drawn-out affair, and the bards told the stories of the past to entertain the audience. Ugrashrava Sauti recited the story of the Mahabharata at Namisharanya during the sacrifice only. Professor Bhattacharya explained the process as

> For ten days one after another different texts are recited as this goes on for a year in the narrative cycles of 10 days. The first day, the history says 'Manu was the son of Vivasvata and men are his subjects' and points out at the house holders sitting down in the sacrificial hall with they (Men as subjects of Manu) are here sitting down.[44]

Thus, consciousness of history was present, and it continued through the recital of these stories or histories during the sacrifices. It was an attempt to connect the past with the present. Bhattacharya points out that on all ten days, different narratives related to various subjects are recited. On the ninth day, some narrative (*Itihasa*) from the *Itihasa* Veda was recited.[45]

According to the historian Romila Thapar, the historical tradition grew out of a variety of literary forms present during the Vedic period. She states:

> Of these, the most significant were the *gathas, Narsamshi, akhyana* and *Purana*. These were often the compositions of priest poets attached to the various tribes. The original tradition was oral and was recited at gatherings. Both the epics include elements of historical tradition. Collecting information and composing it in a literary form was the special function of the *Sutas* and the

---

[43] Bedekar, 'Nature of Mythology', 87–102.
[44] Bhattacharya, *Ancient Indian Rituals*, 17.
[45] Ibid., 18.

Magadhas. They were probably drawing from priest-poet families of the Vedic period.[46]

She further states: 'Chronicles of kings. *Rishi*s and heroes were kept and in the context of new tribal settlement, or intertribal warfare, the genealogies of kings became important for the functional purpose of providing legal rights and social status, not to mention, preservation of tribal identity.'[47]

Thus, there was a close link between the Atharva Veda and *Itihasa* Puranas as the fifth Veda; hence, Kautilya clubbed them together and made Arthashastra a part of the fifth Veda.

During the Vedic and the post-Vedic periods, royal priests played an important role as the society was living in the tribal stage. In this stage, the rituals and sacrifices were considered important to ward off dangers from the natural forces. In the Brahmana period, attempts were made to channelize these natural forces as well as divine forces into a potent power to charge it against the enemy with the help of incantations, magical formulae and sacrifices. The royal priest was instrumental in carrying out these rituals. The ritual became a political weapon. Of course, the rituals and prayers were used for benevolent purposes as well, because the kings and priests wanted harmony, peace, unity and concord in the society. They wanted to use different medicines to cure people of various illnesses.

The Vedic state was not a territorial state but, during the post-Vedic period, the *Janapada* states were in the process of formation. These states consisted of diverse populations and required more secular ideological tools to integrate society. The *Itihasa* Puranas did provide some evidence from the past events, but they were not sufficient to convince the people of the viability of new form. Hence, new ideologies and new concepts were needed. They could be fashioned out of old ideologies.

---

[46] Thapar, *Ancient Indian Society*.
[47] Ibid., 270–71.

During the Vedic period, a few political concepts were developed, including the concepts of Dharma, political authority and its legitimacy and of social contract. Of course, these concepts were in the primary stage of development. The concept of 'Rita' was expounded in the Rig Veda, which was an ordering principle in nature. Because of 'Rita', the order is set in the nature, that is, the rise and fall of the sun and the moon and the time of rains, which appear on the appointed time. Therefore, 'Rita' was called truth; Dharma was based on 'Rita' as it ordered nature. Dharma ordered society and sustained it. Thus, there is a close relationship and continuity between the two.[48] Laxmanshastri Joshi contended that the Vedic thinkers believed that the laws of nature and morality were identical and interdependent.[49]

The second idea was that of political authority. During the early Vedic period, the king was elected by the members of his tribe. However, this practice was slowly discontinued. In the *Shatapatha Brahmana*,[50] there is a description of social contract to create political authority. According to it, gods lost war against the *asura*s because of jealousy and disunity. They decided to create political authority and entered into a covenant to forsake one authority called Tanunapat. They decided to follow truth and vowed. 'May I speak the truth, may I not transgress this covenant. Establish in welfare, for, in welfare of gods indeed, established themselves by speaking truth'.[51] Thus, the *Tanunapatra* is the original social contract between the gods when they surrendered their rights to one single authority. The *Shatapatha Brahmana* said that when there was drought, the stronger seized upon the weak.[52] State of nature, thus hinted at, could be overcome with the help of Dharma only. Therefore, the Brihadaranyaka Upanishad pointed out that after the formation of the society of four *varna*s on the basis of the growing needs of the society, still

---

[48] The Rig Veda, 10.37.2.
[49] Joshi, *Development of Vedic Civilization*, 1996, 110–11.
[50] Muller, *The Shatapatha Brahmana*, Part III, Vol. 26, 93–94.
[51] Ibid., Vol. 26, Part III, 96.
[52] Ibid., Part XI, 1.6.24.

order was not established. Hence, Dharma was created. Dharma was the king of kings, and with its help, even a weak person could rule over the strong. Dharma was based on truth.[53]

The royal authority was legitimized with the help of performance of a large number of sacrifices. Performance of three sacrifices—*Rajasuya*, *Vajpeya* and *Ashvamedha*—was important as the first two bestowed the royal authority on the person consecrated. These rudimentary political ideas were subsequently developed by the Arthashastra and *Smriti* traditions.

During this period, there was a growing disengagement of the temporal from the spiritual, and with the growth of scientific knowledge and rational ideas, the influence of magic and incantations declined. During the Vedic period, people believed that 'Abhichara' and 'yatu' were effective devices, but during the later period, they realized that this belief was based on superstition and the magical formula did not kill the enemy kings. Thus, in the 6th century, great intellectual revolution took place, which ended the influence of Vedic dogma and challenged the efficacy of the costly sacrifices. This new situation posed challenges to the priests and their authority. They met the challenge by using the bountiful resources of the Atharva Veda and the *Itihasa* Puranas. In the next chapter, we shall see how the transformation took place.

Bibliography

Bedekar, D. K. 'Nature of Mythology and Our Heritage'. In *Sanskriti Sugandha* (Marathi), edited by V. Joshi, R. C. Dhere and G. C. Thite, 87–102: Pune: Dastane Ramchandra and Co., 1977.

Bhattacharya, N. N. *Ancient Indian Rituals and Their Social Contents*. Delhi: Manohar Publications, 2005.

Chitrav, S. *Rigvedache Marathi Bhashantar*. Pune: S. R. Date, 1928.

Ghoshal, U. N. *A History of Indian Political Ideas*. Bombay: Oxford University Press, 1966.

Joshi, Laxmanshastri. *Development of Vedic Civilization* (Marathi). Wai: Prajanya Pathshala, 196.

[53] Ibid., 1.4.11–15.

Mirashi, V. V. *Bhavabhuti* (Marathi). Bombay: Popular Publications, 1968.
Muller, Max, ed. *Hymns of the Atharva Veda*. Translated by Maurice Bloomfield, in the series of *The Sacred Books of the East*. Vol. 42. Delhi: Motilal Banarsidass, 2000.
———. *The Shatapatha Brahmana*. Translated by J. Eggeling, Parts I–V. In the series *The Sacred Books of the East*, Vols. 12, 26, 41, 43, 44. Delhi: Motilal Banarsidass, 2005.
Ralph, Griffith T. H. *The Hymns of the Rig Veda* (translation). Delhi: Motilal Banarsidass, 2004.
Saletore B. A. *Ancient Indian Political Thought and Institutions*. Bombay: Asia Publishing House, 1971.
Sharma, R. S. *Aspects of Political Ideas and Institutions in Ancient India*. 5th ed. Delhi: Motilal Banarsidass, 2005.
Thapar, R. *Ancient Indian Society and History*. Delhi: Orient Longman, 1978.
Zimmer, H. *Philosophies of India*. Edited by Joseph Campbell. London: Routledge and Kegan Paul, 1953.

3

The Origin of State and Early Political Speculation in Ancient India

During the post-Vedic period, the old tribal society was disintegrating, and the Vedic chiefship gave way to the establishment of kingships. The disintegration of tribal society had taken place because of change in the production system, and agriculture replaced the old pastoral society as the mode of production. Agriculture required clearing of thick jungles with the help of iron tools to avail the land for farming and settlement. This required a large number of manpower and a regular supply of adequate food to ensure continuous involvement in production activities. The old clan-based society failed to provide a stable labour force. As a result, they had to recruit people from other Aryan and non-Aryan tribal societies and forest bands. Hence, there emerged a complex social order in ancient India. These economic changes caused manifold transformations in Indian society.

In the post-Vedic society, the old clan and tribe-based society faced many challenges, and the most momentous was pastoralism giving way to agricultural society and establishment of village settlements in different parts of North India. It required settled life and identification with the particular territory. The territory occupied by a particular tribe named after that tribe was called *Janapada*. According to Professor Agrawala:

Janapada stands, for country and *Janapadin* for its citizens. The derivative meaning of the term *Janapada* points to the early stage of land-taking by the *Jana* for a settled way of life. This process of first settlement on land had completed its final stage prior to the time of Panini. The *Janapada*s which were originally named after the people settled after them dropped their tribal significance and figured as territorial units or regions.[1]

In the process of change, the *Janapada*s were developed as separate political units, which were dominated by the Kshatriya tribes which formed the majority of the population, and political power was concentrated in their hands.[2]

Although the *Janapada* was dominated by a Kshatriya tribe, it had a diverse population. Some of these *Janapada*s were ruled by the monarchy and some were ruled by the *Gana Sanghas*. Political masters of both the formations were the Kshatriyas. There was Kshatriya hegemony. The Panchala was the name of the *Janapada* as well as the name of the king's lineage. Although there were other castes and classes in the *Janapada*, political power was in the hands of the Kshatriyas. Therefore, the words *Kshudraka-Malava* denoted only a member of Kshatriya clan, and no other sections of population, such as labourers and slaves (*karmakara*s and the *dasa*s) living there. There were Brahmins in the *Janapada*, but political power was not in their hands.[3] Agrawala held that *Janapada* and *Janapadin* were not only geographic but were more of social, cultural and political terms. There was growth of regional and political consciousness. The word *Janapada* was used for a state during the Upanishadic period, as king Janaka of Mithila referred to his *Janapada* as state.[4]

There existed a large number of *Janapada*s in the 7th century BC, which provided support to different types of social and political movements and gave shelter to several heterodox thinkers. The Jaina and the Buddhist sources referred to in sixteen

[1] Agrawala, *India as Known to Panini*, 426.
[2] Ibid., 427.
[3] Ibid., 427–28.
[4] Ibid., 429.

*Mahajanapada*s, which grew out of the numerous *Janapada*s that existed.

Formation of the state is a result of a complex social process as it required a fixed territory or 'rashtra', fertile and large enough to sustain the population that lived on and off it. The territory should be populated by the people who held common affiliations and bonds that were rooted in their cultural traditions. They should have developed political consciousness which enabled them to forge institutions of the state and the government that established control over it and managed affairs of the state by realizing regular taxes and securing obedience of the people.

The emergence of state in ancient India was a neglected subject as far as the history of ancient Indian political ideas was concerned. It was Professor A. S. Altekar who pointed out that, for a long time, the Vedic king did not have a permanent territorial basis. In the later Vedic period, however, the state became territorial. Altekar wrote: 'we have clear references to different tribes' settling down in the different parts of the country and to the kings becoming masters of both of their people as well as their country.[5] Itihasacharya V. K. Rajwade wrote a history of institution of marriage in India, which was first published by a Communist Leader S. A. Dange. In the fourth part of the book, he was to write about the origin of state, but unfortunately, he could not do so.[6]

In his influential book *An Introduction to the Study of Ancient Indian History*, Professor D. D. Kosambi had discussed the material roots of emergence of state. He pointed out that in the post-Vedic period, the tribe had reached the stage of disintegration, and society had to be reorganized on the new basis, which the tribal life could not furnish. A new superstructure beyond that of tribe was needed by the society to cement together its diverse components.[7] New class relations and new institutions were formed and new forms of production emerged. They were

---

[5] Altekar, *The State and Government*, 43.
[6] Dange, *V. K. Rajawade*, 68.
[7] Kosambi, *An Introduction to the Study*, 136.

trade, commodity production, merchant capital and compound interest rate on capital.[8] In Magadha and Kosala, the new state emerged, which replaced the *Mahajanapada*s. They were more integrated as they were ruled by the absolute monarchs. There were rich *grihapati*s, merchants and priests in both urban and rural areas. They were called *paura* and *janapada*. They exercised some influence on the state.[9] According to Kosambi, Magadha ultimately triumphed because it had the metals as well as proximity to river.[10] These states emerged stronger, as they slowly reduced all the *Gana Sangha* formations to the vassalage.

Thus, Professor Kosambi contended that the old tribal society of the Vedic period gave way to the emergence of agriculture-based society, which required a new form of political organization to sustain political institutions which deftly managed the transition from the tribal society to the new agrarian society.

Professor R. S. Sharma has elaborately discussed this problem in his book *Origin of the State in India*.[11] According to him, the *varna*s played a key role in the origin of state as two important *varna*s, Brahmins and Kshatriyas, came together to capture political power and to subordinate Vaishyas and Shudras. This political power was needed to monopolize all the wealth and to exploit the labour power of these classes. Kshatriyas accepted the ritualistic leadership of Brahmins and the latter their political leadership.[12] The development of the agricultural economy and the use of iron implements in agriculture paved the way for rise of new relations of production, and the *varna* order successfully adjusted itself to this situation. Due to development of agriculture, some surplus was created, which was appropriated by the ruling class. There was unequal access to resources and the *varna* system furnished social base to the state.[13]

[8] Ibid., 149.
[9] Ibid., 153.
[10] Ibid., 157.
[11] Sharma, *Origin of State*.
[12] Ibid., 22.
[13] Ibid., 32.

Dr Sharma discussed the origin of state in ancient India in three phases and pointed out that a full-fledged state with all its necessary characteristics emerged in the 5th century BC when the *Mahajanapada*s gave way to the states in the Ganga valley. First, in the pastoral stage of the Rig Veda, a voluntary tribute called 'Bali' was paid to the chiefs by the members who belonged to his kinship. The subjugated sections out of the clan of the chief were forced to pay tributes and were deprived of their cattle. Second, in the later Vedic period, when agriculture began on a large scale, forced tributes began to be collected frequently from the kinsmen. Finally, in the advanced agricultural stage, taxes were periodically and forcibly collected by a group of officials. These stages were overlapping.[14] Sharma opined that the division of labour implicit in the *varna* order was exploited to realize tributes from the Vaishya classes and labour from the Shudra *varna*. The state emerged out of the ruins of earlier tribal chiefships and semi-tribal states. The state apparatus partially appeared to emerge towards the end of the Vedic period and fully around 500 BC in the middle Ganga valley. There appeared a full-fledged state with a sound social base and endowed with the elements of sovereignty, territory, taxation and public officials.[15]

According to Sharma, the *Aitareya Brahmana* enumerated ten forms of governments, such as *Swarajya*, *Rajya*, *Vairajya* and *Bhaujya* in different areas, which showed that the king's power was established over fixed areas. The *Shatapatha Brahmana* called the king 'Rashtrabhrita' or sustainer of the realm.[16] Thus, according to him, the later Vedic state signified four important aspects: (a) formation of the government which realized regular taxes from the people, (b) territorial identity acquired through the clan or tribal names, (c) division of labour in four different *varna*s and dominance of the first two *varna*s and (d) the appropriation of surplus from the agriculture to sustain emerging organs of the state.

[14] Ibid., 34.
[15] Ibid., 34, 38, 39.
[16] Sharma, *Aspects of Ancient Indian*, 360.

According to Professor Romila Thapar, the Vedic period saw a change from the lineage society to a combined lineage and householding economy. In the post-Vedic period, there emerged the sharpest stratification of chiefdoms of the middle Ganga valley. It was in part a continuation of the lineage system but in effect accentuating the tendencies that encouraged the state formation. There were monarchies as well as *Gana Sanghas*, and they were both a contrast to, and in some ways the pointers to, the kingdoms of Kosala and Magadha.[17] In the post-Vedic period, there was disintegration of lineage society as clans separated and organized themselves as households. These households were headed by *grihapati*s who organized production. These *grihapati*s belonged to Brahmin–Kshatriya *varna*s and Vaishya *varna*s. Because of the agriculture development and increase in production new settlements were established as the population grew. There was continuous differentiation in the functions of different classes.

According to Professor Thapar, the class of *grihapati*s played an important role as it organized the production system with help of the workers and slaves. Originally, *grihapati* was an agriculturist, but subsequently he took to trade and invested surplus in trade and commerce. Thus, the growth of trade and agriculture produced the material basis to emergence of state. The rise of Magadha and Kosala in the 5th century BC indicated that now the integrated form of state was emerging. She agrees with Professor Sharma that the state with all seven constituent elements emerged in India in the 5th century BC and the material basis to it was produced by the emergence of new class of people and social relations.[18]

Thus, Dr Sharma laid stress upon the role of Brahmins and the Kshatriyas and *varna* system in the origin of the state. However, Professor Thapar emphasized the role of the lineage system and emergence of class of *grihapati*s in the origin. During the Buddhist period, we could see the emergence of two important factors.

---

[17] Thapar, *From Lineage to State*, 17.
[18] Ibid., 113–14.

There emerged a fairly large state of the Magadha as the Jain sources tell us that the Shishunaga king Bimbisara's state consisted of 80,000 villages.[19] His son Ajatashatru maintained a fairly large army. Second, it is necessary to point out that the old *varna* order was divided on class lines, and a class of *grihapati*s coming from different *varna*s emerged. Hence, the state of the Magadha was dominated by the so-called Shudra kings. The dynasties of the Shishunagas, the Nandas and the Mauryas emerged from the caste of the Shudras.

It is necessary to note here that new intellectual movements that were sweeping the country also played a key role in the formation of political consciousness.

During the post-Vedic period, there was a great social churning in India as the old tribal society disintegrated and new class society dominated by the rich *grihapati*s and the aggressive *Rajanya*s emerged. Old dogmas were challenged, and the old values were questioned. Efficacy of the Vedic rituals and costly sacrifices was challenged by new heterodox schools. They were active in the middle Ganga valley and perhaps in the Sindhu valley as well. However, the Magadha became the centre of their activities. The Buddhist literature mentioned six heterodox schools of thought, that is, Puran Kashyapa, Prakuddha Katyayana, Ajita Keshkambali, Sanjay Belathiputra, Makkhali Goshala and Nigantha Nathaputta or Mahaveer Vardhamana. Apart from these major thinkers, there were *Lokayata* thinkers who were materialists as well as the great Buddha himself, who straddled as an intellectual colossus.[20]

The Buddhist sources indicate there were a large number of wandering teachers who moved about the cities and townships to deliver discourses on the philosophical and spiritual aspects. They challenged the Vedic ideas. Dr B. C. Law points out that the number of such wandering ascetics was more than 47.[21] They

[19] Nagraj, *King Bimbisara and Ajatasatru*, 11.
[20] Basham, *The History and the Doctrines*, 13–18.
[21] Law, *India as Described*, 223–24.

branched themselves off from the existing system and preached new revolutionary ideas. They effected transition from conventional standards of judgment of conduct to later rational or scientific standards. For them, the end was important. In these teachings, god, time, fate and chance had no place. Manliness and self-reliance were the 'raison d'être' of their teaching.[22]

Buddhist literature mentions the existence of a large number of *kutuhalshalas* which provided the platform for these wandering teachers or *parivrajakas* to deliver their discourses. The *Samyutta Nikay* states that these heretical teachers sitting together in *kutuhalshalas* questioned doctrines of Buddha.[23] These *kutuhalshalas* were not only the centres of relaxation and retreat but they attracted the audience of the citizens as the urban life released a degree of curiosity and free thinking. The teaching was open to everyone, and the discourses were popular in nature. Some teachers had a large following, and fringes of large urban centres were useful to them. The subjects debated were varied, but the base question centred on the universality of human experience, knowledge and intuition. These halls were often located in the parks which were demarcated by rows of trees. These *shalas* were maintained by rich traders or wealthy citizens or through royal patronage. They proved to be important locations for debating a variety of doctrines. They discussed the matters of religious and ethical importance. It is repeatedly said that those who frequented and influenced *kutuhalshalas* whether Brahmanas or shramanas were highly respected and had a large following.[24] They admitted into their orders men and women from all social grades, and second, in fact that in varying degrees, their attitude towards the existing social and religious institutions was one of disapproval. The democratization of learning, the evangelization of truth, the social and moral uplift of men and women, the development of living languages and so on were special tasks to which they

---

[22] Barua, *A History of Pre-Buddhistic*, 349–50.
[23] Davids, *The Samyutta Nikay*, 99–100.
[24] Thapar, *From Lineage to State*, 154.

devoted themselves.²⁵ Dr Law further informs us that each of the religious orders of Brahmana *parivrajaka*s was a travelling school of thought. The furtherance of the cause of truth and knowledge in all branches of learning by open discussions was the remarkable feature of their educational and cultural activities.²⁶

Thus, due to these changes, we could see the emergence of new schools of thought and new ideologies. Pointing out the salient features of these changes, Professor Romila Thapar says, 'The centrality of philosophical disputations and the appeal to analytical thinking is at the ideological level reflective of a shift away from the security of the group towards the cutting edge of individual endeavour'.²⁷ Thus, this intellectual ferment created enormous opportunities for different thinkers to expound their own schools of philosophy, which greatly exercised influence on the future course of development.

The ancient Indian state emerged with its seven constituents fully developed in the 5th century BC and that was also the period of the rise of new political science in India. We have seen that the Vedic political ideas were evolved around the problems of pastoral stage of the society and the chiefships in the largely clan-based societies.

The science of politics in ancient India was closely connected with the Atharva Veda and the *Itihasa* Veda. Both were considered the Vedas of Kshatriyas. Regarding this the *Baudhayana Dharmasutra* says, 'Knowledge which Shudras and women possess is completion of all study'. This knowledge is a supplement to the Atharva Veda. The knowledge they possess is the knowledge of acting, dancing, music, other branches of Arthashastra.²⁸ The *Itihasa Purana* tradition has close relations with *Kshatravidya*.²⁹

²⁵ Law, *India as Described*, 284–85.
²⁶ Ibid., 284.
²⁷ Ibid., 154.
²⁸ Muller, Max (2007). Sacred Laws of the Aryas. The *Dharmasutras* (2007), Vol. II, 32.
²⁹ The *Chhandogya Upanishad* (2009), Vol. I 109–10.

According to Dr P. V. Kane, *Itihasa* and *Purana* were two different traditions, and most of the *Itihasa* tradition, except the great epic, was lost but the *Purana*s survived.[30]

The post-Vedic society saw the emergence of the *Janapada* states, which afforded considerable ground for free thinking to different free thinkers. Hence, they provided a lot of material to the thinkers who were developing disciplines such as science of politics. These states had evolved a number of constitutional forms and practices. Ancient Indian political thinkers subjected these states to their critical scrutiny and developed key concepts and theories of political science. It seems that many of the pre-Kautilyan Arthashastra teachers lived in the period when *Janapada* states were giving way to more powerful *Mahajanapada*s and subsequently to powerful monarchies. According to Kosambi, in the midst of 6th century BC, there was a ferocious struggle between the kings of Magadha and Kosala. Simultaneously, both fought against tribal kingdoms. These kings had ministers who were trained in new statecraft. Prasenjit, the king of Kosala, had a minister named Deergha Charayana of Malla tribal origin. He betrayed his king in favour of his son Vidudabha. The Licchavis were brought low by another crafty Magadha minister, Vasskara. He was a student of statecraft. He helped king Ajatshatru to capture the Licchavi *sangha* by sowing the seeds of discord among the members of the *sangha*.[31] Thus, the ministers involved in administration of the state had become students of statecraft.

In the Vedic literature, in some political ideas, as in the Rig Veda, there is discussion on the powers of *Sabha, Samiti* and *Vidatha*. There are also references to Shukra and Brihaspati: royal priests of gods and demons.[32] In the Atharva Veda, in a separate *Raj Karmani* section the functions of the king are described. The *Atharvan* and *Angirasa* aspects of the Veda were meant for the

---

[30] Kane, *A History of Dharmashastras*, 346.
[31] Kosambi, *An Introduction to the Study*, 161.
[32] Griffith, *The Hymns of the Rig Veda*, 373, 587.

welfare of the people and for punishing the enemies, respectively. The *Angirasa* prayers were terrible; hence, they were called 'ghora.'[33] The Veda talked about the duties of the royal priest in performance of various sacrifices, including that of *Sautramani* sacrifice.[34] There were charms of the restoration of the exiled king, charm to secure superiority of the king and prayers to procure power and lustre and battle charms for confusing the enemies.[35] There were prayers to secure harmony and influence in the assembly and to allay discord, strife and bloodshed. [36]

In different *Brahmana*s, especially in the *Aitareya* and the *Shatapatha Brahmana*, there exist a good number of political ideas. In these texts, we could see the growing influence of the royal priest. For example, the *Aitareya Brahmana* says[37] that power is secured through power, strength is acquired through strength and the priest is a protector of the kingdom. The *Shatapatha Brahmana* says, 'He constantly protects and surrounds the king as the ocean surrounds the earth. Kingdom of such a ruler is undisturbed'.[38] Various sacrifices such as *Rajasuya*, *Vajpeya* and *Ashvamedha* were performed to consecrate the king and to enhance his power. The *Shatapatha Brahmana* discusses these rituals in detail. There is rudiment of social contract theory in the Tanunapat.[39]

In the Chhandogya and Brihadaranyaka Upanishad, there are some important passages. For example, in the Chhandogya there is mention of *Kshatravidya*, which was the original name of political science. It has a story of the sage Ushasti Chakrayana who was travelling in the land of the Kurus when there was drought and he had no food to eat. He demanded food from a beggar Shudra who was in possession of some beans. He ate them to

---

[33] Bloomfield, *The Hymns of the Atharva Veda*, 21.
[34] Ibid., 47.
[35] Ibid., 111–35.
[36] Ibid., 134–38.
[37] *Aitereya Brahmana*, 8.99; Mirashi, *Bhavabhuti*, 63.
[38] Muller, Max. (2007). Eggeting, SP.PT I, XIV, 14.
[39] Muller, *The Minor Law Books*, 23–96.

save his life. He justified this transgression of rules saying that, had he not eaten food, he would have died. Now he had saved his life, he could afford to perform merit.[40] This was the basic principle of self-preservation as the fundamental right, which became the basis of Arthashastra–*Smriti* tradition. The concept of *Apaddharma* or the duties to be performed in distress was based only on the right of self-preservation. The *Chhandogya Upanishad* praises the merits of power and says that power could be employed to spread one's own influence and one powerful man defends a hundred men of understanding. If a man has power, he stands firm and beats down all his opponents. Hence, it says that 'by power the world stands firm'.[41]

During the Vedic and later Vedic periods, themes of the performance of different sacrifices and the use of the *Atharvan* and *Angirasa* practices to further the cause of the king dominated the political discourse, but during the Upanishadic period, people realized limited utility of sacrifices, magical formulae and incantations. In the *Chhandogya Upanishad,* this change could be seen as 'Ghora' *Angirasa* told his student Devakiputra Krishna that our daily life was a sort of sacrifice. When one eats, laughs, drinks and delights himself, he does it with hymns recited at the sacrifices. Qualities such as penance, liberality, righteousness, kindness and truthfulness formed his *dakshina* or fee: Ghora *Angirasa* further told him that 'man should realize that his soul was imperishable, unchangeable and then he could see within himself light of the old seed that was truth'.[42] Thus, the transition is pronounced through the mouth of Ghora *Angirasa*!

The Brihadaranyaka Upanishad said that Dharma was the king of kings, and with the help of *dharma* only the weak could rule over the strong. Thus, there is transition to more abstract thinking as new society required not the *Atharvan* practices but the concepts such as *dharma, artha* and *kama* to deal with the complexities of emerging needs of the society. The Upanishad said

[40] Muller, *The Upanishads,* 18–19.
[41] Ibid., 116.
[42] Ibid., 51–53.

that initially, Brahmins subsequently, Kshatriyas and Vaishyas together could not cater to the growing needs of the society; hence, they added three new *varna*s and finally the Shudras were enlisted. But still these four *varna*s could not manage the affairs; hence, Dharma was created, which was considered the king of kings; with its help, even the weak could rule over the strong.[43] Here, the Upanishad clearly identified Dharma with law and argued that it was the ruling principle of the state.

The *Dharmasutras,* which flourished from the 6th century BC to the 3rd century BC, included *Rajadharma* section which dealt with the duties of the king. They also discussed the principles of *Apaddharma.* For example, in the *Gautama Dharmasutra* it is pointed out that in times of distress, Brahmin could transgress his caste duties, perform duties of other castes and save his life. When his life was in danger, a Shudra's occupation could be taken recourse to by an upper caste person.[44]

Thus, in the post-Vedic period, we saw the emergence of territorial state in ancient India as well as the growth of rudimentary form of political speculation. Its growth was accompanied by the development of different forms of political institutions as well as the disciplines such as *Itihasa* Puranas. With the passage of time, more complex forms of state structures and political institutions emerged which required more sophisticated form of political science.

Bibliography

Agrawala, V. S. *India as Known to Panini.* Varanasi: Prithvi Publications, 1963.
Altekar, A. S. *The State and Government in Ancient India.* Patna: Munshiram Manoharlal, 1975.
Barua, B. M. *A History of Pre-Buddhistic Indian Philosophy.* Calcutta: University of Calcutta, 1918.

[43] Muller, *Brihadaranyaka Upanishad,* 1–4, 11–15.
[44] Muller, *Sacred Laws of the Aryas,* 211–13.

Basham, A. L. *The History and the Doctrines of the Ajivikas: A Vanished Indian Religion.* New Delhi: Motilal Banarsidass, 2002.
Bloomfield, M., trans. *The Hymns of the Atharva Veda.* Vol. 42. In the *Sacred Books of the East* edited by Max Muller. Delhi: Motilal Banarsidass, 2000.
Dange, S. A. *V. K. Rajawade: Historian par Excellence—The Problems of Indian Renaissance.* Mumbai: Vichar Bharati, 2000.
Davids, Rhys. *The Samyutta Nikay,* Vol. II. In the *Sacred Books of the East.* Delhi: Motilal Banarsidass, 2001.
Griffith, R. T. H., trans. *The Hymns of the Rig Veda.* Delhi: Motilal Banarsidass, 2004.
Kane P. V. *A History of Dharmashastras* (Marathi). Vol. I. Mumbai: Maharashtra Sahitya and Sanskriti Mandal, Government of Maharashtra, 1969.
Kosambi, D. D. *An Introduction to the Study of Ancient Indian History.* Mumbai: Popular Publication, 1956.
Law, B. C. *India as Described in Early Texts of Buddhism and Jainism.* Delhi: Bharatiya Publishing House, 1980.
Mirashi, V. V. *Bhavabhuti* (Marathi). Mumbai: Popular Publication, 1969.
———. *The Brihadaranyaka Upanishad* with Shankar Bhashya (Hindi). Gorakhpur: Geeta Press, 1966.
Muller, Max., ed. *The Questions of King Milinda,* Parts I and II. in *The Sacred Books of the East.* Vols. 36 and 37. Delhi: Motilal Banarsidass, 2001.
———. *The Shatapatha Brahmana.* Vols. 1–5. Translated by J. Eggeling. In *The Sacred Books of the East,* Part I, Vol. 12; Part II, Vol. 26; Part IV, Vol. 41; Part II, Vol. 43; Part V, Vol. 44, 8. Delhi: Motilal Banarsidass, 2004.
———. *The Minor Law Books.* Vol. 33. In *The Sacred Books of the East.* Delhi: Motilal Banarsidass, 2005.
———, ed. *Sacred Laws of the Aryas.* Vol. 14. Translated by G. Bulher. Delhi: Motilal Banarsidass, 2007.
———. *The Upanishads.* Vol. I, Part I. In *The Sacred Books of the East.* Delhi: Motilal Banarsidass, 2009.
Nagraj, Muni. *King Bimbisara and Ajatasatru in the Age of Mahavir and Buddha.* Ladnun: Jaina Vishva Bharati, 1974.
Sharma, R. S. *Origin of State in Ancient India.* Bombay: University of Bombay, 1989.
———. *Aspects of Ancient Indian Political Thought and Institutions.* Delhi: Motilal Banarsidass, 2004.
Thapar, R. *From Lineage to State.* Delhi: Oxford University Press, 1996.

4

The Origin of Arthashastra Tradition

In Chapter 3, we have seen that political speculation in ancient India had undergone considerable change. The new state that emerged after the disintegration of old tribal society required new political science. The old political science was mired in rituals, sacrifices, black magic and consecration of the king and duties of kingmakers. New political science was needed to address the situation created by the emergence of *Janapada* states and politics of rising powers such as Magadha and Kosala.

In ancient India, the science of politics was known by the term *Kshatravidya*. *Kshatra* meant the ruler, and *Kshatravidya* was the science of ruling. *Chhandogya Upanishad* mentions *Kshatravidya* as one of the sciences.[1] It says:

> The speech makes us understand the Vedas like Atharva Veda and *Itihasa-Purana* and the *vidyas* like *Kshatrvidya* and it is with the help of this knowledge only, we could discern what is true and what is false, what is good and what is bad what is pleasant and what is not pleasant.[2]

The Brihadaranyaka Upanishad held that Dharma was the king of kings, and with the help of dharma, even a weak could rule

[1] Muller, *The Upanishads*, 110.
[2] Ibid., 111.

over the strong.³ Thus, *Kshatravidya* was the science that helped the rulers to rule over the people. In the Buddhist literature also, *Kshatravidya* finds mention.⁴ Buddha held that this was low and inferior type of 'Vidya' as some people used it to predict the victory of a particular king and defeat of the other to earn their livelihood.⁵ Mahabodhi *Jataka* also refers to *Kshatravidya*. This *Kshatravidya* was later developed as Arthashastra.

Kautilya has pointed out that the Arthashastra and *Dharmashastra* belonged to the *Itihasa* Veda, which was considered the fifth Veda. It was mentioned along with the Atharva Veda. The Arthashastra was considered as an Upaveda of the Atharva Veda. The Atharva Veda was considered the Veda of the Kshatriyas.⁶ It was clear that 'trayi' or three Vedas dealt with sacrifices, rituals and duties of different *varna*s and *ashrama*s and the 'Veda' or the Atharva and the *Itihasa* Vedas dealt with *kshatravidya* and other secular sciences. The purpose of the Veda was to ensure the well-being of the people.

The science of politics was known by different names, such as *kshatravidya*, *Dandaniti*, *Nripashastra*, *Rajashastra*, Arthashastra and *Nitishastra*. It seems that the term *kshatravidya* was the oldest of the lot and *Dandaniti* became popular subsequently. Kautilya used both the words. He has given the title Arthashastra but, while describing four sciences, he has used the word *Dandaniti* for political science. He defines Arthashastra as follows: '*Artha* means the land inhabited by the people who provided means of livelihood to the people. The science which teaches how to acquire and preserve that is called Arthashastra'.⁷ Thus, the scope of the Arthashastra is very wide. While interpreting *Dandaniti*, he says:

> *Danda* is a means to maintain Anvikshiski, *Trayi*, *Varta* and the method of proper use of Danda is called Dandaniti. It helps man

---

³ Briaharanyaka Upanishad, 1.4, 14–15.
⁴ Rajwade, *Digha Nikaya*, 27.
⁵ Ibid., 28.
⁶ Bloomfield, *Hymns of the Atharva Veda*, 37.
⁷ Ibid., 15.1.1.2.

acquire the thing not acquired, preserve the thing acquired and bring about its increase, distribute the increased wealth among the needy. It encourages proper well being of the people.[8]

He pointed out that the proper use of *Danda* depended on three sciences, which ensured the *Yoga-kshema* of the people.[9] This description makes it clear that though the meanings of both words are identical, the emphasis within the discipline differs. Arthashastra's scope is wide, and it is closer to the modern discipline of political economy. *Dandaniti* deals with the actual process of governance and the goals it aims to pursue. Ensuring *Yoga-kshema* of the people by properly distributing the wealth among the needy was the goal of *Dandaniti*. *Yoga-kshema* consists of two words '*Yoga*' and '*kshema*'. *Yoga* means the acquisition of the object and *kshema* means peaceful enjoyment of the same. In the later period, due to the growing influence of Dharmashastras, the word 'Rajadharma' was used. Subsequently, *Rajadharma* gave way to *Nitishastra* or *Rajaniti*. Therefore, all later works from Kamandaka through Kshemandra, Somadeva Suri, Shukra, Chandeshvara, Bhartrihari and Malhar Ramrao use the word *niti*.

According to K. P. Jayaswal, the science of politics in ancient India developed during the 7th century BC. He states that the *Apastamba Dharmasutra* recommended that the *purohita* should possess knowledge of *Dharmashastra* and Arthashastra. He also mentioned the name of the Arthashastra teacher called Aditya. According to him, the science of politics must have originated in 650 BC.[10] Agreeing with Dr Jayaswal, Dr A. S. Altekar maintained that the science must have been originated in the 7th century BC and assumed specific form by the 5th century BC. Due to the emergence of the age of specialization, a separate branch of knowledge developed. At that time, the country was studded with a large number of small kingdoms, and the kings required to have specialized knowledge of politics. Altekar wrote, 'If the

---

[8] Ibid., 1.4.3–4.4.
[9] Ibid., 1–5, 1–2.
[10] Jayaswal, *The Hindu Polity*, 4.

quotations from works of predecessors of Kautilya can be taken as representative of these contents, we may well conclude that there was a fairly strong school of politics in India from 500 BC.[11] According to Dr B. A. Saletore, different schools of the Arthashastra represented a distinct phase of development of the ancient Indian political thought. The fact that most of their work had been lost should not hinder our appreciation of their contribution to the subject.[12] Dr D. R. Bhandarkar agreed with Jayaswal that the study of polity in ancient India must have begun in the 7th century BC. He pointed out that the *shastra* was raised to the rank of an Upaveda in the *Parishishtas* of the Atharva Veda; therefore, scholars had to give an early date of its origin.[13]

In his seminal book *A History of Indian Political Ideas*, Dr U. N. Ghoshal does not agree with the early date. According to him, the date given by Dr Jayaswal and Dr Bhandarkar was unacceptable, and even the suggested date of the 5th century BC by Dr A. S. Altekar was well ahead of the mark.[14] He viewed that the *shastra* could have been originated at least 100 years before the Arthashastra, which was probably written in 300 BC. It may be pointed out that in the *Ashtadhyayi* of Panini, there are references to a number of Arthashastra terms, concepts and theories. According to Dr V. S. Agrawala, Panini flourished in the 5th century BC.[15] Agrawala pointed out that some of the terms mentioned by Panini could only be interpreted with the help of the Arthashastra. He held that Kautilya was junior to Panini, and there could be a difference of 100 years between the two.[16] Thus, we could agree with Professor Altekar that the science of politics in ancient India originated in the 5th century BC.

The political situation in the country and the emergence of a large number of states of moderate size and a small number of

[11] Altekar, *The State and Government*, 2.
[12] Saletore, *Ancient Indian Political Ideas*, 49.
[13] Bhandarkar, *Some Aspects of Ancient*, 5–6.
[14] Ghoshal, *History of Indian Political Ideas*, 103–04.
[15] Agrawala, *India as Known*, 467.
[16] Ibid., 474.

large states were conducive to the growth of science of politics, as these states provided virtual political laboratory to the students for learning the discipline of political science or *rajashastra*.

Three versions exist of the origin of political science in ancient India. The two are from the Mahabharata and one from the *Kamasutra* of Vatsyayana. In ancient India, 'trivarga' ideal was considered important, according to which *dharma, artha* and *kama* were the three goals of life. Separate books were written on these goals. These were *Dharmashastras,* Arthashastras and the *Kamashastras. Dharma* stood for righteousness in life, *artha* stood for acquisition of means of livelihood and *kama* stood for pleasure. Earlier, Arthashastra was a part of *Dharmashastra,* but by the 5th century BC, it got separated and the science of politics branched off *Dharmashastra*.

Vatsyayana, in his *Kamasutra,* said that *dharma, artha* and *kama* were three goals of life. These should be properly harmonized and there should be no clash between them.[17] He held that *dharma* means obedience to the command of the *shastras* and proper performance of the duties. *Artha* means the acquisition of arts, gold, cattle, wealth and friends. It also means the protection of what is acquired and increase in what is protected. *Artha* should be learnt from the king's officers and the merchants who were well versed in commerce. Although *dharma* was better than *artha, artha* should be practised by king, for the livelihood of men was dependent upon it.[18] He insisted upon employment of proper means. In the beginning of the *Sutra,* he wrote

> In the beginning the Lord of beings created men and women and in the form of commandments in one hundred thousand chapters laid down rules for regulating their existence with regard to *Dharma, Artha* and *Kama.* Some of these commandments, namely those which treated Dharma were separately written by Swayambhuv Manu; those that related to *Artha* were compiled by Brihaspati;

---

[17] Vatsyayana, *Kamasutra,* 5.
[18] Ibid., 7–8.

and those that referred to *kama* were expounded by Nandi, the follower of Mahadeo in one thousand chapters.[19]

Thus, it was Brihaspati who separated Arthashastra from the divine book.

The second version of the origin of the Arthashastra was expounded in the Shantiparva (12.322) of the great epic. In this chapter, Bhishma tells Yudhishthira that seven great sages prepared the science which was called 'Pancharatra'. It was the essence of the Vedas. Swayambhav Manu developed *Dharmashastra* from it. In this science, three goals of life—dharma, *artha* and *kama*—were described. This divine book contained one lack verses. This included the knowledge about a householder's life and that of ascetics. Manu prepared *Dharmashastra*, and Brihaspati and Ushanasa prepared the Arthashastra from it. The king Vasu followed the teachings of Brihaspati. This book excelled in the world and taught people the essence of dharma and *artha*. It disappeared as soon as Vasu disappeared, but for the benefit of the people, the sage Brihaspati prepared the work, which was meant for welfare of the people.[20] It says that under the guidance of Brihaspati, Vasu performed non-violent sacrifices and refused to sacrifice animals. This angered gods but he persisted.[21]

This chapter throws light on the origin of the Arthashastra. The divine work, prepared by seven great sages, was further interpreted by Manu, Brihaspati and Ushanas. Brihaspati and Ushanas wrote the science of politics. D. R. Bhandarkar opined that the Mahabharata narrative of the origin of the science closely followed that of the *Kamasutra*, which said that Manu separated *Dharmashastra* and Ushanasa and Brihaspati separated the Arthashastra from the divine book.[22]

---

[19] Ibid., XXXII.
[20] Ibid., 322–43.
[21] Ibid., 12–323.
[22] Bhandarkar, *Carmichael Lectures*, 93–94.

Chapter 59 of the Shantiparva discusses the origin of the *shastra*. Here, Bhishma was responding to the question posed by Yudhishthira as to why a single person, who is like other human beings, enjoys power over the multitude of men and why is it that his orders are obeyed by the powerful and wise men of the kingdom.[23] Bhishma answered that in the age of truth or *krita yuga*, there was no king, no kingdom, no punishment and no punisher as everyone managed his affairs with the help of dharma, but gradually due to advent of the *Treta* and the *Dvapar* ages, there was moral decline of the population, and they felt the need for creation of an external agency to control public affairs.[24] For that purpose, the people approached the creator. He first decided to compose a book on the science of politics and subsequently he would institute kingship. He composed a book on *Dandaniti* to provide comprehensive guidance to the king. This divine book on politics consisted of one lack chapters, which was abridged by Vishalaksha (Shankar). It was abridged by Indra (also called Bahudanta) in 5,000 chapters. This book went further abridgment by Brihaspati into 3,000 chapters and by Shukra into 1,000 chapters. As a result, the science was called *Vaishalaksha, Bahudantaka, Barhashpatya* and *Aushanasa*. The abridgement was carried out for the benefit of the people.[25]

This is a popular narrative and names of the four Arthashastra teachers—Vishalaksha, Bahudanta, Ushanasa and Brihaspati—are mentioned. Kautilya in his Arthashastra also mentions the names of these four teachers. The basic principle advocated here is that due to decline of the moral standards of men, the establishment of the institute of the state or the kingship was necessary and a book on *Dandaniti* was composed to guide the king.

The Shantiparva also mentions seven originators of the *Rajshastra*. These were called (12-58-1-3) Manu, Brihaspati, Ushana, Mahendra, Vishalaksha, Bharadvaja and Gaurishiras.

[23] Ibid., 12-59-5-12.
[24] Ibid., 12-59-13-14.
[25] Ibid., 12-59-85-92.

Of these, Kautilya cites the opinions of five teachers, and if Mahendra is identified with Bahadanti-Putra, we can say that six names in both the texts are identical. Only the names and opinions of Gaurishisas are not mentioned in the Arthashastra as well as in the great epic. According to Dr Jayaswal, certain commentators on the books on polity cited the names of these teachers as well as that of Gaurishiras.[26]

In the great epic, the contents of the divine book on *Dandaniti* are discussed. The following are the topics in book:

1. The concept of *trivarga, dharma, artha* and *kama*.
2. Four sciences, including *Anvikshiki, Trayi, Varta* and *Dandaniti*, and training of the king.
3. Nature and aims of the state and calamities befalling it. Three stages are of growth, stability and decline of state.
4. The power, position and duties of king.
5. Council of ministers: composition and their duties.
6. Law and judicial administration: *Dharmasthiya* and *Kantakshodhan* courts.
7. Administration of different departments and regions of state.
8. Inter-state relations: six measures of foreign policy and *Mandala* theory.
9. The army, its composition and functions.
10. Non-monarchical bodies: *Srenis* and *Vratas*.
11. The espionage system. [27]

The Kautilya's Arthashastra consisted of 15 chapters, which were as follows:

1. Concerning the topic of training.
2. Activity of heads of departments.
3. Concerning judges.
4. The Suppression of criminals.

---

[26] Jayaswal, *The Hindu Polity*, 11.
[27] The Mahabharata, 12-59-30-97.

5. Secret conduct.
6. The circle of kings as the basis.
7. Six measures of foreign policy.
8. Calamities befalling the state.
9. The activity of the king about to march.
10. Concerning war.
11. Policy towards oligarchies.
12. Concerning the weaker king.
13. Means of taking a fort.
14. Concerning secret practices.
15. The method of the science.

If we make a comparative study of the topics in both books, we could see that many topics are overlapping. Dr V. S. Agrawal stated that 50 per cent of the contents in both the lists are common. However, a careful scrutiny of the contents reveals that most of them are identical.[28] The topics of the development of 'Sita' land and colonization of virgin territories were omitted in the *Dandaniti* of the Shantiparva, because at the time of composition of the didactic portion of the Shantiparva (1st century AD), these policies were not relevant.[29]

We have seen that Shukra and Brihaspati were considered the originators of science; hence, in the beginning of the Arthashastra, Kautilya saluted both Shukra and Brihaspati. In the Shantipavra too, Shukra and Brihaspati were considered the originators of science. The great epic gives names of seven Arthashastra teachers but there were many more teachers who contributed to the growth of the science. Arthashastra teachers such as Manu, Shukra and Brihaspati wrote their treatises on science; unfortunately, none of them is available now. Therefore, it was a daunting task to reconstruct the tradition.

Three sets of people played a key role in the development of the tradition. These were wandering teachers of political science or

---
[28] Agrawala, *Bharat Savitri*, Vol. III, 52.
[29] Kosambi, *Study of Indian History*, 143.

the *parivrajakas,* the royal priests of the kings and the ministers of the kings.

Kautilya divided these teachers into two categories: *vaktri* and *prayoktri*.[30] The *vaktri* means teachers of *Dandaniti* who were well versed in the science of politics. They were the theoreticians of the science who didn't have practical experience. *Prayoktri* means those who possessed practical experience of administration of the state. In the first category of teachers, we could include the wandering teachers of political science and, in the second category, the royal priests and the ministers of the king. Some teachers such as Kautilya had both theoretical knowledge and practical experience. Hence, according to the Arthashastra, Kautilya held both *shastra* (weapon) and *shastra* (science) with equal felicity.

We shall see the contributions of three set of the people to the science of politics.

As seen in Chapter 2, during the Vedic period, the priest or *purohit* played an important role in the politics of the kings. The priests were experts in the *Atharva* and *Angirasa* rites and worked as the chaplains during the sacrifices that were performed to secure worldly goods. However, in the course of time, the society changed and popular belief in the efficacy of sacrifices, magical formula and incantations declined.

Two of the originators of science, Shukra and Brihaspati were the royal priests. Shukra or Ushanas was the priest of demons and the Brihaspati was the priest of gods. The *Atharvan* aspects of the Atharva Veda were mastered by the *Bharagava*s, and *Shukra* was a *Bharagava*; *Angira* aspects were mastered by Brihaspati, who was an *Angirasa*. In the later period, the influence of the priest declined. However, he held his position. Hence, regarding qualification of his appointment, Kautilya writes:

> [T]he king should appoint a priest who is born in good family and is a man of good character, well-versed in the Vedas, theology,

[30] Ibid., 1.5.8.

Science of divine signs in omens and in the science of politics and capable of counteracting divine and human calamities by means of *Atharvan* remedies. And he should follow him as a pupil does his teacher, a son his father or a servant his master.[31]

He held that the Kshatriya power prospered because of the support he received from the chaplain.

It seems that during the Vedic period, it was sufficient for the priests to be conversant with the *Atharvan* practices, but now they had to be proficient with science of politics as well. Kautilya stated that the calamities were of both of human and divine origin, and the latter could be overcome with the help of the *Atharvan* rites. He performed a royal consecration ceremony to legitimize the king's authority.

Shukra and Brihaspati were *purohita*s, and they wrote their books on politics. In the changed circumstances, the priest lost his preeminent position as one of the ministers in the council of ministers. In the *Kutadanta Sutta* of the *Digha Nikaya*, the royal priest of king Mahavijita is mentioned, who gave advice to the king about the development of his kingdom.[32] The royal chaplain gave the advice consistent with the Arthashastra ideology. This clearly showed that the *purohita*s no longer confined themselves to the rituals, but they started giving advice on political matters as well. In the *Jataka* stories, it is said that the priest was well versed in both *artha* and dharma.[33]

A number of wandering teachers moved about with their disciples and propounded their own ideas. About them, B. C. Law writes:

'[T]here existed in northern India various orders of *Parivrajakas* or wanderers, who were, in the words of Rhys Devids, teachers or sophists who spent eight to nine months of every year wandering about precisely with the object of engaging in conventional

---

[31] Ibid., 19-9-10.
[32] Rajwade, *Digha Nikaya*, 148–49.
[33] Bhagvat, *Sidhartha Jatataka*, 94, 188.

discussions on matters of ethics and philosophy, nature lore and mysticism.

Like the sophists among the Greeks, they differed very much in intelligence, in earnestness and in honesty. They depended on 'Bhiksha' and lived a homeless life. During the rainy season, they took shelter in deserted houses. The Buddhist sources talked about 30 teachers, and each of them carried a group of disciples. Some of them were known by their nicknames such as 'Potthapada who had 300 followers'.[34]

These wandering teachers normally took residence in the public parks and gardens owned by the rich *grihapati*s and were engaged in philosophical discussions.[35] These meeting places were called *kutuhalshala*s. These *kutuhalshala*s were maintained by the kings, the *grihahpatis* or the rich traders. The *Samyutta Nikaya* reveals that these heretical wanderers sitting in the *kutuhalshala*s questioned the doctrines of Buddha.[36] A wanderer, Vatsyagotra, told Buddha that these heretical wanderers were sitting in the *kutuhalshala* and they were debating different doctrines. All six teachers who were opposed to Buddhist doctrines were present there.[37] *Parivrajakas* were interested in different subjects, some of whom were teachers of political science.

Regarding activities of these teachers, Dr B. M. Barua writes:

> The individuals who placed the science of royal policy in an independent footing by gradually separating its province from that of old legal systems were mostly known as *Parivrajakas*. They talked about origin of world, including origin of human institutions, the apparition and distribution of land and water. They cut off connections with the world and passed into new mode of life which admitted no caste system or class bias. They sought to build up a system of moral philosophy on a human and rational ground.[38]

[34] Law, *India as Described*, 223–24.
[35] Ibid., 235.
[36] Woodward, *Book of Kindered Sayings*, II, 99–100.
[37] Ibid., Vol. 4, 279–82.
[38] Barua, *History of Pre-Buddhistic Indian*, 349–50.

The Origin of Arthashastra Tradition / 55

These teachers assumed nicknames which indicated their bodily features. Kautilya mentions names of Vishalaksha, Kaunapadanta, Vatavyadhi and Bahaudantiputra. Vishalaksha means the large eyed, Kaunapadanta means the one who had stinking and decayed teeth, Vatavyadhi means one who suffers from gases and Bahaudantiputra means the son of one whose teeth are as large as hand. In the *Digha Nikaya*, there is a mention of the council of Potthapada who had 300 followers. It writes:

> At that time Pothapada seated with the company of mendicants, all talking with loud voices with shout and tumult all sorts of worldly talk, to wit, tales of kings, of robbers, of ministers of state, tales of war, of terror, of battles, the legends of creation of land, sea and speculation about existence and non-existence.[39]

The wanderers used to make noise and talked on many issues.[40]

Some of these wandering teachers were teachers of *Lokayata* philosophy and, sometime, *the* Arthashastra and *Lokayata* were considered identical sciences.[41] It is said that *Lokayata* was the philosophy of world speculation.[42]

In the '*Sinhanad Sutra*' of *Digha Nikaya*, there is a mention of *Parivrajaka Nigrodha*, who moved along with his 300 followers and lived in the assembly of Potthapada; they were making noise and discussing the issues of sciences such as *kshatravidya*. *Nigrodha* challenged Gautama but, subsequently, he was won over by him.[43] The wanderers always talked about kings, wars, conspiracies, ministers and other secular matters among the gatherings of *bhikkhu*s (ordained male monastic in Buddhism).

According to a teacher who seems to be closer to *Lokayata* thought, there existed no God, soul, karma and the otherworld.

---

[39] Davids, *Gradual Sayings*, Vol. I, 245.
[40] Davids, *Gradual Sayings*, Vol. 5, 128–30.
[41] Rajwade, *Digha Nikaya*, Vol. I, 104.
[42] Davids, *Gradual Sayings*, Vol. I, 146.
[43] Rajwade, *Digha Nikaya*, Vol. III, 28–29.

Self-interest of man was most important, and of all the sources of knowledge, the source of sense-perception was the most important.[44]

Emulating the *parivrajaka*s, the *bhikkhu*s engaged in diverse talks about such things as kings, robbers, and great ministers; armies; panic and battles; other matters such as drinks, clothes, beds, flowers and so on. This was a talk like that of wanderers; 'Buddha rebuked the Bhikkhus for indulging in the empty and useless talk.[45] In the *Samyutta Nikaya*, Mara took the shape of Brahmana teacher and told bhikkhus

> You are too Young to have left the world, black-haired lads that you are. Blessed with the luck of youth, without your prime having had the fun that belonged to the natural desires. Enjoy gentleman, the pleasures of your kind, Do not abandoning the things of the life.[46]

Thus, the heretic *parivrajaka*s, who taught different doctrines as well as political science, were active during Buddha's time. In the Shantiparva of the Mahabharata, references to several teachers are found such as Bharadvaja, Utathya, Vamadeo, Kamandaka and Kalakvrikshiya who delivered discourses on the science of politics.

The third set of people who contributed to the composition of the Arthashastra was the ministers of kings. These ministers knew administration of the state and were experts in *artha* and dharma. They were described as *Prayoktri* by *Kautilya*. Kautilya mentioned a few ministers as Arthashastra teachers such as Katyayana, Deergha Charayana and Gotamukha. The Buddhist sources referred to names of Deergha Charayana, Gotamukha and Vassakara. The last one, instrumental in destruction of the Vajjis, was involved in discussion with Gautama Buddha.[47] In the Mahabharata, different ministers who were proficient in the science of politics were mentioned, namely, Kanika, Vidura,

---

[44] Davids, *Dialogues of Buddha*, 49–50.
[45] Ibid., *Gradual Sayings*, Vol. I, 87–88.
[46] Woodward, *Book of Kindered Sayings*, 147.
[47] Davids, *Gradual Sayings*, Vol. II, 403–41, 186–88; Vol. IV, 10–13.

Kalakvrikshiya and Uddhava. Uddhava was a minister in the Andhaka Vrishni republic. The Ramayana mentions the minister Jabala who delivered a discourse on the science of politics. In Bhasa's plays, the role of Yougandharayan, who was a minister of the king Udayan, is described. Many of these teachers served as ministers in the kingdoms of Magadha and Kosala. In no other work is politics of two ministers—Chanakya and Rakshasa—described more graphically than in the *Mudra Rakshasa,* a play written by Vishakhdatta. He also mentions names of Shukra and Brihaspati.

Thus, along with royal priests and the wandering teachers, ministers of kings also played an important role in making of the Arthashastra.

Kautilya mentions names of ten teachers. In the Mahabharata, the names of several teachers are cited. Dr B. A. Saletore states that twenty-four teachers are mentioned in the Mahabharata.[48]

The names of theme teachers are found in other sources as well. For example, in the original Panchatantra, Pratima Nataka of Bhasa, *Mudra Rakshasa* of Vishakha Datta, Medhatithi's *Commentary on Manu,* Chandeshvara, Vishvarupa's *Commentary on Yajnya Valkya Smriti* and Shankararaya's *Commentary on Kamandaka.*[49] Thus, the Arthashastra teachers were known to the people right up to the 13th century AD.

Bibliography

Agrawala, V. S. *India as Known to Panini.* Varanasi: Prithvi Publications, 1963.

———. *Bharat Savitri.* Vols. I–III. New Delhi: Sasta Sahitya Mandal, 1969.

Altekar, A. S. *The State and Government in Ancient India.* Delhi: Motiram Banarsidass, 1975.

Barua, B. M. *History of Pre-Buddhistic Indian Philosophy.* Calcutta: Calcutta University, 1918.

---

[48] Saletore, *Ancient Indian Political Ideas,* 38.
[49] Ghoshal, *History of Indian,* 106.

Bhagvat, trans. *Sidhartha Jataka*. Vol. 5. Pune: Varada Prakashan, 1997.
Bhandarkar, D. R. *Carmichael Lectures on Ancient History of India*. Calcutta: Calcutta University, 1918.
———. *Some Aspects of Ancient Indian Polity*. Banaras: Banaras Hindu University, 1929.
———. *The Brihadaranyaka Upanishad* (with Shankar Bhashya). Gorakhpur: Geeta Press, 1969.
Bloomfield, M., trans. *The Hymns of the Atharva Veda*. Vol. 42. In *The Sacred Books of the East*. Delhi: Motilal Banarsidass, 2000.
Davids, C. A. F. *A Book on Gradual Sayings*. Vols. I–IV. Delhi: Motilal Banarsidass, 2005.
Davids, Rhys. *The Dialogues of Buddha*. Vols. I–III. Delhi: Motilal Banarsidass, 2005.
Ghoshal, U. N. *A History of Indian Political Ideas*. Delhi: Oxford University Press, 1966.
Jayaswal, K. P. *The Hindu Polity*. Bangalore: Bangalore Printing & Publishing, 1955.
Kangle, R. P. *The* Arthashastra *of Kautilya*. Vols. II–III. Bombay: University of Bombay, 1973–80.
Kosambi, D. D. *An Introduction to Study of Indian History*. Bombay: Popular Publication, 1956.
Law, B. C. *India as Described in Early Texts of Buddhism and Jainism*. Delhi: Bharatiya Publishing House, 1980.
Muller, Max, ed. *The Upanishads*. Vol.1. In *The Sacred Books of the East*. Delhi: Motilal Banarsidass, 2012.
Rajwade, C. V. *Digha Nikay*. Vols. I–III (Marathi). Aurangabad: International Centre for Buddhist Studies, 1999.
Saletore, B. A. *Ancient Indian Political Ideas and Institutions*. Bombay: Asia Publishing House, 1971.
Vatsyayana. *Kamasutra*. Translated by R. Burton and F. F. Arbuthnot. Delhi: Jaico Publishing House, 2008.
Vishakha, Dutta. *The Mudra Rakshasa*, translated by R. Pandit. Bombay: New Book Company, 1944.
Woodward, F. G. *A Book of Kindered Sayings*. 5 Vols. Delhi: Motilal Banarsidass, 2005.

5

The *Lokayata* Philosophy and the Early Arthashastra Tradition

In our discussion in earlier chapters, we have seen that in the Buddhist literature, the *Lokayata* teacher was identified with Arthashastra thinker, as both, perhaps, held identical views.[1] In this chapter, we shall try to examine the relationship between *Lokayata* philosophy and the Arthashastra tradition.

In ancient India, the *Dharmashastra* tradition was considered the *Smriti* tradition. Although the *Smritis* were considered inferior to the *Srutis* or Vedas, as they were based on customs and traditions of the people, they were considered important for providing guidelines to the people. According to Kautilya, both disciplines of the *Dharmashastra* and the Arthashastra belonged to the tradition of the *Itihasa* Veda. It was expected that their teachings would be consistent with the main principles advocated by the Vedas. However, the Arthashastra tradition, which owed its origin to great intellectual ferment of the 6th and 7th centuries BC, showed independence of mind and did not blindly follow the *Smriti* tradition, first enumerated and developed by the *Dharmasutras*. Thus, there emerged the conflict between the two traditions as great religious teachers of the 7th century BC

[1] Rajwade, *The Digha Nikaya*, 27.

disregarded the teachings of the Vedas and opposed the performance of violent sacrifices. The *Lokayata* philosophers who flourished during this period also opposed the Vedas and advocated the pursuit of *artha* (profit) and *kama* (pleasure) in this life. Hence, it is necessary to examine the relationship between *Lokayata* philosophy and the Arthashastra politics.

We have seen that the *kshatravidya* was the oldest name of political science, but according to Dr Law, the Buddhist sources considered it as the science of warfare.[2] There was hostility about this science in the Buddhist tradition. Buddha thought that it was a vulgar science used by the false teachers to earn livelihood. They predicted victories and defeats in the wars, advised kings about the invasions of foreign kings and so on. It was a low science.[3] In the *Mahabodhi Jataka* (No. 528), the *kshatra vidyavadi* minister was condemned for his views as he said that if it was necessary, one must kill his parents to serve his interests. According to Durga Bhagvat, *kshatra vidyavadi* believed that the *vidya* was the only science and held that war, weapon and force determined everything. The *Jataka* tells us that the concerned minister was corrupt and used to take bribes. His ideas were refuted by the Bodhisattva.[4]

Kshatravidya was developed into *Rajshastra, Dandaniti* and *Arthashastra*. *Manusmriti* contends that Arthashastra was *Drishtartha Smriti*, which means it is a science which is based on the direct evidence of senses. Its fruits are visible.[5] The science of politics was considered *Drishtartha* because it is based on the varied experiences that human beings had undergone. Shantiparva, in the Mahabharata, said, unlike the discipline of renunciation whose ends were not sure, politics was the science which was based on the direct evidence of senses and its ends and results were direct.[6] Thus, it was emphasized that the

[2] Law, *India as Described in Early Texts*, 258.
[3] Rajwade, *The Digha Nikaya*, 28.
[4] Bhagvat, *The Siddhartha Jataka*, 171, 180.
[5] *Manusmriti*, 7-1.
[6] Mahabharata, 12-64-5.

Arthashastra was a *Drishartha Smriti*, and it is based on the *pratyaksha praman* or direct evidence of senses.

In India, the concept of *trivarga* was developed during the 5th century BC. *Trivarga* means three ends of life; these were dharma, *artha* and *kama*. Dharma was related to the moral behaviour and the duties of man in the society. *Artha* was concerned with the development of sources of livelihood and political management of the society and *kama* meant enjoyment of pleasures of the life in the well-organized society. Different books were written to explain the meaning of these ideals. The *Dharmashastras* dealt with the ideal of dharma, the Arthashastras the *artha* and the *Kamasutra*s the *kama*. In the Mahabharata, there was discussion on the meaning of these terms. Yudhishthira was a supporter of dharma, Arjuna was of *artha* and Bhima was of *kama*. Arguments of Arjuna and Bhima were designed to refute the opinion of Yudhishthira, who was a supporter of dharma and renunciation.

Arjuna argued that *artha* was the most important *purushartha* because with the help of *artha* only two other ends of life could be successfully pursued. Man became weak not because of loss of physical energy but because of loss of money. As the water from rivers flow to different directions, similarly, the royal policy caused money to flow to different directions.[7] It was necessary for the people to pursue *artha* and *kama*, so that they could exert to earn money and live good life.[8] He held that the earth is the place where all men exerted and secured their livelihood. They developed *varta*—agriculture, trade and cattle breeding and different trades and arts—to promote well-being of the people. The second aspect of *artha* was *Dandaniti*. With the help of *danda*, an order was established in the society. Because of *danda*, people followed the right course of action. Hence, it should be employed judiciously. While using *danda*, violence was inevitable but we could not earn our livelihood taking recourse to non-violence. Human beings lived off animals. Agriculture involved violence.

---

[7] Ibid., 12-08.
[8] Ibid., 12-08.

Hence, perfect non-violence was not possible. He maintained that without necessary regulation of human affairs, civilized human life was not possible. He agreed that it was true that depriving a person of his life was not a good thing but for the sake of self-protection and the interest of the society, we had to do that. Hence, the pursuit of the *artha* was desirable because in this world, different people followed different professions and they had to take recourse to *artha* to make progress.[9] Thus, Arjuna laid emphasis on the importance of *'varta'* (economics) and *Dandaniti* (politics), which were components of *artha*.

Bhima advocated the cause of *Kama Purushartha*. He said that the people always desired pleasures and avoided pains. Therefore, they always tried to control all sorts of diseases.[10] Yudhishthira had lost thinking power like that of the Vedic scholars who recited the Vedic hymns repeatedly without understanding their meaning. Renunciation was talked about by the people who did not want to work. Asceticism of living in jungles was of no use. Animals and birds lived in jungles but they did not achieve salvation. Mountains and trees stood firm as if they were offering penances but of no result. The truth was that everyone should perform action, and without action even ascetics could not live in the forest. This was true about all living creatures.[11] The *kama* was the basic instinct of life and without it no living creature would have been born! It gave inspiration to all human actions. Men pursued agriculture, trade, cattle rearing and other arts and crafts to fulfil the demands of *kama*. All great human achievements such as scaling of mountains and crossing of the oceans were carried out under the influence of *kama*. Not a single individual can escape from its spell. Hence, it was essence of *Trivarga*, and two ends of dharma and *artha* were rooted in *kama* as no worldly course of action was possible without *kama*. Underlying the importance of the end of *kama*, which combined desires, passions and pleasures, he concluded that, in fact, proper

[9] Ibid., 12-15.51-56.
[10] Ibid., 12-10.
[11] Ibid., 12-161.

and judicious pursuit of all three ends of life was desirable as one-sided and excessive pursuit of one end resulted in disaster. A person who had pursued the three simultaneously and with discretion was considered an excellent person.[12]

Although Bhima emphatically laid stress upon the importance of *Kama Purushartha*, ultimately he agreed with Kautilya that excessive pursuit of one end was not desirable. The arguments of both Arjuna and Bhima clearly indicated that the thrust of the position of supporters of *artha* was on *varta* and *dandaniti* that ensured material pleasure. Although Kautilya argued for the primacy of the end of *artha*, he did not favour its one-sided pursuit. He wrote:

> The king should pursue *kama* without contravening *Dharma* and *Artha* because one should not live without pleasures. He should equally devote to three goals of life which are bound up with another. For, if any one of the goals excessively indulged in does harm to itself as to the other two.[13]

The *Lokayata* thinkers held that the pursuit of *artha* and *kama* was necessary because the results were real, and these could be experienced by the senses.

The *Lokayata* or the *Charvaka* philosophy was one of the ancient schools of philosophy which flourished during the great intellectual ferment of the 6th century BC, and we could get references about it from the 7th century BC to the 15th century AD.[14] Most of these authentic texts are now lost, and whatever information we could obtain about them was from their rivals who tended to distort their position. In his 'Sarva Darshan Sangraha', Madhavacharya has described their philosophical position.[15] According to the Charvakas, for the benefit of all living beings, we should take recourse to philosophy of the Charvakas.[16] The

---

[12] Ibid., 12-16.
[13] The Arthashastra, 1.7.3.7.
[14] Saletore, *Ancient Indian Political Thought*.
[15] Madhava (1985), 1–17.
[16] Ibid., 17.

Charvaka philosophers were also called 'Haitukas', who were experts in logic and sophistry. We obtain some information about them from the Buddhist sources as well as from the Ramayana and the Mahabharata. There was an extreme ideological opposition to the *Lokayata* philosophy.

In the Buddhist sources, several references to *Lokayata* teachers exist. In the Brahmajal Sutra of the *Digha Nikaya*, there were some Brahmins who said that when the human soul enjoyed five types of pleasures (born of form, word, fragrance, liquids and touch) to its full satisfaction, it acquired 'Nirvana'.[17] In the *Samanjya Phala Sutra*, Ajita Keshakambali believed that the human body was created of four elements—earth, water, light and air—which merged when a man died. The body turned into ashes. There was no life after death. One should not offer donations as these were misused by fools.[18] Of all the six teachers Buddhist literature talked about, Ajit Keshakambli was closest to the *Lokayata* ideas, though he could not be called the follower of *Lokayata* philosophy, because there was profound pessimism in his philosophy.[19] The teachers in the *Digha Nikaya* argued that there was no god, heaven or karma and of all the sources of knowledge, the source of direct evidence of senses, was the most important.[20]

The *Khabbagiya Bhikkhus* learnt the *Lokayata* system, which was described like those who enjoyed pleasures of the world. Buddha advised his followers not to learn the *Lokayata* system. He said, 'Now can a man who holds the *Lokayata* as valuable reach up, Bhikhus, to the full advantage of or to attain growth in, to full breadth of this doctrine and discipline? If he did so, he will be guilty of Dukkata'.[21] In the Buddhist literature, *Lokayata* is considered closer to Arthashastra and a low science.[22]

[17] Rajwade, *The Digha Nikaya*, 47–48.
[18] Ibid., 66.
[19] Chattopadhyay, *Lokayata*, 518.
[20] Davids, *Book of the Kindred*, Part I, 49–50.
[21] Muller, *The Vinaya Texts*, Vol. III, 151–52.
[22] Rajwade, *The Digha Nikaya*, 203.

The Patanjali mentions a *Lokayata* teacher called Bhaguri. The Charvakas of the *Lokayata* school were mentioned as the models of dialectical proficiency and for convincing exposition of their doctrines.²³

In the Ramayana, Rama was warned of Brahmins who believed in direct evidence of senses and rejected the *Dharmashastras* that were considered authoritative. They followed the method of logic and reasoning to expound their useless science.²⁴ Also, there is a discourse of the minister Jabala, who was a *Lokayata* follower and an Arthashastra teacher.²⁵

In the Mahabharata, there are several references to the *Lokayata* philosophy, which was called 'the Barhaspatya mata', or the opinion of Brihaspati. Brihaspati was believed to be the originator of the *Lokayata* philosophy.

In the Shantiparva, a *Charvaka* Brahmin opposed Yudhishthira when he was entering Hastinapur after registering victory over the Kauravas. The Brahmin argued that Yudhishthira had committed sin by killing his kith and kin and even his teachers for the sake of kingdom.²⁶ This ethical position of the *Charvaka* was interesting because it laid stress upon the clan solidarity and opposed the use of violence for taking kingship. In the Shantiparva, the *Hetuvadi* Brahmin said that he followed logic, which was based on inference and did not accept the authority of Vedas. He was an atheist and used to condemn Vedas in the assembly by advancing the logical arguments.²⁷ In the *Bhrigu*–Bharadvaja dialogue, Bharadvaja asked some pertinent questions about the efficacy of the Varna system and validity of the Vedic positions as they proved to be against the known human experience.²⁸

---

²³ Agrawala, *India as Known to Panini*, 394.
²⁴ Valmiki. *The Valmiki Ramayana*, Vol. I, 440.
²⁵ Ibid., 459–60.
²⁶ Mahabharata, 12.39.
²⁷ Ibid., 12–174-45-47.
²⁸ Ibid., 12–181.

The *Lokayata* position was clearly stated in ancient India and the following were the basic principles enunciated in it:

1. Direct evidence of senses is the only true source of knowledge.
2. Soul is not immortal, and soul and body decayed because of old age, diseases, exertion and death.
3. There exists no heaven as its existence cannot be established with the help of inference and, in fact, heaven means the imagined highest happiness of man.
4. The real happiness in the world accrued due to fulfilment of desires.
5. Inference and '*Aptavachan*' or opinions of the wise are not separate sources of knowledge as they are based on the direct evidence of senses. We cannot accept their authority if they are contrary to the direct evidence of senses. We cannot use inference to prove the existence of god, soul or heaven.
6. There is no consciousness or life outside the human body. There is nothing supernatural in consciousness as it is created out of combination and synthesis of four basic elements such as earth, water, light and air. There is a variety in the world, and it arose out of one cause. The seed of banyan tree gave birth to a huge banyan tree with all its branches and leaves. The entire tree is hidden in a microform in the small seed, and it assumed huge form at the right time. The spirit is germinated through fermentation of different chemicals; semen of man is responsible for the birth of human body, mind, intelligence and consciousness. Human consciousness was luminous, and light is produced when it is in human body. The magnet creates movement in the iron articles. It is the inherent character or 'Svabhava' of magnet. There is no external agency to produce consciousness.
7. Four material elements generate and sustain the human body, and after its death, it merges back into the elements.[29]

---

[29] Salunkhe, A.H., Charvaka Darshan, 56-58 and The Mahabharata 12.211 and Vol. 6. 454-455.

In the epic, according to *Hetuvadins,* the direct evidence of senses is the only authoritative source of knowledge. They contend that the atoms have the properties of permanence and the entire world is produced by it. There does not exist supernatural beings such as *Parabrahma.*[30] A Chinese scholar, Ting Pin, held that the *Lokayata* accepted only atom as the cause of entire universe and four elements as a cause of all forms, sense organs and intellect.[31]

In the *Kamasutra,* the Lokayatikas held that religious ordinances should not be observed, because they bear fruits in the future, and it is doubtful whether they will bear fruits at all. Therefore, it is a foolish thing to give away one's possessions to others. Moreover, it is better to have a pigeon today than to have a peacock tomorrow.[32]

In the 'Sarva-Darshan Sangraha', Madhava has elaborately discussed the basic principles of the *Lokayata* philosophy. According to Dr D. R. Shastri, *Lokayata* philosophy developed in four different phases: (a) *Barhaspatya* phase, (b) *Swabhvavadi* phase, (c) hedonism and (d) Purandara, who accepted inference and sky or space (Akash) as the fifth element.[33]

Normally, the Charvakas did not accept the validity of inference because they held that because of differences in circumstances, time, place and things differed in their power and capacity. The experience of a large number of cases cannot eliminate the possibility of failure of agreement in the future. Both inference and 'Aptopadesh' were rooted in direct experience of senses. Second, there were no universals, and hence there was no scope for inductive reasoning. Since they did not admit the validity of inference, then the probability, other sources such as testimony of the wise, scriptures, analogy, comparison and

[30] Mahabharatha, Vol. 7, 498–99.13.147.
[31] Joshi, '*Lokayata* in Ancient India', 398.
[32] Vatsyayana, *The Kamasutra*, 7.
[33] Shastri, 'History of Ancient Indian', 33–72.

implication were not admitted. Third, the *Lokayata* ontology was based on 'Swabhava vada' as it was the basic character or 'Swabhav' of a particular thing that acted as the prime cause, but they did not allow 'Swabhav vada' to grow as a principle of determinism. Fourth, they held that human body was the constant perceiver or the enjoyer of all experiences. Consciousness in the body was produced through the operation of vital functions of 'Prana' and 'Apana' and other bio-motor facilities. Consciousness, memory and intellectual functions could be experienced in human body and not beyond it. Fifth, there is no god, soul, heaven or rebirth. Hence, prayers to gods brought no results. The rituals were empty practices designed to procure monetary gains for the priests. Hence, they were opposed to performance of sacrifices, idol worship, prayers and questioned authority of the Vedas. Sixth, they were opposed to caste and Varna distinctions and believed that no lineage had remained pure due to irrepressible sex desires of men and women. Hence, the observances of caste distinctions were useless and fruitless.[34] Seventh, they believed in the dignity of women and said that in the *Ashvamedha* sacrifice, the woman was forced to recite obscene dialogues, embrace the dead horse and hold its genetical organ in her hand. These sacrifices degraded human dignity and were based on the religious superstitions. Eighth, they held that there was no god and he did not dispense with justice. If indeed he dispensed justice, then who was responsible for injustice and cruelty in the world? In fact, god should be blamed for it. There existed no universal power and only authority man should accept was that of the sovereign king, who with the help of *Dandaniti* ensured '*Yogakshema*' of the people. Ninth, they wanted the people to enjoy pleasures and avoid pains and pleasures arose in men due to contacts with different objects. They wanted the people to enjoy pleasures by organizing pleasure festivals such as *Madanotasvas*.[35] However, the Lokayatas did not distinguish between the mental and the physical pleasures. They were not the individual hedonists, because they were the supporters of

---

[34] Dasgupta, *History of Indian Philosophy*, 548.
[35] Reipe, *The Naturalist Thought in India*, 63–73.

artha and *Kama Purusharthas* that ensured the well-being of the society. The *artha* provided the material basis to human life and the *kama* ensured its continuity as well as enjoyment. In order to consummate these two ends, the *Lokayatikas* supported the sciences of *Varta* and *Dandaniti*. *Varta* meant acquisition of means of livelihood, with the help of the proper development of agriculture, trade and cattle breeding. *Dandaniti* was required for the orderly management of public affairs of men who wanted to live in the civilized society.[36] They were supporters of equality. Hence, they said, 'All men are equal. There is no purity or superiority of caste. Social equality is the supreme philosophy. *Lokayata* declared that there was no milk in the veins of Brahmins and blood only in a Shudra. Hence all are equal'.[37]

The opponents of the *Lokayata* philosophy criticized it for its moral relativism and hedonism. Madhava said that the Charvakas taught people to drink *ghee* even by borrowing money from others. The truth was that though they believed that true pleasure was enjoyed with the help of sense organs, they never said that these material pleasures should be enjoyed at the cost of others.

Charvakas or the Lokayatas were supporters of 'Swabhav vada', which believed that sharpness of thorn, sweetness of sugarcane and bitterness of lime are the result of their own inherent character, and they assumed peculiar form according to their own inherent property.[38] A great tree emerged with all its characters out of a small seed of the same but it required soil, water, light for its growth. Hence, they were not determinists as they held that employment of human reason and exertions were necessary for the emergence of cities, village settlements and townships. They rejected the theory of Karma and provided enough space for the human will and endeavour.[39] According to Riepe, they were not amoral relativists as they maintained that by adopting only those means which were seen to be practical such as agriculture,

---

[36] Shastri, 'History of Ancient Indian', 53.
[37] Joshi, '*Lokayata* in Ancient India', 400.
[38] Shastri, 'History of Ancient Indian', 71–72.
[39] Tucci, 'A Short Introduction', 90.

cattle breeding and trade, politics and administration, a wise man should endeavour to enjoy pleasures of this world.[40] He further pointed out that the *Lokayata* commended truth, integrity and consistency and esteemed freedom of thought, which they most exercised it in their time.[41]

Thus, it would not be correct to call the Lokayatikas amoral as they denied a distinction between men on the basis of birth. They sought to protect dignity of women by opposing immoral and obscene practices in the rituals. They opposed the evil and selfish behaviour of the priests and blind superstitions propagated by them. They opposed performance of violent sacrifices, killing of animals for food, and killing of one's own kinsmen for the sake of kingdom. They upheld the cause of truth, reason and integrity and decried deceit. Their philosophy was worldly, and they valued material pleasures and happiness. They sought to promote spirit of scientific inquiry and held that the continuity of life cycle is ensured as we receive it from one generation to another. The atom was pregnant with different forms.[42] They thought that life on the earth could be made happy, by the pursuit of *artha* and *Kama Purushartha*s. They visualized the establishment of an order in the society where everybody would live a happy and prosperous life, free of priestly deception. In this system, the 'Matsya-Nyaya', or anarchy, would be overcome with the help of proper application of *Danda*. The 'Yoga-Kshema' of the people, which is rooted in 'Varta', is ensured by the correct pursuit of science of politics. Hence, it would be wrong to condemn *Lokayata* philosophy as amoral and hedonistic as it sought to improve life of man on the earth.

There was a close relationship between the Arthashastra and the *Lokayata,* as in the Buddhist literature both the words were interchangeably used. Both the thinking traditions believed in the efficacy of direct evidence of senses. The minister Jabala in the Ramayana was a *Lokayata* thinker as well as an expert

[40] Riepe, *The Naturalist Thought in India,* 74.
[41] Ibid., 76.
[42] Salunkhe, *The Charvaka Darshan,* 56–58.

The *Lokayata* Philosophy and the Early Arthashastra Tradition / 71

in the science of politics. *Lokayata*'s viewpoint was also called 'Barhaspatya mata', similar as the viewpoint of Brihaspati, considered the founder of *Lokayata* philosophy as well as science of politics. Kautilya in his Arthashastra argued that the king should study four disciplines, such as philosophy, theology, economics and politics. Later, in the Mahabharata, with the growing influence of idealism, philosophy was called knowledge of the spirit or *atmavidya*. Kautilya wanted the king to study the *anvikshiki*, which included three philosophies—*Samkhya*, *Yoga* and *Lokayata*.[43] Why should the king study these three philosophies?

In the Arthashastra, Kautilya has used the concepts of *anvikshiki* and *yukti*. *Anvikshiki* included the study of philosophies of *Samkhya*, *Yoga* and *Lokayata*. Explaining its utility, he wrote:

> Investigating by means of reasoning, what is *Dharma* and *Adharma* in *Trayi*, what is material gain and loss in the *Varta* and what is good and bad policy in *Dandaniti* as well as the relative strength of and weaknesses of these sciences, philosophy confers benefits to the people, keeps mind steady in prosperity and adversity and brings about proficiency in thought, speech and action.[44]

Hence, he says, 'philosophy ever thought about as the lamp of all sciences, as the means of all actions and support of all laws and duties'.[45] We can say that there could be no better explanation of philosophy than that of Kautilya. With the help of *Samkhya* and *Yoga* philosophy, the mind of a person could be kept steady in prosperity and adversity and it provided moral standards to decide what was good and bad. The study of *Lokayata* philosophy was to sharpen intellect and reasoning power of the person. The study provided proficiency in thought, speech and action. Thus, it helped an intelligent person to acquire *Vijnyan-bala*, which was described in the Shantiparva of the Mahabharata.[46]

---

[43] The Arthashastra, 1.2.1.
[44] Ibid., 1-2-11.
[45] Ibid., 1.2.12.
[46] The Mahabharatha, 12–127.

The king should study *Samkhya* philosophy to discipline his mind and to give strength to his reasoning power. It taught people how to stand firm by correctly disciplining their minds by proper concomitance of three *gunas*: *Sattva*, *Rajas* and *Tamas*. According to Dr Walter Ruben, the *Samkhya* ethic taught Kshatriya to perform disinterested action in the spirit of selflessness.[47]

The meaning of philosophy of *Yoga* was controversial. Some scholars identified it with *Yoga-Darshana*, which was developed by Patanjali. D. Chattopadhyay opined that *Yoga* was another name of *Vaisheshika* philosophy, which believed that the combination and concomitance of two atoms furnished new creation. The *Vaisheshikas* were known for their proficiency in logic.[48] If we go by the Bhagavata Geeta, *Yoga* meant the philosophy of *Karma Yoga*. This philosophy enjoined the actor to perform disinterested action in the spirit of equanimity. It asked the Kshatriyas to perform the duty without aspiring for its fruits. Dr Ruben contented that due to incorporation of the Kshatriya ethic in his *Karma Yoga*, the moral dilemma of action was resolved. Hence, Kautilya recommended it as one of the philosophies to be studied by the king.[49]

According to *Lokayata* philosophy, *artha* and *kama* were the two *Purusharthas* that should be pursued by the king. There was a close relationship between the *Lokayata* and *Dandaniti*, as the former held that *Dandaniti* was the only science.[50] The *Lokayata* teachers were experts in logic and reasoning; hence, they were called 'Haitukas'. Therefore, it was thought that the study of this philosophy would sharpen the intellect of the prince.

Similarities and differences between *Lokayata* philosophy and the theory of Arthashastra are as follows:

1. Both Lokayatikas and Arthashastra thinkers agreed that direct evidence of senses is the principal source of

[47] Ruben, 'Beginning of the Epic', 175–80.
[48] Chattopadhyay, 'Indian Materialism', 491–508.
[49] Ruben, 'Beginning of the Epic', 189
[50] Shastri, 'History of Ancient Indian', 53.

knowledge. Therefore, Arthashastra was called *Drishtrtha Smriti* as it draws its results from the visible world and its fruits were visible. But Arthashastra was essentially a social science; hence, it used the sources such as inference, analogy, historical experiences, legends and events of the past and comparison to secure knowledge. In order to develop political theory, it was not averse to using inductive reasoning to arrive at broad conclusions which had the universal validity. Thus, the Arthashastra did not confine itself to direct evidence of senses as the only source of knowledge. Both the schools agreed that the knowledge thus perceived needed to be properly processed with the help of logic and reasoning; hence, the use of *yukti* was important. *Yukti* was a method of analysis and reasoning. Kautilya has mentioned 32 *tantra yukti*s which were used to compose the Arthashastra.[51]

2. One does not know whether *Lokayata* would have accepted the validity of '*Itihasa*' as the source but the Arthashastra was dependent upon historical events of the past to draw some useful conclusions. Evidence gathered from history was used as an illustration to arrive at some conclusions.

3. The Arthashastra thinkers belonged to different schools of thought; therefore, for Manu, '*Trayi*' was an important science, but Brihaspati and perhaps Ushanasa did not accept the validity of the Vedas. Kautilya quoted Brihaspati, who condemned the Vedas by using the *Charvaka* terminology. Bharadvaja agreed with Brihaspati and condemned three Vedas as 'samvaran'.[52]

4. Both the traditions agreed that self-aggrandizement should not be the goal of the king and the purpose of science of politics was to ensure the overall welfare of the society. Both of them laid stress upon the development of the sources of livelihood or *Varta*.

5. *Lokayata* philosophers did not believe in the existence of god, soul and karma and rejected the validity of rituals

[51] The Arthashastra, 15.
[52] Tucci, 'A Short Introduction', 89.

and caste system. They regarded sovereign king as the final authority in this world. Arthashastra thinkers differed while taking position on these points. They accepted the sovereign authority of the king. But some of them asked king to perform religious rituals, without believing in them, to hoodwink people. Since the *varna* system proved useful to stabilize the government, Kautilya supported the *varna* system and, for that purpose, accepted the authority of the Vedas. In contrast, the *Lokayata* thinkers adopted a principled position.

The difference between the two traditions occurred because the Arthashastra was a social science based on the direct human experiences and had a practical application. It had to continuously revise its doctrines in the light of their practical application in different countries and in different circumstances and, as a result, its form and content were flexible and, at times, varied, though it was rooted in realism and rationalism. Thus, the relationship between the two traditions was complex and, at times, the Arthashastra recommended the policy that would not be approved by the *Lokayata*, for example, the performance of religious rituals by the king.

Bibliography

Agrawala V. S. *India as Known to Panini*. Varanasi: Prithvi Publications, 1963.
Bhagvat, Durga. *The Siddhartha Jataka*. Vol. 5. Pune: Varada Books, 1978.
Chattopadhyay, D. 'Indian Materialism'. In *New Indology*, edited by W. Ruben. Felicitation volume in honour of H. Cruger. Berlin: Verlag, 1975.
Chattopadhyay, D. *Lokayata: A Study of Indian Materialism*. New Delhi: Peoples Publishing House, 1973.
Dale, Reipe. *The Naturalist Thought in India*. Delhi: Motilal Banarsidass, 1961.
Dasgupta, S. N. *A History of Indian Philosophy*. Vol. III. Delhi: Motilal Banarsidass, 1975.
Davids, Rhys C. A. F. *The Book of the Kindred Sayings* (Samyutta Nikay). Vol. I. Delhi: Motilal Banarsidass, 2005.

Ghoshal, U. N. *A History of Indian Political Ideas*. Bombay: Oxford University Press, 1966.
Heesterman, J. C. *The Inner Conflict of Tradition*. Delhi: Oxford University Press, 1985.
Joshi, R. V. 'Lokayata in Ancient India and China'. *Annals of Bhandarkar Oriental Research Institute* (R.G. Bhandarkar 150th Birth Anniversary Volume) (1988): 393–405.
———. *The Manusmriti with the Commentary by Kullukabhatta*. Pune: Niralnaya Sagar, 1946.
———. *Kautalya Studies*. Delhi: Oriental Publishers, 1975.
Law, B. C. *India as Described in Early Texts of Jainism and Buddhism*. Delhi: Bharatiya Publishing House, 1980.
Muller, Max, ed. *The Vinaya Texts*. Parts I–III. Translated by T. W. Rhys Davids and H. Oldenberg. In *The Sacred Books of the East*. Vols. 16, 17, 20. Delhi: Motilal Banarsidass, 2007.
Rajwade, C. V. *The Digha Nikaya*. Vol. I. Aurangabad: Buddhist Research Centre, 1999.
Ruben, W. 'The Beginning of the Epic Samkhyas'. *The Annals of Bhandarkar Oriental Research Institute* 37 (1956): 175–89.
Saletore, B. A. 'Historical Notices of the *Lokayata*'. *ABORI* 23 (1942): 386–97.
———. *Ancient Indian Political Thought and Institutions*. Bombay: Asia, 1971.
Salunkhe, A. H. *The Charvaka Darshan* (Marathi). Bombay: Keshav Gore Trust, 1987.
Shah, K. J. 'Of Artha and Arthashastra'. In *Comparative Political Philosophy*, edited by A. Parel and R. Keith, 160. Delhi: SAGE, 1992.
Shastri, D. R. 'History of Ancient Indian Materialism and Hedonism'. In *Charvaka Manthan* (Marathi), edited by U. Kumathekar, 33–72. Pune: Paramarsha Prakashan, 2001.
Tucci. 'A Short Introduction to Indian Materialism'. In *Charvaka Manthan*, edited by U. Kumathekar, 81–92. 2001. Pune: Paramarsh Prakashan.
Valmiki. *The Valmiki Ramayana*. Translated by Kashinath Shastri Lele. Vols. I and II. Pune: Varada Publications, 1986.
Vatsyayana. *The Kamasutra*, edited and translated by R. Burton and Arbuthnot. Delhi: Jaico Publication, 1989.
Vidya Bhushan, S. C. *A History of Indian Logic*. Delhi: Motilal Banarsidass, 1978.

6

The Arthashastra Teachers

As discussed in the previous chapter, there was a close relationship between *Lokayata* thinkers and the Arthashastra teachers, and some similarities existed between the two because the minister Jabala in the Ramayana and 'Barhaspatya' teachers in the Mahabharata belonged to the same traditions. In this chapter, we shall provide insight about the Arthashastra teachers.

We have seen that during the 6th century BC, a grim struggle existed for political power and dominance between Magadha and Kosala kingdoms and, ultimately, the Magadha kings succeeded in absorbing Kosala kingdom and in subordinating the *Vajji* confederacy. This success was achieved with the help of material resources, courageous and cunning leadership, and new political science, which taught kings how to acquire enemy's kingdom and how to develop it as a prosperous region. According to Professor D. D. Kosambi, a cold, inexorable, grimly calculating, logically formulated and carefully reasoned political theory laid behind the prolonged political struggle between two states. There was never a least pretence of morality or specious excuse of doing good to others. The theorists of this new policy were as important in their own way as the contemporary religious leaders.[1]

---

[1] Kosambi D. D. (1966), 120–21. Bhagvat (2003), Siddharth *Jataka*, Vol. I. 72.

We have seen that the royal priests, ministers and wandering ascetic teachers were the originators of the science of politics, and of the three, the wandering *parivrajaka*s were the most creative. A few Buddhist passages gave some information about these thinkers. According to B. C. Law, 'Examining carefully, the import of all these Buddhist passages, we may perhaps go so far as to maintain that these wanderers, quasi-wanderers were the Sophistic predecessors of Chanakya to whom tradition ascribes the authorship of Arthashastra.[2]

There is some information about the Arthashastra teachers in Kautilya's Arthashastra. He gave information about three sets of teachers.

1. Four schools of political science were those of Manu, Parashara, Brihaspati and Shukra. Some referred to the fifth school of the Ambhia, whose opinion is cited only once.
2. Individual teachers' opinions have been cited many a time in the Arthashastra as along with those of ministers who left the royal court after witnessing bad omens.
3. The opinions of the teachers who were called Acharyas. Professor Kane has convincingly proved that the term 'Acharyah' did not mean the teacher of Kautilya but it meant the body of the Arthashastra teachers whose views have been cited. They might have represented opinions of pre-Kautilyan teachers as well as views prepared by Kautilya himself whenever the composition needed it. He cited their views 56 times on many crucial issues.[2a]

Apart from Manu, Parashara, Brihaspati and Ushanasa, Kautilya mentioned the names of the following teachers: Bharadvaja, Vishalaksha, Kaunapadanta, Vatavyadhi Bahaudantiputra, Pishuna and Pishunaputra. Kautilya also mentions the names of Katyayana, Deergha Charayana, Ghotamukha, Kaninka Bharadvaj and Kinjalaka.

[2] Law, 'A Short Account', 229–30.
[2a] Kane, The meaning of ABORI, 207–13.

In the Mahabharata, the names of Manu, Shukra, Brihaspati, Bharadvaja and Mahendra are mentioned. These five and Vishalaksha and Gourishiras are called originators of the science of politics. At other place, the names of Vishalaksha, Bahudantaka, Shukra and Brihaspati are mentioned. Except Gourishiras, other names are common in both the texts. Apart from these thinkers, the Mahabharata includes the discourses on political science delivered by some teachers, namely, Utathya, Kalaka Vrikshiya, Vamadeo and Kamandaka. These are the teachers of Arthashastra, but their names are not found in the Arthashastra. A good number of political ideas in the epic are attributed to Narada, Vidura, Bhishma, Arjuna, Bhima, Yudhishthira, Draupadi, Krishna, Hanuman and Dhritarashtra. These are important heroes in the great epic, and the author of the Mahabharata expressed many important political ideas through them. There is no doubt that sages such as Narada, Vidura, Bhishma and kings such as Yudhishthira and Dhritarashtra were experts in political science, but it is difficult to say that the ideas they expounded were their own ideas. It is possible that some of the experts in the Arthashastra, who contributed to the redrafting and redaction of the great epic, must have incorporated them in the text. It is possible that many of these ideas belong to the post-Kautilyan and some of them may belong to the pre-Kautilyan periods, but it is difficult to distinguish them as they are intricately enmeshed with and integrated in the main body of the text. The influence of the *Dharmashastra* tradition on them is quite evident.

In the Arthashastra, Kautilya refers to some of the cases of ministers who immediately left the royal court after observing changes in the behaviour of non-human beings. Most of these names are historical, as they were mentioned in the Buddhist and Jaina literature. Professor D. D. Kosambi has written a long article on the line of Arthashastra teachers, which was republished in 2007.[3] These ministers were the teachers of Arthashastra.

[3] Kosambi, 'The Line of the Arthashastra', 260–78.

In the Arthashastra,[4] Kautilya referred to some historical cases when the ministers left the royal courts after sensing danger to their lives because of abnormal behaviour of human and non-human beings. He was discussing the proper behaviour of the courtiers. He wrote, 'And he should observe the change in behaviour even of non-human beings'. He gave the following examples:

1. 'He is sprinkling water from high' with this thought Katyayana left the court of the king.
2. 'The heron is flying towards left' with this Kaninka Bharadvaja left.
3. 'Ah!grass' with this Dirgha Charayana left.
4. 'The garment is cold' with this Ghotamukha left.
5. 'The elephant has sprinkled water' with this Kinjalka left.
6. 'He has praised the chariot and horses' with this Pishuna left.
7. At the barking of dog, Pishuna's son left.[5]

Thus, here Kautilya mentioned seven ministers or courtiers who were wise enough to read the signs of danger and left the scene to save themselves. Who are these teachers and what is the meaning of the signs mentioned by Kautilya? In the note on the topic, Professor Kangle sought to explain the meanings of these signs. According to Professor D. D. Kosambi, such a brief reference would have been a complete waste unless the original context of each saying was known to the contemporary reader.[6]

According to Kangle, Katyayana saw the gardener watering from on high instead of the usual low level, thus making him wet, which served a warning that the king wanted to kill him. It could be an indication of his displeasure; hence, he left the royal court.[7]

---

[4] Arthashastra, 5-5-10-11.
[5] Ibid., 5-5-10-11.
[6] Kosambi, 'The Line of the Arthashastra', 262.
[7] Kangle, 1963, Arthashastra II, 352.

1. Heron's flying left was a bad omen, indicating danger; therefore, Kaninka Bharadvaja left.
2. Dirgha Charayana saw the grass appeared where it was not expected. He thought it abnormal and left.
3. Ghotamukha expected a warm garment from the king; instead, he received wet garment, indicating displeasure of the king and as a result he left.
4. Kinjalka left because the elephant sprinkled water on him unexpectedly. He thought the behaviour of the elephant unusual.
5. Pishuna left because the king praised horses and the chariot. Pishunaputra probably went on a campaign and registered victory, but instead of praising him, the king praised horses and the chariot, indicating his displeasure.
6. Barking of dog was considered a hint of king's displeasure, Hence, Pishunaputra left. Perhaps, it was a pet dog of the king and whenever king was displeased with the person, it would bark or king might have encouraged it to bark.

It seems that all these seven persons were ministers or high officials of the king, and they were teachers of political science as Kautilya refers to ideas of Bharadvaja and Pishuna in his Arthashastra. Dr D. D. Kosambi observed that some of these ministers were Kshatriyas and Brahmins. The following is a very little information available about these thinkers.

Katyayana was another name for the great grammarian Vararuchi who flourished during the age of the Nandas in the 4th century BC.[8] In the *Katha Sarit Sagara* of Somadev, he is called the minister of the Nandas. He was an expert in all sciences, including grammar and Arthashastra.[9] According to Rajaram Shastri Bhagvat, Katyayana flourished in the 4th century BC. He was a minister of the Nandas and had written a commentary on the *Ashtadhyai* of Panini.[10] He left the royal court when he saw

---

[8] Saletore, *Ancient Indian Political*, 48.
[9] Bhagvat, 2003, Vol. I, 72.
[10] Bhagvat, *Rajaramshastri Bhagavat*, Vol. II, 80.

water being sprinkled from high. He is mentioned in both the Arthashastra and the Mahabharata.[11] According to Jain sources, Katyayana was assassinated in the court.[12] Thus, Katyayana must be a great intellectual, expert in many disciplines, but we did not have information about him and his work on politics.

Bharadvaja was one of the most famous Arthashastra teachers of ancient India, whose ideas are often quoted in different books on politics. Normally, he is called Bharadvaja or Bharadwaja. He belonged to the *Bhrigu* family of Bharadvaja *gotra*. Dronacharya, a teacher of the Kauravas and the Pandavas, also belonged to Bharadvaja *gotra*. In the Mahabharata, Drona was called an expert in Arthashastras of Shukra and Brihaspati[13]; therefore, some commentators have identified him with Dronacharya.[14] However, it is difficult to agree with this view because the Mahabharata separately included two discourses of Kanika and Kaninka Bharadvaja. Similarly, he is considered one of the originators of the science of politics or *rajshastra*.[15] In the great epic, he is identified as Kanika, Kaninka and Bharadvaja, and in the Arthashastra he was called Kaninka Bharadvaja as well as Bharadvaja. Perhaps, these different names referred to the same person called Bharadvaja as there is a similarity in their ideas.[16]

In the Mahabharata, two discourses of Bharadvaja are found. The first discourse is delivered in the Adi Parva[17] of the great epic to king Dhritarashtra by his minister Kanika, which is called Kanika—Niti. This is not included in the text of the critical edition of the epic, but we have taken it as an authentic specimen of the Arthashastra thought. The second discourse is included in the Shantiparva,[18] where 'Muni' or sage Kaninka–Bharadvaja

---

[11] Dikshitar, 'Katyayana: A Jurist', 353–56.
[12] Bhagvat, *Saskriti Sanchit*, 86–87.
[13] The Mahabharata, 5-5.
[14] Bhandarkar, *The Carmaechel Lectures*, 93–94.
[15] The Mahabharata, 12.58-1-3.
[16] Kangle, 'Bharadvaja: An Ancient Indian', 333.
[17] Adiparva, 140, Mahabharata, 12.138.
[18] Ibid., 138.

delivered the address to the Sauvira king Shatruntapa. Kautilya has cited the opinions of Bharadvaja on several important issues. He was closer to *Lokayata* philosophy, as he advocated the efficacy of *artha* and *kama*. He was known for his cold-blooded realism and had represented the extreme tendencies of the Arthashastra tradition.

According to Professor Kosambi, Kalinga Bharadvaja, mentioned in the *Jataka* (No. 479)[19] is the same person as the Arthashastra teacher Kanika. Kalinga was a *purohita*, or royal priest, of the Kalinga king, and his advice was consistent with the Buddhist teaching, which was contrary to the ideas of Bharadvaja.[20] Therefore, it is difficult to believe that Kalinga Bharadvaja had anything to do with Kaninka Bharadvaja.

Dirgha Charayan was a Kshatriya minister of the king Presenjit of Kosala. He was a nephew of great Kosala general and minister Mahabandhula, who was treacherously killed along with his thirty-two sons on the orders of the king. However, Charayana continued to serve as a minister in Presenjit's ministry. Once Presenjit decided to meet Buddha and left his royal insignia with Charayan. Charayan handed it over to his aspiring son Vidudabha, who went back to the capital and, using the royal insignia, captured political power and declared himself the king of Kosala. The deposed king ran to Rajgriha to seek protection of his nephew Ajatshatru but before the opening of the gate, he died of cold.[21] In the *Bhaddasala Jataka* (No. 465) and in the Mahavagga (1.118.25), this story is narrated. Thus, Charayana took the revenge of his uncle's death. According to Dr Kosambi,

> The brief note from Charayana or Karayana is to be perhaps interpreted as 'even a bit of chaff is enough to show which way wind blows. Presumably, the remark was made when the minister was convinced that Presenjit meant to dispatch nephew like the uncle, and then took steps to get rid of the king first.[22]

[19] Bhagvat, *The Siddhartha Jataka*, 268.
[20] Kosambi, 'The Line of the Arthashastra', 161–78.
[21] Ibid., 263.
[22] Ibid., 264.

In other words, we can say that after seeing the unusual growth of grass where it should not have grown, he took it as a bad omen and left the court. Meanwhile, the king killed Mahabandhula and his 32 sons. Though Charayana was restored to the office, he used to move about condemning killing of his uncle.[23]

In the *Kama Sutra* of Vatsyayana, Dirgha Charayana was mentioned as one of the teachers of the *Kamashastra*. Charayana explained the first part of the *Kamashastra* or the science of erotics.[24] Vatsyayana quoted Charayana's views on different matters in verses 1.4.20 and 1.5.22 of the *Kama Sutra*.

Thus, Charayana was a scheming minister as well as an erudite expert of *Rajshastra* and *Kamashastra*, but we do not have any quotation of his political ideas.

Ghotamukha or Ghotaka Mukha was an Arthashastra teacher, and his nickname was Ghota Mukha, which meant one who had the horse's mouth. In the Mazzim Nikay, it is said that Ghotamukha was a Brahmin who denied existence of virtuous life[25] and was given a discourse by Udena. He constructed a hall at Pataliputra for the Buddha *bhikshu*s. Neelmani Chakravarti opines that he was a predecessor of Kautilya.[26] On Kautilya's testimony, he seemed to be a minister who left the court when he was offered wet clothes instead of the warm clothes which he expected. He thought that this was an indication of the displeasure of the king and departed.

Ghotamukha or Ghotaka Mukha was one of the teachers of erotics and, according to Vatsyayana, he composed the third part of the *Kamashastra*.[27] He quotes the opinions of Ghotamukha at four places, that is, in verses 1.1.14, 1-5-24, 3-13 and 3-1-10. According to him, a man should not marry any time he liked. His discourses were of general nature.

[23] Bhagvat, *The Siddhartha Jataka*, Vol. 4, 134.
[24] Vatsyayana, *The Kama Sutra*, 34.
[25] Bhagvat, *The Siddhartha Jataka*, 157.
[26] Chakravarti, 'Ghotakmukha: A Predecessor', 275.
[27] Vatsyayana, *The Kama Sutra*, 34.

Much information about Kinjalka does not exist, but according to Kautilya he left the royal court when the elephant sprinkled water on him. He thought that this was an unusual behaviour of the animal, which indicated a bad day for him in the kingdom. Hence, he left the court.

Similarly, we do not have much information about Pishuna and Pishunaputra, who left the court when the behaviour of the king's dog was unusual and hostile. Dr D. R. Bhandarkar observes that Pishuna was another name for Narada. In the *Sabha Parva* of the epic, Narada delivered a discourse on politics and he was considered an expert in Arthashastra. Bana, in his *Kadambari*, called Narada an expert on politics. Hence, Bhandarkar had likened him with Pishuna.[28] However, the relationship is tenuous because the Arthashastra of Narada in the Naradniti of the great epic represented the post-Kautilyan phase when it had synthesized and integrated the *Dharmashastra* influences in great detail.

Manu was one of the most famous political science teachers, and his views are quoted in the Arthashastra as well as in *Dharmashastra*s and the epics. There were fourteen Manus, as each Manu was chronologically distinct and consisted of four ages, such as Krita, Treta, Dvapara and Kali. Each age consisted of 10,000 years. Once an age completed 10,000 years, it was called 'Manvantar'. Swayambhav Manu separated dharma from other sciences and wrote *Dharmashastra*.[29] Prachetasa Manu wrote the Arthashastra, was a very famous exponent of the Arthashastra and there was a school named after him. Professor Kangle observes that the text of *Manava* Arthashastra must be existing in ancient times. Therefore, a large number of verses from it were quoted by various authorities.[30] According to him, the two Manus–Swayambhav and Prachetas—were different, whose ideas differed on many important issues.[31]

---

[28] Bhandarkar, *The Carmaechel Lectures*, 95–96.
[29] Vatsyayana, *The Kama Sutra*, 33.
[30] Kangle, *The Kautilya* Arthashastra, 42.
[31] Kangle, 'Manu and Kautilya', 48–54.

Kautilya refers to views of Parashara in the Arthashastra and observed that a school was developed after his ideas. He need not be confused with Parashara of the Parashara Smriti. However, his name is not included as one of the originators of the science of politics in the great epic. There is not much information available about him.

Shukra is considered one of the promulgators of the science, and Kautilya saluted him along with Brihaspati. In the great epic also, he is considered the originator of the Arthashastra. He was called Ushanasa as well as *kavya* or son of Kavi. He was considered the royal priest of the *daitya*s or demons. His name could be traced back to the Rig Veda. A school was named after Ushanasa, which was called Aushanasa; his views on science are quoted by Kautilya, the Mahabharata and other authorities. He was a political scientist who came from the family of royal priests. In the Rig Veda, Indra was called a friend of Ushanasa.[32] It was said the *Angirasa* first won power, which was followed by Ushanasa.[33] Kavya Ushanasa gave weapon to slay Vritra.[34] Ushanasa belonged to the Bhargava clan. Kavya was called the strengthener.[35] Thus, Shukra was a priest who helped his supporters and disciples to win wars.

Shukra's science of politics was the most famous, verses from which are often cited. The later work, the *Shukra Nitisara*, attributed to Shukra was perhaps written in the 18th or 19th century; hence, it could not be considered the authentic version of the political ideas of Shukra.

Along with Shukra, Brihaspati was called the originator of the science and was saluted for the same. The Mahabharata (12-395) said that it was Shukra and Brihaspati who separated Arthashastra from *Dharmashastra*. This view was corroborated by Vatsyayana, who said that Brihaspati separated *Artha* from

---

[32] Griffith (1989), 34.
[33] Ibid., 52.
[34] Ibid., 83.
[35] Ibid., 297.

dharma. He was considered the founder of *Lokayata* philosophy, who held radical views on many subjects, only because of which there was a close identification between the two.

Brihaspati belonged to the family of the Angirasas who developed expertise in the *Angira* aspects of the Atharva Veda. With the support of priestly craft of Brihaspati, the gods won many battles against enemies. Hymns in the Rig Veda admired the intellectual powers of Brihaspati. It said that Brihaspati punished the spiteful and his mantras were as sharp as the arrows of a hunter.[36] In the Rig Veda, he was admired as follows: 'With thee as our own rich and liberal ally, may we, Brihaspati, gain highest power of life. Let not the guileful wicked man be lord of us still we may prosper singing goodly hymns of praise!'[37] He was called consumer of foes and victorious in the strife.[38]

Brihaspati was the author of Arthashastra, and his views were often cited in the Arthashastra. In the great epic, there are several discourses attributed to Brihashati. His Arthashastra was written in the verses. It is rightly pointed out by Professor Kangle:

> It would be unreasonable to suppose that Brihaspati and Ushanasa were real persons who served as *purohita*s to some kings and instructed them in the art of government and regular instruction in this art was unknown before their time. Even if we suppose, however, that Brihaspati and Ushanasa were purely mythical beings and cannot be regarded as historical personages, there can be no denying that these two names were very closely associated with the founding of this *shastra* since very early times.[39]

Vishalakasha was considered as one of the seven originators of science, and according to the epic, he played a key role in the evolution of science.[40] His views are often quoted in the Kautilya's

---

[36] Ibid., 127.
[37] Griffith, *The Hymns of the Rig Veda*, 145.
[38] Ibid., 146.
[39] Kangle, *The Kautilya* Arthashastra, 7–8.
[40] Ibid., 12–59.

Arthashastra, as well as in other science books. The Mahabharata states that Vishalaksha was the other name of Shankara. One can say that it was a nickname. His name was also referred to in the inscriptions of Cambodia.[41] He must have written the text of political science which was used by the people.[42] Therefore, his ideas were quoted in distant places such as Cambodia.

Bahudantaka or Bahudantiputra is an Arthashastra teacher whose views are cited both in the Arthashastra of Kautilya and the great epic. According to the Mahabharata, Bahudantaka was another name for Indra,[43] and Indra or Mahendra was considered one of the originators of the *Shastra*. Bhandarkar states that Bahudantin was a nickname for Indra. Indra's elephant, Airavat, had four tusks; hence, it was called Bahudanta. Because Indra owned it, he was called Bahudantin, and the science composed by him was called Bahudantaka. Bahudantiputra meant Indra's follower.[44] Some scholars opine Bahudantin was a nickname as it showed physical character of persons such as Potthapada, Digha Nakha, Vishalaksha, Kaunapadanta and Vatavyadhi. Hence, Bahudantin meant a person who had large and protruding teeth like hands![45]

These were two important thinkers whose views had been cited by Kautilya in his Arthashastra. The Mahabharata does not refer to their views. According to Dr Bhandarkar, the commentators were of the view that Kaunapadanta meant one whose father had stinking and decayed teeth. It was Shantanu, father of Bhishma, who had decayed teeth. Bhishma was considered an expert in the science of politics, and his discourses in the Shantiparva bore witness to his ability as a teacher of the *shastra*. However, according to Professor Kangle, on the basis of this fact, one could not suppose that the *Shanti Parva* contained his original ideas. The

---

[41] Sahai, 'Rajyashastra in Ancient Cambodia', 151–63.
[42] Kane, 'Rajshastras of Brihaspati', 270.
[43] The Mahabharata, 12-59.
[44] Bhandarkar, *The Carmaechel Lectures*, 94–95.
[45] Kangle, *The Kautilya* Arthashastra, 47.

opinions attributed to Kaunapadanta in the Arthashastra cannot be traced in the Mahabharata.[46]

Vatavyadhi's views are cited by Kautilya, and Vatavyadhi meant the one who was suffering from acidity and gases. He must be occasionally farting, hence this nickname. According to commentators, this was the nickname for Uddhava, who was one of the closest advisers of Shri Krishna. The Sabhaparva of the great epic stated that Uddhava was appointed as one of the ministers in the government of *Andhaka-Vrishni Samgha*. He was a warrior minister and expert in science of politics. Uddhav is more famous for his spiritualism and devotion. It was Uddhava who advised the use of the powers of Bhimsen to kill Jarasandha in a single combat to avoid a great loss of life in the battle.[47] Kautilya has quoted opinions of Vatavyadhi but no separate text of his ideas was found.

Gaurishiras was the seventh teacher of political science mentioned by the great epic as the originator of the *Rajshastra*. His views are not cited either in the Mahabharata or in the Arthashastra.

Jabala was a Brahmin minister of king Dasharatha. He continued to work in the council of Bharata also. He had delivered a discourse on politics to Rama requesting him to accept the offer of Bharata as he was in exile. Jabala was an Arthashastra teacher trained in the science of politics as well as in the philosophy of *Lokayata*.[48]

Arthashastra teachers are mentioned in the Buddhist literature. In the *Digha Nikaya*,[49] there is *Potthaapada Sutra*, in which the Arthashastra teacher Potthapada and his assembly are described. In *Mahabodhi Jataka* (No. 528), a *Kshatra Vidya Vadi* minister believed that this world was real, and it was held together by the weapons and physical power and, if necessary, we must kill our

---

[46] Ibid., 47–48.
[47] Menon, *Krishna: Life and the Song*, 210.
[48] Ram II, Ayodhakand, 2007), 108.
[49] *Digha Nikaya*, Vol. I, 107.

parents to safeguard our interests.⁵⁰ In the *Mahaumagga Jataka* (No. 546), the king said that by whatever means—modest or extreme—we should protect ourselves and then pursue dharma.⁵¹ In the *Bhooridatta Jataka*,⁵² the *trayi* and *kshatra vidya* were compared, and the Bodhisatva said that both of them were identical in their viewpoint because their meanings were not clear, and out of self-interest, they blindly pursued the object. As far as their benefits and losses were concerned, they equally adversely affected all the castes, including the Brahmins.⁵³

Thus, the Buddhists did not hold the *kshatravidya Vadi* ministers or *purohita*s in high esteem as they held that *kshatravidya* was the science of low type and it held self-interest and success in the worldly affairs more important.

It seems that most of the teachers of political science assumed nicknames that indicated their peculiar physical characteristics. They assumed names such as Vishalaksha, Kaunapadanta, Bahudantaka, Vatavyadhi, Pishuna, Potthapada, Dighanakha and several others. Even Kautilya could be a nickname. According to Professor B. M. Barua, '(these) Brahmin wanderers were known to their contemporaries generally by some nicknames. Let us consider for instance the names Potthapada, Uggamana, Deeghanakha—by the nicknames we trace some of the teachers whose views are quoted and discussed in Kautilya's Arthashastra'.⁵⁴ According to Professor A. D. Pant

> one likely reason why these nicknames came to be given appeared to their contemporaries as unconventional, therefore, strange in dress, in manners and also in their ideas. The occurrence in the Arthashastra of some of these names, which we also come across in the early Buddhist canonical literature, certainly cannot be considered mere accidental.⁵⁵

⁵⁰ Bhagvat, *The Siddhartha Jataka*, Vol. 5, 171, 180.
⁵¹ Ibid., Vol. 6, 324.
⁵² Ibid., 543.
⁵³ Ibid., Vol. 6, 180–81.
⁵⁴ Barua, *A History of Pre-Buddhist*, 351.
⁵⁵ Pant, *An Introduction to Theory*, xxxviii.

Thus, the teachers, including Kautilya, assumed these names to indicate their unconventional ideas as well as their distinctiveness as free thinkers.

Thus, in this chapter, we have briefly discussed biographical details of some of the Arthashastra teachers and, in the next chapter, we shall discuss their political ideas.

Bibliography

Barua, B. M. *A History of Pre-Buddhist Indian Philosophy*. Calcutta: University of Calcutta, 1918.
Bhagvat, D. *The Siddhartha Jataka* (Marathi). Vols. 1–6. Pune: Varada Books, 1980–81.
———. *Saskriti Sanchit*. Mumbai: Shabala, 2015.
Bhagvat, R. R. *Rajaramshastri Bhagavat Yanche Lekh* (Marathi). Vol. 2, edited by Bhagvat D. Pune: Varada Books, 1979.
Bhandarkar, D. R. *The Carmaechel Lectures on Ancient History of India*. Calcutta: University of Calcutta, 1918.
Chakravarti, Neelmani. 'Ghotakmukha: A Predecessor to Kautilya and Vatsyayana'. *Journal of Royal Asiatic Society of Bengal* (1930): 275.
Davids, Rhys, ed. *The Buddhist Vinaya Texts*. Part I, Vol. 13. In *The Sacred Books of the East*. Delhi: Motilal Banarsidass, 2008.
Dikshitar, V. R. R. 'Katyayana: A Jurist'. *Indian Historical Quarterly* 11 (1935): 313–16.
Griffith, R. T. H. *The Hymns of the Rig Veda*. Delhi: Motilal Banarsidass, 2004.
Jayaswal, K. P. *The Hindu Polity*. Bangalore: The Bangalore Printing & Publishing, 1955.
Kane, P. V. 'Rajshastras of Brihaspati, Ushanasa, Bharadvaja and Vishalaksha'. *Journal of University of Bombay* 2 (1942): 79–80.
Kane, P. V., 'The Meaning of the 'Acharyah', Annals of Bhanderkar oriented Research Institute, Vol. 23, 1942, pp. 207–13.
Kangle, R. P. 'Bharadvaja: An Ancient Indian Teacher of Political Science'. *Bharatiya Vidya* 20–21 (1961): 330–36.
———. 'Manu and Kautilya'. *Indian Antiquary* 1 (1964): 48–54.
———. *The Kautilya* Arthashastra, Part III. Bombay: University of Bombay, 1965.
Kosambi, D. D. 'The Line of the Arthashastra Teachers'. In *Combined Methods in Indology and Other Writings*, edited by B. D. Chattopadhyay, 260–78. Delhi: Oxford University Press, 2007.

Law, B. C. 'A Short Account of Wandering Teachers at the Time of Buddha'. *Journal of Royal Asiatic Society of Bengal* 14 (1918): 229–30.

Menon, Ramesh. *Krishna: Life and the Song of Blue God*. Delhi: Rupa and Co., 2009.

Pant, A. D. *An Introduction to Theory of Government in Ancient India by Beni Prasad*. Allahabad: Central Book Depot, 1968.

Sahai, Sacchidanand. 'Rajyashastra in Ancient Cambodia'. *Vishveshvarand Indological Journal* 9 (1971): 151–63.

Saletore, B. A. *Ancient Indian Political Thought and Institutions*. Bombay: Asia, 1971.

Vatsyayana. *The Kama Sutra*, edited by R. Burton. Mumbai: Jaico, 2009.

7

Political Thought of Early Arthashastra Thinkers

In Chapter 6, we have studied biographical details of some of the Arthashastra teachers. In this chapter, we shall study political ideas of major teachers that are found mainly in the Kautilya Arthashastra, the great epic and the Ramayana. In this chapter, we shall discuss (a) political ideas of major Arthashastra teachers and (b) two dialogues of Jabala and a *Barhaspatya* Brahmin and the *Kootdanta Sutra* of the *Digha Nikaya*.

As we have seen, it was Prachetasa Manu who wrote a book on the Arthashastra. In the Arthashastra as well as in the great epic, his views have been cited. The following are the opinions of the school of Manu cited by Kautilya:

1. According to the followers of Manu, three Vedas, *varta* and *dandaniti* are the only three sciences, as *Anvikshiki* or philosophy was the branch of three Vedas.[1]
2. 'There should be 12 ministers in his council of ministers'.[2]
3. 'Among the causes of loss of revenue, the fine is as much as loss of money increased by one fold in the each succeeding cases, according to the order dated above'.[3]

---

[1] The Arthashastra, 1.2.3-5.
[2] Ibid., 1.15.47.
[3] Ibid., 2.7.11.

4. 'The false witness who bring into being a non-existing thing or ruin an existing thing shall pay ten times that thing'.[4]
5. 'In case of forcible seizure of Jewels, articles of high value, of low value and foreign produce, the fine shall be equal to their value'.[5]

Manu omits the study of philosophy as he thinks that it is a part of the discipline of theology or three Vedas. This clearly shows his ideological bias as perhaps he does not want to include non-Vedic philosophy like *Lokayata* in the curriculum of the king.

In the Ramayana, two verses of Manu are quoted, in which he said that if a particular person had committed sin and if he had been rightly punished for the same by the king, both the king and the sinner had expiated the sin and gone to heaven. However, on the other hand, 'if the king did not punish the sinner due to negligence, he invited the sin of the sinner'.[6] Here, Manu is supporting the *Shankha-Likhita Nyaya* of the *Smritis*.[7]

In the Mahabharata, the opinions of Manu are quoted at several places.

In the Adiparva of the great epic, Manu's ideas are cited. He said, 'A person who looked after well-being of the people, and especially if the person is the king, he is greater in merit than 10 Brahmins who were well-versed the Vedas'.[8] In the Aranyaka Parva, both Draupadi and Bhima cited the opinion of Manu. Draupadi said that it is the opinion of Manu that human beings should constantly exert.[9] Bhima referred to *Rajshastra* of Manu.[10] The following are the quotations from the Shantiparva:

---

[4] Ibid., 3.11.46.
[5] Ibid., 3.17.35.
[6] The Ramayana, 1986, Vol. II, 56, 84–85.
[7] The Mahabharatha, 12–24.
[8] Ibid., 1.41.
[9] Ibid., 3.33.
[10] Ibid., 3.34.

1. The king who has vowed to follow Dharma should punish the person trained in the Vedas, if he opposed him on the battle ground. He really understood the essence of Dharma who protected it. While doing so he is not transgressing principles of Dharma because here anger is destroying anger.[11]
2. The fire is derived from water, Kshatriyas from Brahmins and the iron from rock. All the three are full of energy and they get absorbed in the place of their origin. But due to lust and avarice, if fire began hitting water, iron began hitting rock, the Kshatriya started hitting Brahmana, fire, Kshatriya and rock got destroyed.[12]
3. You have to abandon leaky boat when you are travelling in the sea. Similarly the man should abandon the *purohita*, who did not study the scriptures, the king who did not protect and the wife who did not speak sweet words, cowherd who wanted to go in the town and the barber who loved to stay in the jungle.[13]
4. It is with intelligence that the victories are won, the achievements secured through knowledge are of superior nature, that of force of the arms is of middle nature and through the pedestrian efforts is of lower nature. If we had to personally strive hard to achieve it, it is of the lowest order. The king who is committed to his duty and who had achieved self-control could only maintain his kingdom. The king who wanted to secure more wealth could do so with the help of intelligence only.[14]
5. Everything depends upon *Danda*. *Danda* kept constant vigil on the people who were appreciated or not appreciated and when it is properly employed, it protects the people. Hence, it is called Dharma.[15]
6. One should fight war righteously. Injured enemy shouldn't be killed. Ultimately Dharma resides in the heart of good men.[16]
7. If the king used *Danda* with non-violence there would be intermixing. *Danda* has to be used to protect truth, keeping

---

[11] The Mahabharata, 12.55.16–17.
[12] Ibid., 12.56.23.24.
[13] Ibid., 12-57-43-45.
[14] Ibid., 12.113–17.
[15] Ibid., 12.121.9–10.
[16] Ibid., 12-96-13-14.

in view consideration of one's own life, strength and time. It is stated by Swayambhav Manu that if we take recourse to this policy, we do not abandon the cause of *Dharma*.[17]

8. Vyavahara' (Judicial transactions) are so called because it is a means of protection of the kingdom of the duty conscious and the cautious king. It is Dharma which carefully controls behavior of the people whether they are loved ones or not and *Danda* has to be employed to ensure justice and protection of the people.[18]

These are some of the stray ideas from the *Rajshastra* of Manu, which was a very famous text on politics. These ideas clearly showed that he was ideologically very close to *Dharmashastra* tradition. The following are some of the important ideas of Manu:

1. Philosophy had no independent existence as it was the part of the Vedas.
2. There had to be a close alliance between the Brahmins and the Kshatriyas, as the Kshatriyas were dependent on the Brahmins.
3. It is the right of the king to punish the guilty, and by exercise of that right, both the king and the guilty would get expiated. This was consistent with the *Shankha-Likhita Nyaya* of *Dharmashastra* tradition.
4. Manu does not seem to be agreeing with amoral realism of other Arthashastra teachers as he valued truth and dharma. Hence, he would agree with Manu of the *Manusmriti* that, 'What is given by force, enjoyed by force and what is written by force; indeed all matters that are done by force, Manu has declared to be undone'.[19] The Mahabharata does not make proper distinction between Prachetasa and Swayambhav Manu, as both names are used interchangeably. According to Professor Kangle, in the matter of punishment, the followers of Manu appeared to have been more

---

[17] Ibid., 12-259 34-35.
[18] Ibid., 12-121-8-10.
[19] 86–168.

moderate and reasonable.[20] There are a number of identical quotations in the Mahabharata and the *Manusmriti,* and Dr U. N. Ghoshal stated that probably both of them borrowed these verses from a common Arthashastra source.[21]

Political Thought of Shukra

Along with Brihaspati, Shukra is considered one of the originators of the Arthashastra.[22] Kautilya saluted him. He was born in the *Bhrigu gotra* and was a royal chaplain of the *asura* kings like Prarhad, Virochana and Bali. In the Arthashastra and the great epic, several of his ideas are quoted. First, we shall discuss his ideas as cited in the Arthashastra.

1. Discussing the comparative importance of four sciences, the followers of Ushanas say that *'Dandaniti* or science of politics is the only science, for, with that it is bound up all undertakings connected with all sciences.'[23]
2. The king should appoint twenty ministers in his council of ministers.[24]
3. 'Among those cases of loss of revenue the fine should be as much twenty times of the loss of money.'[25]
4. 'In case of divergent replies to questions through the folly of witnesses themselves, they should be fined the lowest, middle most and the highest fines with regard to testimony about time, place and the matter respectively.'[26]
5. 'In case of forcible seizure of jewels, articles of high value or low value and the forest produce, the fine should be the double the value.'[27]

---

[20] Kangle, *The Kautilya* Arthashastra, Vol. III, 64.
[21] Ghoshal, *A History of Indian Political Ideas,* 86.
[22] The Mahabharata, 3–150.
[23] The Arthashastra, 1-2.7-8.
[24] Ibid., 1-15-49.
[25] Ibid., 2-7.14.
[26] Ibid., 3-11-44.
[27] Ibid., 3.17.4.

6. 'Among the sons of the same wife, share is to be given in the form of animals. In the absence of animals, the eldest shall receive one part of every ten articles with the exception of Jewels. For he has fetters of duty of offering oblations in the manes tied around him.'[28]
7. 'Regarding the arrangement of the battle array, there should be two wings—a center and reserve.'[29]

The Mahabharata and several texts referred to Shukra as a thinker. His greatness is recognized by Krishna, who in his Bhagavad Geeta declared in the tenth chapter that he was Shukra among 'Kavis' or thinkers.[30]

The following quotations are cited in the Mahabharata from the *Rajshastra* of Shukra:

1. 'Enmity of the powerful is dangerous'.[31]
2. 'To protect a family a person should be shunned, to protect a village, a family could be abandoned and to protect country a village could be abandoned'.[32]
3. 'The king who cares for growth of Dharma should kill a person who is well versed in the Vedas if he has attacked him in the battlefield. A person who protects Dharma really knows what it is. By killing a person who harms the cause of Dharma a king doesn't commit sin'.[33]
4. 'A king who does not exert is devoured by the enemy king as a rat sleeping in his hole is devoured by the snake. The king who didn't oppose enemy and a Brahmin who did not travel is destroyed'.[34]

---

[28] Ibid., 3-6-1-5.
[29] Ibid., 10.6.1.
[30] The Bhagavad Geeta, 10.37.
[31] Ibid., 2.55-10-11.
[32] Ibid., 2.55-10-11 and 5-39-16-17.
[33] Ibid., 12–56, 23–25.
[34] Ibid., 12-57-2-3.

5. 'One should first secure a king, and wife and wealth in train. If there is no king to rule over the world, whence can there be a wife and wealth?'[35]
6. 'One should be afraid of remnants a hostile army which turned back to fight though broken which desires to take life since they are bent upon one object only.'[36]
7. 'As regards a purpose which is common to a king and his powerful enemy, the former may enter in to an alliance with stronger, act with care and stratagem and after the purpose is carried out, he may not repose too much trust in him. We should not trust one who does not trust us and not to trust one who has trust in us. We should see to it that others trust us but are as not trust them.'[37]
8. 'He who trusts words of the enemy meets the destruction like the people who fell down from mountain mistaking honey for dry grass.'[38]
9. 'Shukra told the *Asuras* that knowledge which does not remove doubt is no knowledge. The knowledge which is tested on the criterion of reason is true knowledge.'[39]
10. 'At the time of emergency, the king should exterminate his enemies and protect the good people.'[40]
11. 'The enemy once defeated but ready to fight could return to war with renewed vigour, even though small in number, is dangerous because due to annihilation of their kith and kin, they single-mindedly fight to take revenge. Hence, they should be taken seriously.'[41]

Thus, Shukra's political ideas were a part of political discourse in India and perhaps due to their realism and rationalism, they were

[35] Ibid., 12-57-41.
[36] Ibid., 12-138-68.
[37] Ibid., 12.136.184-87.
[38] Ibid., 12-137-66-67.
[39] Ibid., 12-140-22-23.
[40] Ibid., 12.140-33.
[41] Ibid., 9-57.12-13.

not carefully heard.[42] Shukra gave importance to the state, and Somdeva Suri who wrote a text called '*Nitivakyamrita*' saluted the state instead of Jain Teerthankaras because it facilitated pursuit of dharma and *artha*. Why did he salute the state? The commentator explained: 'The *Barhaspatya* and the *Aushanasa shastras* are the main authorities of Somedeva and Brihaspati had saluted "Muni" and Shukra had saluted the state. While opening the text, the *Aushanasa shastra* said, 'नमो स्तु राज्यवृक्षाय षाडगुण्याय प्रशाखिते! सामादि चारूपुष्पाय, त्रिवर्ग फलदायिनी:'. Salute to the state (tree) which had branches of six expedients of foreign policy and four devices like conciliation as flowers, and its pursuit accrues fruits in the form of *trivargra*: dharma, *artha* and *kama*.[43]

Shukra was a radical thinker who held that *Dandaniti* is the only science that should be studied, as all the sciences are parts of *Dandaniti* and its pursuit included all undertakings in the world. Thus, he not only valued politics but also state as it facilitated the pursuit of dharma and *artha*. Although Shukra was not considered a follower of materialistic philosophy of *Lokayata* such as Brihaspati but their ideologies seemed to be identical, as both of them were hard realists and rationalists and rejected the Vedic dogma. They held pursuit of *artha* and *Kama Purushartha*s most important. He held that politics was the most important science, and operations of all sciences were part of it. The other sciences (according to Shankararya, commentator of *Kamandaki Nitisara*[44]) are like the spokes in the nave of a chariot wheel. According to Dr Ghoshal, 'Politics, according this ultra-political school was master science providing key to all sciences'.[45] According to him, 'this constituted the land mark in the history of Indian political thought, for, they mark a fresh instance of early application of the spirit of rationalism to politics'.[46] Apart from

---

[42] Ibid., 2–66, 7–8.
[43] Jayaswal, *The Hindu Polity*, 10.
[44] The Mahabharata, 111.5.
[45] Ghoshal, *A History*, 84.
[46] Ibid., 84.

above-mentioned facts, the following are some key principles of his political ideas:

1. Knowledge has to be tested on the crucible of reason, and one-sided morality was no good.
2. Self-preservation is the fundamental principle of human life, and interest of the state should be the key element while taking decisions.
3. The king should not trust his enemies because trusting untrustworthy person may prove fatal to him. The best policy is not to trust anyone.
4. The king should not ignore the remnants of defeated army, as it could bounce back and destroy the unwary king.

Shukra's *Rajshastra* was popular and it is the opinion of Soma Dev that he was the originator of the Mandala theory but he had not given any evidence to prove it.[47] He was greatly respected for his erudition; hence, he was called 'Bhagvan'. No other political scientist enjoyed this much respect.

The school of Parashara was one of the ancient schools of political science, and in the Arthashastra, its views have been cited at six places. However, the great epic does not make mention of his ideas, though there is a long dialogue on the issues of social order and spiritualism with king Janaka. He is not included as one of the originators of science.

The following are some his ideas:

1. Regarding the appointment of ministers, Bharadvaja said that he should appoint his fellow students as ministers, and Vishalaksha said that he should make people like his own nature ministers. Opposing this, Parashara said,

   > Defect of divulgence of secrets is common to both. For through the fear that they too are conversant with his

[47] Ibid., 94.

secrets, he would acquire in what they do and what they omit to do. To as many people the lord of men communicates a secret; to so many does he become subservient, being helpless by that act of his. He should make those of his ministers who may have helped him in calamities involving danger to his life, since their loyalty is thus proved.[48]

2. While refuting the argument of Vishalaksha regarding keeping of counsel, who said that he should listen to the opinion of everyone, Parashara said,

> This is the ascertainment of counsel, and not guarding of counsel, He should ask councilors concerning the matter exactly similar to the undertaking he has in mind, 'this work was done like this', or if it were to happen like this, how then should it be done. As they might advise, so should he do that work. In this way is the counsel ascertained and secrecy maintained at the same time.[49]

3. Vishalaksha said that the royal princes should be kept confined in one place. But the Parasharas said, 'This is the danger as from the snake, for, the prince realizing that through the fear of my valour my father has confined me might get himself in his power. Therefore, making him stay in the frontier province is the best'.[50]

4. 'Among the cause of the loss of revenue, the fine should be eight times as much as the loss'.[51]

5. On calamities, he said,

> Of the calamities befalling the country and the fort, calamity of the fort was more serious says the school of the Parashara. For, it is the fort that the treasury and the army spring up and a place (secured) for the country people in times of trouble and city dwellers are stronger than the country people and being steadfast (in loyalty) are helpful

[48] The Arthashastra, 1.8.7.10.
[49] Ibid., 1.15.23.26.
[50] Ibid., 1.17-9-11.
[51] Ibid., 2-7-12.

to the king in times of trouble. Country people on the other hand are common to the enemy.[52]

6. 'As between the violation of property and physical injury, violation of property is worse, for spiritual good (Dharma) and pleasure (Kama) are rooted in money (Artha). Its destruction is a greater evil'.[53]

In the Shantiparva, Parashara makes some observation about politics. It is his opinion that the king who did not protect his subjects and plunders his cows is worse than a thief.[54] He exhorted the king to follow dharma and avoid violence.[55]

According to Professor Kangle, Parashara was of later origin than Shukra or Brihaspati. His ideas were cited by Kautilya in a series of arguments, when one authority rejected the views of other authorities and finally Kautilya reconciliated their ideas.[56] Parashara had a keen mind and he made three observations:

1. He asked the king to appoint such persons as ministers who had helped him at the time of distress.
2. He did not favour confinement of the prince and advised king to keep him confined in the frontier fortress.
3. Calamities befalling the fort (i.e., the capital city) were more dangerous because it was the city dwellers who helped the king in times of distress as the country people (*Janapada*) might switch loyalty when there was calamity.

In the Arthashastra, there is one quotation of Ambhies which is regarding the treatment to be meted out to the prince. They say, 'And one of the secret agents should tempt him with hunting, gambling, wine and women (suggesting to him) attack your father

---

[52] Ibid., 8.1.24-27.
[53] Ibid., 8-3-30-32.
[54] The Mahabharata, 12-282-8-9.
[55] Ibid., 12-283-23-25.
[56] Kangle, *The Kautilya* Arthashastra, 43.

and seize the kingdom. Another secret agent should dissuade him from doing that'.⁵⁷

Along with Shukra, Brihaspati is considered one of originators of the science of politics. He was a royal chaplain of gods and was born in the famous *Angirasa* family. He was considered the exponent of *Lokayata* philosophy, which was also known as 'Barhaspatya Mata.' We have citations of Brihaspati's opinions six times in the Kautilya's Arthashastra, and there are several quotations and three discourses of Brihaspati on the science of politics in the Mahabharata.

The following are statements in the Kautilya's Arthashastra.

1. According the followers of Brihaspati, '*Varta* and *Dandaniti* are only two sciences, for, the Vedic lore is only a cloak for one conversant with the ways of the world'.⁵⁸
2. 'The strength of the ministers in the council should be 16'.⁵⁹
3. 'For the loss of revenue, the compensation ten times that of loss of money should be realised'.⁶⁰
4. 'In case of divergent replies for a question through the folly of the witnesses themselves, and if the folly led to wrong Judgment death by the torture should be the penalty!'.⁶¹
5. 'He who causes others to commit act of force, saying, "I accept the responsibility" shall pay the money as stated as well as fine'.⁶²
6. Regarding arranging of counter arrays, there should be two wings, two flanks, a centre and a wing.⁶³

In the Mahabharata, there are a number of quotations of Brihaspati, and they are as follows:

⁵⁷ The Arthashastra, 1.17.28.29.
⁵⁸ Ibid., 1.24.5.
⁵⁹ Ibid., 1.15.48.
⁶⁰ Ibid., 2.17.13.
⁶¹ Ibid., 3.11.47.
⁶² Ibid., 3.7.13.
⁶³ Ibid., 10.6.2.

1. 'There is bound to be a difference between the royal behavior and the behavior of the ordinary people. Therefore, the king should continuously seek his own self-interest. He should not think about moral or immoral nature of the action as he had to secure victory in the war.'[64]
2. 'We should take help of war or peace to tackle the enemy who wanted to act against our interests.'[65]
3. 'Good wishes of gods, intelligence of the wise, humility of the learned and destruction of the sinners is the essence of the policy.'[66]
4. 'The king should start a war against enemy when he had confirmed himself that the enemy's strength is 1/3 less than his own.'[67]
5. 'One should kill a person even if he is his teacher if he is working against the seven constituent elements of the state.'[68]
6. 'The king should exert because with the help of exertion only, Amrita was won, demons were defeated and lordship was secured by Indra. Like a snake bereft of its poison, a king devoid of exertion, even if intelligent, becomes constantly vulnerable to enemy's attack.'[69]
7. 'The wise king should avoid the expedient of war and use three other expedients to attain his goal.'[70]
8. 'As the snake swallows the rats sleeping in its hole, the earth swallows these two: a Brahmin who does not want to go on journey and the king who does not want to exert.'[71]
9. 'Having performed the work of protecting his subjects, the king easily prospers in the next world. Of what use is of penance to the king or of what use are even sacrifices to

---

[64] The Mahabharata, 2.50-13-14.
[65] Ibid., 2-66.7-8.
[66] Ibid., 5.38.69.
[67] Ibid., 5-54.62-63.
[68] Ibid., 12.57.5-6.
[69] Ibid., 12-58-13-16.
[70] Ibid., 12.69.22.23.
[71] Ibid., 12-23-16.

him, who has well-guarded his subjects. He is sure to be the one who knows his Dharma.'[72]
10. 'Canon as well as human reason should be used to find out true nature of Dharma.'[73]
11. 'If the king continues to tolerate the offences of the people, then the people of inferior quality would also insult him and would nurse desire to mount on the head of the king like that of the mahout of an elephant.'[74]

Apart from these 11 verses, there are three dialogues of Brihaspati. The first is between Brihaspati and Vasumana.[75] The second is between Brihaspati and Indra[76] and the third is again between Brihaspati and Indra.[77] These discourses were perhaps borrowed from the *Rajshastra* of Brihaspati. According to Dr Kane,

> The *Rajashastra* of Brihaspati was a work in the mixed prose and verse like the Arthashastra of Kautilya, it embraced all the topics that fall to be treated under the Rajdharma and it was one of the most popular works on the Rajdharma in the time of the Mahabharata and several centuries afterwards.[78]

According to Jayaswal, the commentator of the Nitivakyamrita quotes a verse from the *Barshaspatya Shastra*. It says:

वाचा कायेन मनसा प्रणम्य शिरसां मुनीं ।
नीतिशास्त्रं प्रवक्ष्यामि भूपतिनां सुखावहः ॥

The author praises his teacher muni *Angirasa* and says that he has composed this work on the *niti* for the benefit of the kings.[79]

---

[72] Ibid., 12.69.70-71.
[73] Ibid., 12-140-16-17.
[74] Ibid., 12.56.38.9.
[75] Ibid., 12–68.
[76] Ibid., 12–85.
[77] Ibid., 12–104.
[78] Kane, *Rajshastras of* ..., 73.
[79] Jayaswal, *The Hindu Polity*, 11.

In his book, Shukra saluted the state but Brihaspati saluted his teacher.

In the first dialogue in the Shantiparva, Brihaspati discusses the problem of divinity of the king as well as need of the state. This was called 'ancient dialogue' by Bhishma who facilitated the discussion.

Brihaspati was responding to a question posed by king Vasumana that why the king is called divine by Brahmins? In his reply, Brihaspati returned to the original theme of the Arthashastra tradition, which held that it was due to fear of the king that the people did not annihilate each other. Dharma that was observed by the people was rooted in the king. If there was no state, the strong would devour the weak and destroy order in the society. There would prevail logic of fish and in the absence of *Danda*, fish in the water would fly in the air like birds and destroy each other.[80] In the absence of king, the people would be reduced to rudderless ship or there would be sheep without shepherd. If there is no *Danda*, the strong would take away the property, wives and cattle of the weak. If the latter opposed the abduction, they would be kicked. It is because of the king that the people slept in the night without worry. The state came into existence to check the strong and to protect the weak. Hence, the king was called *raja, bhoj, virat, samrat, kshatriya, bhoopati and nripa*.[81] He represented the mature understanding of the people. With the help of the king only, the people could afford to live good life. The king assumed forms of different gods to punish the persons who worked against the country and people.

This dialogue forms the central theme of the ancient Indian concept of *Dandaniti*, which maintained that due to establishment of kingship only, the law of nature was prevented, the logic of fish overcome and order in the society established. No civilized life was possible without state, and because of that only

[80] 12.68.11.13.
[81] 12.68.54.

the king was considered god by the people on the earth as the king assumed the sovereign power (*Eishvarya*).

In the second dialogue, which took place between Indra and Brihaspati,[82] the importance of expedient of *Sama* or conciliation is emphasized. Brihasapti told Indra that he should always use the method of conciliation, and it was the expedient in which all qualities existed. The king who employed this method was appreciated by the people. Even for the use of the method of *Dana* or bribery, the method of conciliation was needed. At the time of collection of taxes, the king could moderate its impact by speaking sweet words. Even the method of force could be used by applying the method of conciliation simultaneously.[83]

The third dialogue also took place between Brihaspati and Indra in which the former told the latter that he should use all the four expedients intelligently as he had to use them in a peculiar political situation. He should not trust his enemy and wait for a right opportunity to defeat him. He should continuously increase his strength and should not start hostilities with the enemy. When the enemy was more powerful than him, he should behave with him with at most humility, but in his heart's heart, he should nurse hostility. There should be no overt display of hostility. He should not get involved in acts like assassination because that brought bad name to him. He should wait for the right opportunity to defeat his enemy. It is always difficult to predict the outcome of war, but valour and strength tilted the balance in favour of the industrious person. He should use his expert ministers to break the secrets of the enemy. He should not destroy the food grains and not to mix poison in the rivers and water sources. He should use different secret methods to defeat his enemy but should not do it openly because that would adversely affect his reputation. He could use different magical formulae through the experts to harm his enemy![84]

---

[82] 12-85.
[83] The Mahabharata, 12-85-8-10.
[84] Ibid., 12-104-38-44.

Brihaspati's teachings are consistent with the amoral realism of the Arthashastra tradition in which the no foul means advocated, it was advised to defeat the enemy by all means at his disposal. But the golden rule is that you should use the cruel methods but the people should feel that you are not doing so. He also wanted the king to use the various 'Abhicharas' prescribed by the Atharva Veda against the enemy king as he belonged to the house of *Angirasa*. He sought to use reason and discouraged one-sided pursuit of the Vedas. What he insisted was the use of intelligence and industry as there was no set formula of success. He was a proponent of *Lokayata* philosophy; hence, he laid stress on the use of reason, argued in favour of human exertion, need of the state to pursue *artha* and *kama* effectively and employment of various means to secure victory against the enemy. He gave importance to *varta* and *Dandaniti* which were necessary for the proper consummation of *artha* and *kama*.

Bharadvaja is considered one of the promulgators of political science, and his ideas are cited in different books of politics. It is the opinion of Jayaswal that the later commentators also quote verses from his Arthashastra.[85] He was called Kanika, Kaninka, Kaninka Bharadvaja and Bharadvaja. There are two discourses of Bharadvaja in the Mahabharata and several passages in Kautilya's Arthashastra are attributed to him.

The following passages are presented from the Arthashastra:

1. 'The king should make his fellow students ministers, their integrity and capacity being known to him, for, they enjoy his confidence'.[86]
2. Regarding maintenance of secrets, Bharadvaja is of the view that

    > The divulgence of the secrets is fatal to the security and well-being of the king and the officers appointed by him.

---

[85] Jayaswal, *The Hindu Polity*, II.
[86] *The* Arthashastra, 1-8-1-2.

Therefore, he should deliberate alone over confidential matters, for, even councilors have (other) councilors and these have other still. Thus the series of councilors leads to the divulgence of secrets. Therefore, 'others should not know any work sought to be done by him. Only those who undertake it should know (about it) when it is begun or even when it is actually completed.[87]

3. Bharadvaja is of the opinion that 'the king should guard against the princes right from their birth, for the princes devour their begetters being of the same nature as crabs. Before the love of them produced in the father, the silent punishment for the same is the best'.[88]
4. Regarding the role of minister in the succession crisis, Bharadvaja says,

> When the king is dying, the minister should make members of the royal family, princes and principal officers fight against one another or against principal officers. If any one of them fights, he should get him slain by rising of the subjects. Or getting the rid of the members of the family, princes and principal officers by silent punishment, he should seize the kingdom for himself. For the sake of kingdom, father fights with sons and sons fight with father, what is to say then of the constituent the minister the only support of the kingdom? He should not disdain that when it has come to him of its own accord. A woman approaching her own accord curses, if discarded such is the saying among the people. Time comes only once to a man waiting for an opportunity; that time is difficult for that man to get again when he wants to do his work.[89]

5. Bharadvaja held that calamities befalling the minister were more dangerous than the king because deliberation in counsel, securing fruits of deliberations, carrying out undertakings, managing the income and expenditure,

---

[87] Ibid., 1-15-13-17.
[88] Ibid., 1.17.4-6.
[89] Ibid., 5.6.24-31.

infliction of punishment, warding off enemies and forest tribes, protection of the kingdom, taking steps against calamities, guarding of princes and installation of princes are all dependent on ministers. In the absence of these, these activities are lacking, and there is loss of activities on the part of the king as a bird with clipped wings. And in the calamities of these, secret instigations by the enemy are close at hand. And if 'these are hostile, there is a danger to king's life since they move near the person of the king'.[90]

6. According to Bharadvaja,

> Anger is behavior proper for good man, a means of requiting enemy, extirpation of insults and keeping men in dread. And reason to anger is ever needed for putting down the evil. Lust is a means of attainment of success, conciliation, generosity of nature and being lovable. And resort to *Kama* is ever needed for enjoyment of the fruits of work done.[91]

7. 'A weak king, attacked by a stronger king should everywhere remain submissive showing the characteristic of a needy person. For, he submits to Indra, who submits to strong king'.[92]

Bharadvaja is referred to in the Arthashastra as Kaninka Bharadvaja along with Katyayana and Pishuna who left the court when the crane was flying left.[93] Here, he seems to be the minister or councillor in the court.

There are two dialogues of Bharadvaja in the Mahabharata. In the Adiparva,[94] there is a dialogue between king Dhritarashtra and his minister Kanika and the second dialogue took place between the Sauvira king Shatruntapa and the sage (*muni*) Bharadvaja or Kaninka Bharadvaja. This was included in the

[90] Ibid., 8.1-6-11.
[91] Ibid., 8.3-8-12.
[92] Ibid., 12-1-2.
[93] Ibid., 5-5-10-11.
[94] The Mahabharata, 1.140.

Shantiparva[95] of the Mahabharata. Though there is considerable similarity in the approach of the two dialogues, the emphasis differed. The Adiparva dialogue was omitted by Dr V. S. Sukatankar from the critical edition of the epic but because of its uniqueness, we have included it for our discussion, as this dialogue is derived from the host of material on the Arthashastra that existed in the ancient India. In the Adiparva chapter on the Kanikniti, there are 93 verses, and in the Shanti Parva's chapter called 'Kaninka-Shatruntapa Samvad', there are 70 verses, both the dialogues are interesting for throwing light on the realistic political theory in the ancient India.

Kanika was a Brahmin minister of king Dhritarashtra who was alarmed by growing power and influence of the Pandavas. He feared that due to popularity of Yudhishthira, he would be forced to anoint him as the crown Prince instead of his son Duryodhana. Hence, he sought the advice of Kanika who was an expert in science of polities. He was called an expert in counselling and science of politics.[96]

At the outset, Kanika told the Kuru king that his advice was very harsh, and at times, he might feel uncomfortable and he might not like it, but nevertheless, it was beneficial to him. He said, 'You have asked me about the possibility of peace or war between the Kauravas and the Pandavas but it is my opinion that due to enmity between Duryodhana and Bhima and Karna and Arjuna, peace and conciliation between them is not possible'. Hence, the war is the only alternative. If you want to start a war against the enemy, you must know everything about him. Broadly speaking there are three types of enemies: the weak enemy, the enemy of equal strength and the powerful enemy. The king should design different policies for each one of them. The purpose should be to completely subjugate him and deprive him of all his wealth and property. As far as weak enemy is concerned, he should suppress him in such a manner that he would not be in a position

[95] 12.138.
[96] The Mahabharata, 1-140.1-2.

to raise his head again. By using different weapons, he should strike terror in his mind. He should be cautious and careful while dealing with the enemy of equal strength. He should gradually increase his own strength and once he is confident of his superior strength, he should attack and destroy him.[97]

While dealing with powerful enemy, he should conceal his secrets and weak points like tortoise and at the same time try to find out the weak points of the enemy, and once the weakening hole is discovered, he should enter the enemy's territory with ease and destroy it. He should constantly use force and annihilate the enemy because the remnants of the thorn and the enemy are dangerous and if the thorn is not removed at a right time, it created a corn in the foot. The defeated enemy could also regroup and destroy. Even though enemy is brave and powerful, he could be destroyed by striking at him at right time and right moment. At the same time, he should never neglect a weak enemy as fire even if small could assume dangerous proportions when supported by the fuel. The weak enemy would bend his knees, beg your kind indulgence, meekly tolerate insults and insolence, but when his time comes, he would ferociously launch his counter attack, like a hunter killing an unwary dear, and hence, he should be properly exterminated, so that there would be no worry of him.[98]

He said,

> It would be difficult to overcome powerful enemy with the help of force, hence, the method of bribery should be secretly used to weaken his position. He should see to it that by employing the method of dissension, he wins over important persons of the enemy camp. Once this is achieved, five important constituent elements of his state such as army, treasury, ministers, fort and territory should be destroyed. Principal ministers and the councilors of the enemy camp should be poisoned or assassinated. It is like slowly eroding the roots of the tree which ultimately gets uprooted.

[97] Ibid., 1.140-12-16.
[98] Ibid., 1-140-17-18.

Kanika told Dhritarashtra to perform rituals and sacrifices to show people that he was religious because normally fools believe in the promises of the religious people. Once the enemy is convinced of his religious nature, he should immediately pounce upon him like a wild wolf and kill him. He should not show any mercy to the enemy when caught and destroy him without any remorse.[99]

While delivering his discourse, Kanika narrated an animal fable which purported to teach the weak and intelligent person how different expedients of conciliation, bribery, dissension and force could be employed to secure the desired goals. Once upon a time, there lived five friends in a jungle: tiger, wolf, fox, mongoose and mouse. The tiger wanted to kill a powerful deer for his consumption, but it could not do it. It sought help of friends. The fox told the mouse to nibble at its foot so that it would not be in a position to run fast. The mouse did it successfully and the tiger killed it. Because the fox wanted to eat the deer all alone, it played a trick. It told the tiger that the mouse claimed that only because of its help the tiger could kill the deer. As a result, the tiger left the place in disgust. It told the wolf that tiger was angry with it and wanted to kill the wolf. As a result, it ran away. The fox told the mouse that the mongoose wanted to eat it because it did not like the flesh of deer. The mouse left the place in fear. Lastly, the mongoose came. The fox told it that it had already defeated the two in the battle and it was ready to fight with it. Mongoose realized that it could not fight duel with the fox and left the place. After that, the fox ate away the flesh of deer all alone. The moral of the story was that an intelligent person could defeat his more powerful adversaries if he used his intelligence properly. Hence, Kanika called fox-स्वार्थपंडित an expert in serving self-interest.[100]

Kanika told Dhritarashtra that he should kill his father, son, friend, brother or a teacher if any one of them had become his

[99] Ibid., 1-140-19.
[100] Ibid., 1-140-38-47.

enemy.[101] The enemy should be killed by deception, poisoning or by rioting. He should not neglect his enemy. He should kill his enemy and after his death, he should express profound grief over his sad demise! The king should practice religious rituals to conceal his dangerous plans! He should deport thieves, vagabonds, atheists and irreligious people from his kingdom to show that he did not tolerate irreligious behaviour.[102]

Kanika is of the view that the king should always suspect injury from the sources which he considers friendly because otherwise they could strike at him at an opportune moment in the most harmful way. He should appoint his spies at all places and keep all his 18 principal officers under surveillance. If he has given promises, he should fulfil only half and tell the person that the remainder would be given in due course of time. But he should not do that! He was of the opinion that the king should not expect permanent friendship with the enemy, as he would harm him when he was unaware of the danger. Hence, one should always be alert, industrious and be prepared for any eventuality. He should be realistic and rational. While taking the decision, he should take into consideration, three stages of power, time and place. He should take into account the time and place because ultimately, they decided the outcome of the endeavour.[103]

He pointed out that the pursuit of dharma, *artha* and *kama* brought a good number of benefits as well as pains. One must properly select the pleasures and avoid pain. All the three goals should be enjoyed in such a manner that they do not clash with each other. They should not be excessively enjoyed. For example, *kama* is the principle of pleasure, but if it is enjoyed excessively, it would produce pain. Thus, enjoy pleasures and avoid pains.[104] The king should maintain stability of his mind. He should not get disturbed by other's prosperity and he should take a particular

---

[101] Ibid., 1-140-52.
[102] Ibid., 1-1-40-62-63.
[103] Ibid., 1-140-63-66, 73-76, 83-85.
[104] Ibid., 1-140-69-73.

harsh action only to save himself from danger and once the emergency is over, he should behave righteously. But the message of Kanika was loud and clear. The king should conceal his anger and intentions like a sharpened razor which is kept in the sheath of leather bag and should be willing to strike at his enemy when the right opportunity arises. 'Dhritarashtra should not allow the Pandavas to grow strong and should destroy them before they acquired more power' was the counsel which the king followed and sent the Pandavas to Waranavata to burn them to death.

In the *Apaddharma Parva* of the Shantiparva, there is a dialogue between Kaninka Bharadvaja and Sauvira king Shatrumtapa. Bhishma quoted this 'ancient dialogue' between the two to tell Yudhishthira how a king should behave when he was in distress. Shatrumtapa asked Bharadvaja how the acquired object should be maintained and how it should be enhanced, protected and enjoyed. In his reply, Bhardvaja told him that the king should constantly uphold the rod of punishment in his hand and punish the guilty. Of all four expedients, the expedient of *Danda* is the most useful. At first, he should cut at the roots of his enemy and after his annihilation, he should bring under the control the allies and his partisan elements. He should renounce lust and anger, speak sweet and mild words but at his heart, he should be sharp like a razor. He should sever the head of the enemy by his own hands and then shed tears for him! When the time is unfavourable, he should carry his enemy on the shoulder and when the opportune time comes, he should break him into the pieces like an earthen pot. He should conceal his defects like a tortoise, think on financial matters like a crane, show prowess like a lion, live in ambush like a wolf and attack and pierce his enemy like an arrow! He should understand the exact nature of time and place, evaluate strength and weakness of his enemies and then only attack. He should completely exterminate the enemy because remnants of fire, foe and debt always increase and endanger the concerned person. He should trust no one and kill his near relatives and friends if they acted against his interests. In fact, there is no separate order of friends and foes, and persons become friends and foes on the trend of circumstances. The king should be foresighted like a vulture, stable like a heron, watchful like a dog, brave like a lion, dreadful like a crow and enter into enemy's territory like a snake with ease and without anxiety. He should first see that his adventures bring about desirable results and then he should act. This advice which is tainted with sin should be used to counter the evil designs of the enemy, and it should not be always pursued.[105]

There is considerable similarity between the discourses of Kanika and Bharadvaja. But Kanika's advice was directed against the extermination of the enemy; hence, it was more devious and cruel. As against this, Bharadvaja advises the king regarding acquisition, preservation and increase of the kingdom. Some part of the advice of Kanika is repeated by Bharadvaja and both share amoral realism and extreme hostility towards enemy. There are at least 12 stanzas identical in both the texts. The story of the crafty fox is not included in the Shantiparva discourse.

From the seven extracts of the Kautilya's Arthashastra and two dialogues of the Mahabharata, it emerges that Bharadvaja was the most ruthless teacher of political science who gave self-interest of the king or the minister of the state primacy while deciding the course of action. Though he was not averse to using other expedients of the policy, he advocated the methods of dissention and punishment. He is not averse to using soft methods if they are effective. For example, he says,

> The king should become soft or sharp depending upon the situation. He should be soft against soft targets and sharp against the hard targets. Soft methods could be used to destroy soft objects as well as the most dreadful enemies. Therefore, there is nothing unachievable through soft methods.[106]

He considered the minister as the most important constituent element of the state and wanted him to capture power if there

---

[105] Ibid., 12.138.69.
[106] Ibid., 12.138.64-66.

was a succession crisis. He should do it out of personal interest as well as for the interest of the state. He is a political scientist, who gave importance to *artha* and *Kama Purusharathas*. Following are some of the important principles of his political theory:

1. Enjoying pleasures and avoiding pains should be the goal of the king and he should pursue 'trivarga' ideal in such a manner that the pleasures are enhanced and the pains are minimized. Excessive pursuit of *kama* did not bring pleasure but pain.
2. The king should take the policy decisions on the basis of reason, time and place. Current understanding of the situation is important.
3. He should see to it that his own interests as well as that of the kingdom coincided and should use all fair and foul means to safeguard his interests.
4. All the devious measures should be employed by the king during emergency but in normal circumstances, he should not always use them. In both the texts of the epic, this stanza is repeated.

"कर्मणायेन तेनेह मृदुना दारूणेत वा।

उद्धरेत् दीनमात्मानं समर्थो धर्ममाचरेत् [107, 108]

It is not incorrect to say that Kaninka Bharadvaja represents the extreme tendencies in the Arthashastra tradition which is based on calculated policy of treachery, deceit and murder, practised by some kings and ministers. According to Dr Ghoshal:

> It not only involves undisguised sacrifice of moral principles for political ends but also lacks the saving grace of the appeal to the necessity of the state, On the contrary, the author parades his creed of unbridled selfishness and holds up the state itself as a standing example of its free play.[109]

---

[107] Ibid., 12-138-38.
[108] Ibid., 1-140-72.
[109] Ghoshal, *A History*, 101.

Kosambi held that the treachery preached by this school was practised by the ruling monarchies of the 6th century BC. It is practised by them to spread their empire against elected tribal oligarchies.[110] Kangle is of the opinion that

> The echoes of teaching of Bharadvaja are to be found in such respectable works as the Manusmriti. And in the teaching of the shastra, it is not Bharadvaja alone who can be charged with unscrupulousness, though he perhaps represents the most extreme example of this tendency.[111]

Bharadvaja's amoral realism is so stark that even Machiavelli may blush.

We have so far discussed those political thinkers whose ideas found place both in the Arthashastra and in the Mahabharata. We shall now study political ideas of those thinkers whose ideas are cited by Kautilya only. They included Vishalaksha, Kaunapadanta, Vatavyadhi, Pishuna, Bahudantiputra and Pishunaputra.

Vishalaksha is a cryptic name, which means a person with big eyes. It is the name of Lord Shankara. Vishalaksha was a famous teacher of politics as his name is cited in the Arthashastra as well as in the great epic. Kautilya cited his ideas six times, which are as follows:

1. About the appointment of ministers. Bharadvaja said that he should appoint his fellow students as ministers,

   > No! Says Vishalaksha, having been his playmates, they treat him with disrespect. He should make those, ministers who are of like nature to him, in secret matters since they have the same character and vices. For, through fear that he is conversant with their secrets, they do not offend him.[112]

---

[110] Kosambi, 2007, 268.
[111] Kangle, 'Bharadvaja: An Ancient Indian', 333–39.
[112] The Arthashastra, 1-8-3-6.

2. Bharadvaja said that the king should deliberate alone on secret matters but

> There is no attainment of deliberation by a single person says Vishalaksha. For, the affairs of the king are threefold: directly perceived, unperceived and inferred. Coming to know about what is not known, definite strengthening of what has become known, removal of doubt in a case of two possible alternatives in a matter, finding out the rest in a matter that is partly known, this can be achieved only with the help of ministers, Therefore, he should sit in counsel with those who are mature in intellect. He should despise none but should listen to the opinion of everyone. A wise man should make use of sensible words of even a child.[113]

3. He opposed Bharadvaja's view that the princes should be killed when they were young. He said, 'This is cruel as it involves killing of innocent persons and the destruction of the *kshatriyas* race. Therefore, confinement (of the princes) in one place is the best'.[114]
4. Of the calamities befalling minister and the country, the latter is more serious according to Vishalaksha because, 'the treasury, the army, the forest produce, laborers, means of transport and stores spring from the country. In the absence of the country, there would be a lack of these and disappearance of the king and the minister would follow immediately thereafter'.[115] (Here, country means Janapada or rural areas of kingdom.)
5. 'As between verbal injury and violation of property, verbal injury is worse. For, a spirited man, spoken to harshly, retaliates with energy. The barb of offensive speech, embedded in the heart inflames the spirit and afflicts senses'.[116]
6. 'A weak king should not submit to the stronger, he should fight with all the mobilisation of his forces, for, valor

---

[113] Ibid., 1-15-18-22.
[114] Ibid., 1-17-7-8.
[115] Ibid., 8-1-19-21.
[116] Ibid., 8.3.24-26.

overcomes a calamity. And this is *kshatriya*'s special duty, whether there be a victory or a defeat in the war'.[117]

Vishalaksha is more moderate than Bharadvaja, and he refutes extreme views of Bharadvaja with his own views. He is of the view that the king should deliberate with a larger body of the people as he says that the sensible words of even a child should also be heeded. He thinks that calamity befalling the country or *Janapada* is more serious because it provides material and human resources to the state; however, he is not correct in saying that the weak king should not submit to the strong and should prefer to go down fighting because it is the policy of sure disaster.

Vatavyadhi is considered the cryptic name of Uddhava. His ideas on different issues are cited five times by Kautilya, as follows:

1. Regarding the qualifications of ministers, he did not agree with Kaunapadanta's view that he should appoint his hereditary servants as ministers. He said

    For bringing under their control, everything belonging to him, they behave like masters themselves. Therefore, he should make new men well versed in politics his ministers. New men, indeed, looking upon the wielder of the rod as occupying the position of Yama, do not give offence.[118]

2. Opposing Kaunapadanta's view that the prince should be kept with kinsmen of his mother, he said,

    This in the position of the flag for the prince, for, with him as the flag his mother's kinsmen would be making demands like Aditikaushikas (mendicants earning their livelihood by showing images of gods) they will misuse the possession. Therefore, he should let him free to indulge in vulgar pleasures. For sons kept engrossed in pleasure do not become hostile to the father.[119]

[117] Ibid., 12.1.3-5.
[118] Ibid., 1.8-20-23.
[119] Ibid., 1.17.19.21.

3. Of calamities befalling the ally and the army, calamity on the ally is more serious. The ally does the work without being paid and at a distance, repels the enemy in the rear, his ally, the enemy and the forest chief and helps with treasury, army and territory, remaining united in the conditions of calamity.[120]
4. Of the vices of women and drink, indulgence in women is worse, for harmful among women is of various kinds (as explained in the rules of royal residence) In the drink on the other hand, there is enjoyment of pleasures of senses such as sound and other, making gifts of love, honoring attendants and the removal of fatigue caused by work.[121]
5. 'There are only two measures, for, out of peace and war only, six measures come into existence'.[122]

In the Mahabharata, Uddhava said, 'The path of Politics is very devious and it consists of *Sama, Dama, Bhed* and *Danda* these have to be used when we are attacked by the enemies.' *Danda* should be used when the enemies are weak, when he is of equal strength, *Sama* should be used. When he is more powerful than we are, *Dana* should be employed, and when all these expedients could not be useful, *Bheda* should be used.[123]

They say that Kaunapadanta is the other name of Bhishma. Following are the political ideas of Kaunapadanta:

1. Refuting the view that the financial expertise cannot be the sole criterion for the appointment of ministers, he says,

   For these are not endowed with other qualities necessary for minister. He should make those his ministers who have come from hereditary servants from his father and grandfather, since their pure conduct is known. They do not desert him, even when he misbehaves, being of the same kin. This

---

[120] Ibid., 8.1.53-54.
[121] Ibid., 8.3.55-57.
[122] Ibid., 7.1-3-4.
[123] The Mahabharata, Vol. 9, 746–47.

is observed even among the animals, for, cattle, passing by a herd of cattle not their kin abide by only with those that are their kin.[124]

2. Refuting Pishuna's opinion that the prince should be confined to the fortress of a neighbouring prince, Kaunpadanta said, 'This is the position of the calf for the prince. For, the neighboring prince might milk his father as one milks the cow with the help of the calf. Therefore making him stay with the kinsmen of his mother is the best'.[125]

3.
Of the calamities befalling the territory and the army, the calamity of the army is more serious. For, dependent on the army are restraint of allies and enemies, rousing alien troops to action and reinforcement of one's own troops. And in the absence of an army, the loss of treasury was certain. And in the absence of treasury, it is possible to collect an army with forest produce or land or by allowing seizure of enemy's land by each for himself and to collect treasury, when one has an army. And being in the close proximity to the king, the army has the same characteristics as ministers.[126]

4.
Of the vices of gambling and women, vice of gambling is worse for continuously at night or in lamplight and even when mother has died, the gambler goes on playing. And if questioned in difficulties, he becomes enraged. But in the case of indulgence in women, questioning concerning spiritual and material well being is indeed possible on occasions of bath, toilet and meals. And it is possible to employ a woman in what is beneficial to the king or to turn her away by means of silent punishment or make her go away.[127]

---

[124] The Arthashastra, 1-8-14-19.
[125] Ibid., 1-17-15-17.
[126] Ibid., 8.1.41-45.
[127] Ibid., 8-3-47-51.

Kaunapdanta had a practical bent of mind; hence, he realized that the prince could not be confined to the fortress of the neighbouring king. He also pointed out the importance of the army to the king.

Pishuna, according to the commentators, was other name of Narada. Kautilya cites views of Pishuna four times, which are as follows:

1. Pishuna does not agree with the view that the person who had helped the king in calamities should be appointed as minister, he said, 'This is devotion and not a trait of intellect. He should make those his minister who, when appointed to tasks, the income from which is calculated, (beforehand) would bring in the income as directed or more, since (thus) their qualities are proved'.[128]
2. He opposed the policy of confining the prince to frontier fortress because this is danger as from fighting ram, for, realizing that alone to be means of his return, he might become the ally of frontier chief. Therefore, making him stay in the fortress of neighbouring prince, far removed from his territory is the best.[129]
3. Of calamities befalling the fort and treasury, the calamity befalling treasury is more serious. For, dependent on treasury are building of the fort, protection of the fort, control over the country and the allies and the enemy's incitement of those away from the land, and the use of armed forces. A fort is susceptible to secret instigations by enemies with money. And in a calamity, it is possible to go away with treasury and not with fort.[130]
4. He held that among them of gambling and hunting, hunting is worse for in it the danger of robbers, enemies, wild animals, forest fires and stumbling and the loss of way as

[128] Ibid., 1-9-11-13.
[129] Ibid., 1-17-12-14.
[130] Ibid., 8-1.33-36.

well as hunger and thrust constitute a danger to life. In gambling, however, there is only winning for one expert in dice as it was for Jayasena and Duryodhana.[131]

Thus, Vatavyadhi, Kaunapadanta and Pishuna represent different viewpoints on controversial issues.

According to Kangle, Bahudanti is a name of Indra's mother, hence he is called Bahudantiputra.[132] There is one quotation of this teacher in the Arthashastra.

Regarding the qualifications of persons for appointment as ministers he said, 'one conversant with science but not experienced in practical affairs would come to grief in carrying out undertakings. He should appoint as ministers such persons as are endowed with nobility of birth, intellect, integrity, bravery and loyalty because of the supreme importance of qualities in this matter'.[133] Here, Bahudantiputra specifically mentions that merit alone should be sole qualification for the minister.

Kautilya constantly mentions the opinions of Acharyas. It is the contention of ShamShastri and Ghoshal that 'Acharya' means the teacher of Kautilya. He was a single person. However, Professor Kane did not agree with this. He was of the opinion that 'Acharyas' meant the previous teachers of political science.[134] Kautilya refers to the ideas of these teachers 56 times. In most of the cases, first, he puts forward their ideas as a *Purvapaksha* and then refutes them by putting forward his own ideas. It is the opinion of A. B. Keith that these ideas were artificially prepared by Kautilya in order to put forward his own views. Endorsing his view, Heesterman is of the opinion that these ideas of the former teachers were visualized by Kautilya to train students in the art of argumentation.[135] According to Professor Kangle,

---

[131] Ibid., 8-3-39-41.
[132] Kangle, 1963, Arthshastra Vol. II, 18.
[133] The Arthashastra, 1-8-24-25.
[134] Kane, *The Meaning of Acharyah*, 213.
[135] Heesterman, *The Inner Conflict*, 130–31.

Now it cannot be denied that there is an element of artificiality in the manner in which the opinions of the earlier teachers are presented in this text. It would, however, be hardly right to conclude from this that the opinions themselves are all invented by Kautilya.... Moreover, many of the opinions attributed to the predecessors can be shown to have been conceivably held, before this text was written.[136])

He further pointed out that all these views were held by different authorities, and Kautilya converted their ideas in his own language, worked up and schematically presented. It is superhuman to think that all these ideas were conceived by the author. In fact, he himself said that his work was composed on the basis of the works prepared by earlier masters on the Arthashastra. As far as the term 'Acharyas' is concerned, it could be the opinion of some of them, it could be opinion of majority of them.[137] Kautilya has cited the ideas of many of these Acharyas by taking their names. Hence, it was easier to attribute these ideas to them. In the case of 'Acharyas', no names or the names of schools are given and nor do these ideas present a coherent ideology. Therefore, knowing it very well that many of their ideas represented political ideas of pre-Kautilyan thinkers; we have decided not to include them for our consideration.

In the Ramayana, there is a full-length chapter on the discourse of Jabala who was considered one of the experts in the Arthashastra. There are 40 verses of the dialogue which is included in the *Ayodhyakand* of the Ramayana. Bharat, young brother of Rama, came to jungle to request him to assume kingship but he refused to accept it. Jabala, a minister and expert in politics and logic, moved forward to convince Rama. He exhorted him not to follow Dashratha's order and assume kingship.

Jabala said that there was no brother or anyone else, as man is born alone in the world and he would leave it alone. The relationship with our father and mother was temporary,

[136] Kangle, *The Kautilya* Arthashastra, III, 50–51.
[137] Ibid., 51.

and our stay with the fathers was just like a stay in the guest house, as we occupy it in the evening and leave it in the morning in the course of travel. Father sowed the seed in the womb of mother and the son was born. There was nothing special in the death of Dashratha as every human being had to leave the world. There was no other world such as heaven and hell. All the religious ceremonies such as sacrifices and rituals were false as they were designed by the crafty priests to earn their livelihood. Performance of the last funeral rite was waste of food grains, as it did not reach dead parents. If it were so, we could have served food to our close relatives, when they were travelling to the distance places, sitting in our homes. Instead, we gave them food to eat during the journey. Hence, there was no other world and Rama should believe in the direct evidences of senses as true source of knowledge. Those people who followed dharma instead of *artha* suffered a great deal in their life.

He maintained that considering these hard facts of life, Rama should not grieve for sad demise of his father and accept kingship as suggested by his brother Bharat. He should not abandon his traditional kingdom and follow the path which was full of sufferings and miseries. It is wrong to follow the advice given by clever priests. This is the road approved by the people (लोकसंमत) and by the good men who followed the testimony of direct evidence of senses.[138]

Jabala's discourse is based on the *Lokayata* philosophy as he advocated the validity of sense perception, discounted the existence of other world and condemned the Vedic sacrifices and rituals. It is rightly pointed out by Dr Walter Ruben that Jabala did not advocate the use of force and overlooked human weakness of old king. He briefly treated only the political motive of the act without reference to pure moral scruple. Ruben wrote,

> Against this prompting of the conscience of pious Rama, Jabali puts forth the materialist outlook, denies the supra sensuous other

[138] Valmiki. *The Ramayana*, Vol. I, 459–60.

world and sanctity of holy scriptures with the arguments typical of the materialist, to be repeated later on, which were presumably not the personal intervention of Valmiki but were found by him in the polemics against the materialists.[139]

His arguments were clear. He pointed out that there was nothing wrong and immoral in accepting kingship because Dashratha's authority to send him to exile was questionable, and religious sanctions and Vedic injunctions supporting it were of dubious authenticity. The path of so-called dharma was full of thorns and unhappiness. It is better for Rama to abandon the exile in forest and return back to Ayodhya. His teaching was consistent with *Lokayata* philosophy which held that the *artha* was the only goal of life, and 'Loksammat' king was the only authority to be accepted. Jabali was prophetic in telling Rama that the path he wanted to follow was full of dangers, unhappiness and miseries.

Jabala was the Arthashastra teacher who was influenced by *Lokayata* ideology; hence, he used their ideas to convince Rama that the Vedic rituals and performance of religious rites were useless. Also, he should not respect his father's order if it was not reasonable because our relationship with our parents was temporary. He should not get emotional and consider his interests as well as interests of the state more important. He told him that he had to consider consequences of his action, and his decision to obey the orders of the father was not going to benefit the state, because the state would be without an effective ruler for 14 years.

In the Aranyaka Parva of the Mahabharata, there is a rare discourse on politics delivered by a teacher who belonged to the school of Brihaspati. In the great forest where the Pandavas were exiled, there was a heated discussion between the Pandavas and Draupadi. Yudhishthira was a supporter of dharma who declared that he performed dharma not for the sake of fruits that accrued of but he performed it as a part of his duty. He advocated the policy of restraint and did not want to break exile. Draupadi

[139] Ruben, *The Minister*, 456.

did not accept his arguments and said that if dharma stood for universal beneficence, why did it not support her when she was in distress. Why did Duryodhana enjoy sovereignty earned by fraud and why did Yudhishthira suffer exile when morally he was right? In the course of discussion, she quoted a discourse of a *Lokayata* teacher who delivered it in the court of Drupad. She heard it sitting in the lap of her father. There are 59 verses in the chapter.[140]

The 'Barhaspatya' teacher told the king that in this world, everybody had to exert to earn his livelihood as only the trees in the Jungle survive without exertion. Nobody could hope of a better life without exertion as the great Himalaya mountain would get exhausted if we continued to consume without adding anything to it. Performance of action was necessary because we could witness its fruits in our life. We must continuously acquire, maintain and enhance the sources of livelihood. Action gave us immediate rewards; therefore, people exerted. It is possible that sometimes an action might not bring desired results but still the people performed their functions and received rewards in due course of time.

He pointed out that human effort was superior to the fate. Due to human efforts only, cities were built, townships were established and villages and houses were developed. It is through the instrumentality of human body that men exerted. Men secured oil from sesame, milk from the udder of cow and fire from wood sticks with exertion only. Men used their intelligence to understand this fact and exerted to extract the desirable things to live their life comfortably. Ultimately, the skill of the performer mattered. It is not the fate but human efforts that are important. If there was no reward for the action, the students would not have worked under their teachers. Man is admired on the successful performance of his duties and is condemned for his failure. He maintained that there were three theories of action. The first theory held that it was the fate that decided everything and human

---

[140] The Mahabharata, 3.33.

efforts were of no use. The second theory argued that it is due to human efforts that everything is achieved in the world and the third theory held that it was the 'svabhava' or the quality inherent in a particular thing that decided everything. Size and growth of a tree are decided by the character of the seed. Human efforts act as the efficient cause. He quoted Manu who said that human beings must exert.[141]

Continuing his arguments, the teacher said that if a man does not perform his duties, he would live miserable life. Men should realise that after performing particular action only, they would know whether it is fruitful or not. He gave an example of a farmer, who ploughed his land, cleared it and sowed the seed, but his success was dependent upon the proper rainfall. If rainfall is good, he would get good crops and if it is not good, he would not get it. But it would be wrong to blame the farmer for failure.[142] He had done what he ought to have done. He should not blame himself for the failure. It is true that human efforts alone do not bring desired results as the success depends on many factors such as time and place.[143] But taking into account time, place and the purpose of the action, man has to endeavour. What is important is human efforts, human endeavour and the desire to excel in different situations and circumstances. Men had achieved great successes as they had crossed the oceans and scaled mountains with the help of the courage. Hence, he should not curse himself but repose confidence in his abilities. He should not lose heart if he has not achieved success but he should ceaselessly work hard. Human efforts aided by time and place factors achieved great things in life.[144]

The arguments of Draupadi spilled over in Chapter 34, in which Bhimsena forcefully enunciated efficacy of *artha* and *kama* Purusharathas. In this dialogue, Draupadi presented the authentic

[141] Ibid., 3-33-17-21.
[142] Ibid., 3-33-44-45.
[143] Ibid., 3-33-49.
[144] Ibid., 3-33.53-54.

account of ethics of Brihaspati who was a prominent *Lokayata* thinker. She puts forth four important principles of his ethics:

1. Human efforts are more important than the fate or 'Dishti' as its fruits were directly experienced.
2. It is through human efforts that the cities and towns were built. Villages settled and the natural resources husbanded for human use. It is through efforts that the great oceans were crossed and the mountains scaled.
3. Sooner or later, every human action brings its own rewards. It is possible that man may not achieve success in his every endeavour but in due course of time, he would get its rewards. Inaction is no substitute for action because its result is living a miserable life.
4. Though the human efforts are important, they alone do not decide the outcome of an action as the factors of time and place also play an important role in it. But for successful accomplishment of a particular task, human energy, force and enthusiasm are needed.

Dr Agrawala is of the view that in this chapter, the *Barhaspatya* teacher was refuting the arguments of Makkhali Gosala (supporter of *Dishti* or fate) Ajita kesh kambli (swabhavavadi) and Prakuddha katyayana (philosophy of inaction or Akriyavada). In this discourse, he advocated both validity of sense perception or validity of direct evidence of senses and the importance of human action.[145] He considered human action as the efficient cause that shaped events along with time and place. He shared with Bharadvaja importance of factors: time and place and primacy of *artha* and *kama*.

In the *Digha Nikaya* (Vol. I), there is '*Kootdanta Sutra*' and in this famous *sutra*, Buddha discounted the path of violent sacrifices. There is a story of the king Mahavijita who was advised by his royal chaplain (who belonged to *Lokayata* School) about the alternative path to perform violent sacrifices. In ancient

[145] Agrawala, *The Bharat-Savitri*, Vol. I, 216.

times, there lived a king called Mahavijita who was very rich and wealthy. The king had a *purohita* who was well versed in *Lokayata Vidya* or science of politics.[146] He used to perform costly sacrifices. Due to that, slaves and workers were not happy, trees were cut and many animals sacrificed.

King Mahavijita expressed a desire to perform a big sacrifice, which would bring great happiness and pleasure to him. His *purohita* told him that in his kingdom, there were robberies and other disturbances as the people were not happy. The robbers plundered people in cities, towns and villages. If the king imposed extra taxes on the people for the sake of the sacrifice, that would be against the interests of the people. If the king thought that he could bring robberies under control by killing, imprisoning or deporting the robbers, then that would not bring about desirable result because some robbers who escaped the punishment would continue to plunder the country. If they were pacified by bribing that would be an added incentive to plunder. The real remedy to overcome this situation was to support the poor people by giving them jobs, and other means of livelihood. Those who wanted to pursue agriculture and cattle breeding, they should be given land, seeds, loan and the cattle. He should provide necessary capital to the traders, and to those who wanted to serve the government, he should give them salaried jobs. Once these people get involved in their profession they liked, they would not create disturbances in the state. Due to these steps, the production would increase, so would revenue and there would be peace in the state. There would be no theft and robbery, and the people would live in their family with their children, enjoying pleasures without fear.[147,148]

King Mahavijita accepted his advice and implemented it immediately. He provided seeds and land to farmers, capital to traders and service to the people. As a result, income of the people increased, so did revenue of the kingdom. There were no robberies and the people lived happily. They kept their houses

---

[146] Rajwade, *The Digha Nikaya*, Vol. I, 29.
[147] Ibid., 149–50.
[148] Kosambi, Darmanand, Buddha-Leela, 2007, 244–45.

open during night!¹⁴⁹ There was no sacrifice and because of that *Das-karamakaras* (the slaves and workers) were happy because they had to perform excessive work during the sacrifices. No trees were cut, no animals were killed and everyone was happy because of termination of the sacrifices. The *purohita* provided new alternative to costly sacrifices.¹⁵⁰

This sutra is an excellent example of synthesis between the *Lokayata* and the Buddhist ideas. It is well known that both of them were opposed to performance of violent sacrifices and pretentions of selfish priests. In the first part of the story, the *Lokayata* ideas of peaceful development of the state with the growth of *Varta* and *Dandaniti* are emphasised. The development of sources of *artha* was their answer to the robberies and the pillage that people took recourse to because of poverty and lack of sources of livelihood. In the second part of the story, the Buddhist elements are discernible. After the success of his policy, the king still wanted to perform sacrifice. The *purohita* allowed him to do so with following five conditions:

1. The sacrifice should be performed after taking consent of the officers appointed in the cities and provinces, ministers, rich Brahmins and moneylenders.
2. There will be no animals sacrificed; only butter and food grains will be used as offerings.
3. *Dasas* and *Karmakaras* will not be forced to do hard physical labour which made them extremely unhappy. Their participation in the sacrifice will be voluntary.
4. No trees will be cut and no wealth of forest will be destroyed.
5. The king would not accept the gifts brought by the *kshatriya* officers, rich Brahmins, ministers and moneylenders, and he would advise them to utilize the wealth for the construction of public works such as rest houses, roads, wells, and tanks for the benefit of the people.¹⁵¹

---

¹⁴⁹ Ibid., 150.
¹⁵⁰ Kosambi, 2007, 254.
¹⁵¹ Rajawade, *The Digha Nikaya* 151–54.

In the *'Kootdanta Sutra'*, we could see amazing ability of Buddha to put new meaning in old concepts and practices. He virtually changed the old concept of sacrifice. He preached non-violence, protection of environment, expenditure of the money meant for the royal consumption for construction of public works.

It is the opinion of Dr Kosambi that the royal priest's advice was an excellent example of modern political economy. He wrote,

> To gain prosperity for his people, to abolish banditry and thieving, the *purohit* suggested instead that the king should furnish seed to the peasants, capital to the trader, suitable employment for those who wished to serve the state. In this way, all would be busy with their own duties, there would be no revolt, taxes would be properly collected and the treasury full. This surely is a modern approach to the problem.[152]

In our discussion, in the first part, we have studied political ideas of major pre-Kautilyan Arthashastra teachers such as Manu, Ushanasa, Brihaspati and Bharadvaja. We have seen that Bhardvaja represented the most radical of the *Arthasthastra* ideas and Manu was closer to the *Dharmashastra* tradition. Ushanasa and Brihaspati represented the rationalistic tradition as they gave more importance to human reason.

In the later part, we have discussed three distinct Arthashastra approaches in three different dialogues, all of which presented a new way to life. It was a more positive approach towards life. In the discourse of Jabala, he sought to persuade Rama to accept the office, which he was entitled to hold. He should not be misled by misplaced idealism flowing from false religious teaching. He wanted him to think about consequences of his action. Brihaspati sought to emphasize the importance of the *Lokayata* ethic, which stood for continuous and ceaseless human action to achieve the goal. It is because of human efforts that great cities and townships were established and land was brought under cultivation. In the 'Kootdanta sutra', the *purohita* showed a new way to the people and asked them to develop sources of *artha* instead of

---

[152] Kosambi, *An Introduction to Study*, 170.

spending money on the performance of useless sacrifices. These three dialogues have their origin in *Lokayata* philosophy and they presented the positive aspects of political activities. The purpose of politics was not engaged in the self-aggrandisement and catering to self-interest, but it was to bring about all-round development of the people through the development of sources of *artha*, by adopting right course of action and employment of correct policy.

Bibliography

Agrawala, V. S. *The Bharat-Savitri*. Vol. I. Varanasi: Sasta Sahitya Mandal, 1966.
Ghoshal, U. N. *A History of Indian Political Ideas*. Bombay: Oxford University Press, 1966.
Heesterman, J. C. C. *The Inner Conflict of Tradition*. Delhi: Oxford University Press, 1985.
Jayaswal, K. P. *The Hindu Polity*. Bangalore: Central Press, 1955.
Kane, P. V. 'The Meaning of Acharyah'. *Annals of Bhandarkar Oriental Research Institute* 23 (1942a): 206–13.
———. 'Rajashastras of Brihaspati, Ushanasa, Bharadvaja and Vishalaksha'. *Journal of University of Bombay* (New Series) 2 (1942b): 79–80.
Kangle, R. P. 'Bharadvaja: An Ancient Indian Teacher of Political Science'. *Bharatiya Vidya*—K. M. Mamshi Felicitation Volume) 21–22 (1961): 333–37.
———. *The Kautilya* Arthashastra. Vol. III. Bombay: University of Bombay, 1965.
Kosambi, D. D. *An Introduction to Study of Ancient Indian History*. Bombay: Popular Publication, 1956.
———. *Combined Methods in Indology and Other Writings*. Delhi: Oxford University Press, 2007a.
Kosambi, Dharmanand, *Buddha Leela*. Mumbai: Maharashtra Sahitya and Sanskrit Mandal, 2007b.
Rajwade, C. V. *The Digha Nikaya*. Vol. I. Aurangabad: Buddhist Study Center, 1999.
Ruben, W. 'The Minister Jabala in the Ramayana'. *Indian Studies: Past and Present* 6 (1964): 445–65.
Valmiki. *The Ramayana*. Vol. I. Pune: Varada Books, 1986.

8

Vijnyan Bala and *Apaddharma*

In the Arthashastra tradition, the concept of *Apaddharma,* or the duties that are to be performed at the time of emergency, played an important role because thinkers such as Manu, Brihaspati, Ushanasa and Bharadvaja declared that self-preservation was the fundamental duty of an individual. In the *Dharmashastra* tradition also, duties performed during emergency are discussed.

In the *Chhandogya Upanishad*, Ushasti Chakrayana had to eat beans at the hut of a beggar, which were left over by him to save his life because there was drought in the land of the Kurus. He ate the beans but refused to drink water. Explaining his position, he told, 'I should not have lived if I had not eaten the beans, but the drinking of water would be a mere pleasure'.[1] The *Upanishad* puts forward three important principles.

1. It is the supreme duty of the man to preserve his cheerless self at all cost and, for that purpose, he could eat forbidden food.
2. Eating leftover food was an exception to save his life, but drinking leftover water was a luxury because pure water was easily available. Hence, he would not transgress the rule.
3. After saving his life, he could use it for earning merit.

[1] Muller, *The Upanishads*, 18–19.

The same arguments were put forward by sage Vishvamitra in the Mahabharata when he had to eat forbidden food in similar conditions.² The *Apastamba Dharmasutra* accepted it and said, 'One who taken intentionally forbidden food, when he is in danger of his life, shall not be held guilty'.³ The *Gautama Dharmasutra* said that during emergency, one could change his profession to save his life as a Brahmin could take to a Shudra's profession.⁴ Thus, Dr U. N. Ghoshal observes that the right of self-preservation was a fundamental right, which was accepted by the Arthashastra-*Smriti* tradition.⁵

In the Arthashastra tradition, the concept of self-preservation was important. How to protect one's own self and one's own kingdom was one of the key considerations of the thinkers. According to Dr V. S. Agrawala, in ancient books on political science, a chapter called 'Atma rakshitavyam' discussed ways and means to save one's own self as well as kingdom in the most difficult situation.⁶ In the Kautilya's Arthashastra, this problem was discussed as the *Vyasanas* or the calamities befalling the state.⁷ He held that revolts in the interior and external regions constituted a real danger to the state.⁸ He objectively tried to analyse various situations that constitute calamity, so that the king might avoid it.⁹ However, he does not study it through the concept of *Apaddharma*.

The Shantiparva of the Mahabharata contains three sections: the first section deals with the duties of the king and the problem of governance; the second section deals with the duties to be performed in an emergency, and the third section deals with the problem of salvation. Hence, these sections are called

²The Mahabharata, 12.139.
³Muller, *Sacred Laws of the Aryas*, 169.
⁴Ibid., 227.
⁵Ghoshal, *A History of Indian*, 231.
⁶Agrawala, *Bharat-Savitri*, Vol. III, 119–20.
⁷Arthashastra, 8 and 9-4-7.
⁸Chousalkar, 'Contemporary Relevance', 29–41.
⁹Bowls, *Dharma, Disorder and Political*, 77.

Rajadharmanushasan, Apaddharma, and Moksha Dharma Parva, respectively. In the *Apaddharma parva of the Shantiparva*, the problem of preservation of the state at the time of distress is elaborately discussed. According to Bowls, on the one hand, *Apaddharma* denoted a behaviour that was, in some way, exceptional; on the other hand, it also argued that this behaviour was, in some way, legitimate. This sense of legitimacy was carried by the word 'dharma'.[10] Some important Arthashastra dialogues are included in the second section of the Shantiparva, which are extremely thought provoking, original and, at times, startling.

Three important characteristics of the political ideas included in the second part of the Shantiparva are as follows:

1. There is application of principle of rationalism to politics, which is one of the rare instances in the history of Indian political thought.
2. Bhishma expounds the concept of self-interest as the defining principle of political theory and exhorts an intelligent king to survive in the politics of *Matsya-Nyaya*.
3. Self-preservation was the fundamental duty of the individual, and he should save himself even by taking recourse to questionable means in the hope that once he survived, he would follow the principle of dharma. Thus, the *Apaddharma* has to be pursued as an exceptional practice to be followed at the time of distress.

Those who constituted the present version of the Apaddharma Parva should be congratulated because they have brought together rare pre-Kautilyan Arthashastra material in this section. Most of the material in the Apaddharma belonged to the pre-Kautilyan Arthashastra tradition, especially three animal fables: a fable of three fish, the story of a wise mouse and a cat, and a dialogue between Brahmadatta and Poojani as well as the discourses of Bharadvaja and Chapter 140 on the nature of

[10] Ibid., 81.

dharma. It is possible that these Arthashastra ideas are adapted to the narrative form of the great epic. Some of the chapters in the *Apaddharma Parva* belonged to the ancient tradition of the Arthashastra, and by placing them in the text of the Shantiparva, ancient editors of the epic had saved them for posterity.

While responding to the question of Yudhishthira regarding the survival of the king during distress when he had lost his treasury, when his army was depleted and demoralized and his allies and friends had deserted him, Bhishma told him that it was the responsibility of the king to save his kingdom by strengthening his treasury and army because the kingdom could be retrieved only with their help. The state had to be retrieved and freed from the calamities or *vyasana*s. He held that there was no greater morality than that of the different activities of the state, as ultimately the pursuit of dharma depended upon the state.[11] No dharma could be pursued in anarchy. It is the responsibility of the people to protect the state by giving it necessary financial support. The king should approach people and enlist their support in mobilizing public debt.[12] Bhishma suggested different methods to save the kingdom when the king was in distress.

In one of the animal fables, Bhishma narrated a story of three fish. He expounded the old Arthashastra principle of three types of intelligence: (a) *Anagata-Vidhata buddhi*, (b) *Pratyutpanna buddhi* and (c) *Deergha sutra buddhi*. *Anagata buddhi* meant the intelligence that constantly studied the time and place factors, perceived the approaching dangers in advance and was ready to meet the eventuality in advance. The 'Pratyutpanna mati' was intelligence that was ready to respond to any eventuality because it had the capacity to immediately perceive danger and devise methods to resist it. 'Deergha sutra' intelligence took time to decide and, hence, was overwhelmed by the dangers and consequently suffered. According to Bhishma, 'Anagata Vidhata' and 'Pratyaptanna mati' correctly visualized dangers and resisted

---

[11] The Mahabharata, 12-128-47.
[12] Ibid., 12-128.30-32.

them.[13] The first two understood the exact nature of time and place and, as a result, they correctly responded to the danger and survived. The Arthashastra teachers such as Bharadvaja frequently used these two terms while explaining their viewpoints. Thus, the intelligent use of human reason was important.

In the course of discussion, Bhishma has expounded the concept of *Vijnyana bala*. *Vijnyana* means the phenomenal world that could be understood with the help of sense perceptions. A variety of human experiences and multiplicity of human practices had to be understood and analysed. An intelligent person should not rely on the scriptures or on the testimony of the wise alone, but should make his own judgement by making critical assessment of the situation. Men learnt many things from the experiences as well as from natural phenomena. A discerning mind should draw right conclusions. He should possess either 'Anagata buddhi' or 'Pratyatpanna mati'. Thus, *Vijnyana bala* meant the wisdom and strength derived from a variety of human experiences. As bees gather honey from different flowers, similarly, the wise should draw wisdom from different sources.

According to Bhishma, the nature of dharma was complex; as at times, dharma looked like *adharma* and vice versa. The more we pound the soil, the finer it gets; similarly, the more we discuss dharma, the subtler it becomes. It is as difficult to understand dharma as to find out the feet of a snake. Therefore, the wise king with a discerning mind really knew that dharma and *artha* were clear issues and there could be no subterfuge or camouflage regarding these. Our current understanding of dharma does not admit direct proof. The appeal is always to the judgement of the wise man and not to brute majority or sheer prosperity.[14] Thus, the concept of *Vijnyana bala* enables the king to draw fresh conclusions on the basis of multiple practical experiences. According to Bowls, *Vijnyana bala* meant discrimination judgement by which a person would be able to discern the proper application of

---

[13] Ibid., 12-135.
[14] S. K. Belvalkar quoted by Goshal, *A History of Indian*, 230.

dharma in respect of limitations and circumstances.¹⁵ He quotes Bhishma: 'Who can say anything about him who is resolute and endowed with the ability to discriminate between proper modes of living even if he lives among the despicable, purified as he is by power of his discriminatory judgement.¹⁶ This discerning judgement is acquired by intelligently studying a variety of human situations and experiences and analysing them with the help of 'Anagatabuddhi' and 'Pratyuptanna mati'. While taking judgement, the basic criterion is self-preservation and welfare and well-being of the people.

Bhishma said that the king or a Brahmin who was in distress should live by *Vijnyana bala* as great royal sages had followed this path. He said:

> One should live by *Vijyanabala* and sometimes he may have to follow immoral ways and he is not deserved to be censured for that. The men of middling intelligence followed the canon without modification, but the wise men make special application of the same as while practicing *Dharma* he should be in secure confidence that the people always supported good and not evil. Hence, he should avoid evil and practice merit.¹⁷

He should know that the final authority of dharma was approved by one's own conscience.¹⁸

There is an example of Vishvamitra, who saved his life relying upon *Vijnyana bala*. He was extremely hungry as there was drought in the area. He wanted to eat the haunch of the dog kept in the house of an outcaste. The outcaste asked him to follow the injunctions of Vedas and not to eat the dog's meat. The sage told him that self-preservation was the supreme right of the individual and when an intelligent man faced calamities, he should use every

---

[15] Bowls, *Dharma, Disorder and Political*, 219.
[16] The Mahabharata, 12-130-3-8.
[17] Ibid., 12-130.
[18] Ghoshal, *A History of Indian*, 230.

means at his disposal to save himself because only by saving his life he could practice dharma and earn merit.[19]

In Chapter 140 of the Shantiparva, Bhishma sought to explain the meaning of *Vijnyana bala*. He said:

> I do not instruct you regarding the duty taught by the Vedas alone, what I have told is the result of wisdom and experience. This is the honey the learned have gleaned. The kings should collect wisdom from various sources. One cannot go successfully through the worldly course of action with one sided morality. Duty must originate with reason and understanding that makes him triumphant.[20]

Wisdom had many facets, like a stream with devious undercurrents. Bhishma has quoted two Arthashastra teachers—Ushanasa and Brihaspati—who proclaimed that man had to use his intelligence to secure victory, because human endeavour was ultimately important. Brihaspati suggested that both reason and cannon are important, but one should not indulge in its one-sided pursuit. According to Ushanasa, knowledge that confused person was no true knowledge.

He pleaded for the use of intelligence and reason to arrive at truth. For the Kshatriya, his job was clear. He had to protect the people at all costs. He was a wretch among the Kshatriyas in whose kingdom the robbers go about plundering the property of other people, like crows picking up fish out of water. If the king did not establish order in the society, people would prowl upon each other like wolves.[21] Shukra advised that during distress, the king should control unscrupulous people and protect good people, so that his kingdom would flourish.[22] In this discourse, Bhishma had stressed the importance of reason and criticized the supporters of one-sided morality. Dr U. N. Ghoshal contends that this was the highest watermark of rationalism.[23]

[19] The Mahabharata, 12-139-93.
[20] Ibid., 12-140-5-7.
[21] Ibid., 12-140-27-28.
[22] Ibid., 12-140-33.
[23] Ghoshal, *A History of Indian*, 233.

In the Appadharma Parva are present three important dialogues: those of of Palita and Lomasha, Brahmadatta and Pujani and Kaninka Bharadvaja and Shatrumtapa. Bharadvaja's teaching represents certain extreme tendencies in the Arthashastra tradition. He preached the king to follow immoral ways to defeat his enemies, but, at the same time, he said, उध्दरेत् दीनमात्मानं समर्थो धर्ममाचरेत् ।[24] One should save his self-fallen position in distress by following these methods, but once he becomes strong, he should follow principles of dharma. In the previous chapter, we had elaborately discussed the political ideas of Bharadvaja. The remaining two animal fables are important because they contain the basic principles of pre-Kautilyan Arthashastra tradition.

In Chapter 135, Bhishma described three types of intelligence: (a) one which takes into account the present and the future and is ready for any eventuality, (b) one who understands the present and is quick to apprehend impending events and is ready to respond to it and (c) one who is slow to understand and the slower to act upon it. He said that the first two understand time and place factors and impending changes in it and take appropriate decisions. According to him, time meant hour, day, month, seasons and the year, day and night, *kalp* and the entire earth might be considered as place. Time is abstract. First two types of intelligence succeed in the world as corroborated by the sages. Hence, Bhishma said, 'intelligent and active man through his intelligence and exertion brings about changes in time and place and secures desirable benefits of them'.[25] A person who completely prepares himself for the approaching time and place wins rewards![26] In Chapter 136, Yudhishthira asked Bhishma how an intelligent person could protect his own self as well as his kingdom when he was surrounded by all sorts of enemies and was facing a number of dangers. Bhishma narrated him the story of Palita and Lomasha, which tells us how a 'Pratyutpanna mati' mouse ensured his security in the most difficult period. It

[24] The Mahabharata, 12-138-38.
[25] Ibid., 12-135-23.
[26] Bowls, *Dharma, Disorder and Political*, 249.

is one of the biggest dialogues in the Shantiparva as it contains 211 verses. It discusses certain basic principles of politics. The dialogue belonged to the 'Atmarakshitam' section of ancient political science and its contents are expressed through the dialogues of the mouse Palita.[27]

In his famous book *Philosophies of India*, a great German Indologist, Heinrich Zimmer, has discussed the philosophy of power in ancient India. When the Berlin pact between Hitler and Stalin—two sworn enemies—was signed in 1939, Zimmer remembered this remarkable fable. He wrote:

> Yet as soon as I learnt of this startling alliance between two powers that had been thought to be natural enemies, professing conflicting interests and the ideas of life, I was reminded of a Hindu tale, a beast fable figuring in the epic Mahabharata that unique and inexhaustible treasury of spiritual and secular wisdom. It was a parable of a cat and a mouse. And its teaching was two sworn and deadly enemies, such as Hitler's Germany and Stalin's Russia might very well enter into an alliance and present a united front, if such arrangement suited the temporary interests of both.[28]

He further stated that the fable gave an idea of the cold-blooded cynical realism and sophistication that was the very life sap and flavour of the ancient Indian style of political theory. The quick-witted mouse was bold, unprejudiced in the forming of an alliance to ward off the danger. He was a master of art of timing.[29] He wrote:

> The Hindu beast fables ran parallel in doctrine to the moral technical treatises. The vivid case histories presenting under the entertaining guise of animal kingdom, perplexing situations and issues of policy that everywhere confront king, states and private individuals, both in the great struggle of survival and lesser emergencies of life have been the delight of many generations in the West.[30]

---

[27] Agrawala, *Bharat-Savitri*, Vol. III, 119–20.
[28] Zimmer, *Philosophies of India*, 87.
[29] Ibid., 89.
[30] Ibid., 92.

In the Appadharma section of the Shantiparva, two different animal fables delivered the moral discourse on the nature of dharma and *artha*. The animal fables represented the pitiless world of animals that were locked in the fierce struggle of survival. It was the world of jaws and claws. In these fables are put forward political ideas of per-Kautilyan Arthashastra teachers who preached moral and political ideas to secure political goals.[31] In the animal fables, for the animal, the death or survival was the only issue and the fittest survived, as big fish always tried to devour the small. Hence, it was contended that the small fish should use its intelligence and find out a device to survive in the law of the jungle. There was no possibility of external moral intervention, because in the last instance, power and force prevailed. One had to be extremely cautious all the time because even if one enemy was exterminated, there was always a potential enemy to challenge the victor.

In the animal fable of Palita and Lomasha, Bhishma sought to show how a person of 'प्रत्युत्पन्नमती'—a man of quick-witted wisdom—responded to the danger.

Yudhishthira asked Bhishma to tell him about the relationship between enemies and friends during an emergency. Bhishma told him that during the emergency, self-interest of the king was more important than friendship, because in politics, friends and enemies change according to the exigency of time. Keeping this fact in view, the king should decide his course of action.[32] He narrated an old story to drive home the point.

There was in a jungle a very big fig tree that gave shelter to a large number of birds and animals. There lived a cat named Lomash in one of the branches of the tree. There also lived a mouse in one of the mouse pits near the tree. Every day a ferocious-looking hunter used to lay a trap near the tree to catch birds and carried the trapped birds home. One day, Lomash—the cat—got caught in the trap. At the same time, Palita—the

---

[31] Pant, *Introduction to Beniprasad's Theory*, 1–52.
[32] The Mahabharata, 12.136.12.14.

mouse—came out in search of food. It saw its enemy caught in the trap. However, at the same time, it saw two enemies ready to pounce upon it. One was a mongoose called Harin and another was an owl called Chandraka. Palita, a student of politics, realized that its life was in danger and it had to take quick decision. It realized that now it should use intelligence to find out a device to survive, because if it could survive this calamity, it would be in a position to live a full life of 100 years. Palita realized that in this difficult situation, it could save itself by forging an alliance with its 'natural' enemy, Lomasha. Palita approached Lomasha and requested it to give shelter in its net and in lieu of that Palita would free Lomasha from the bondage. Lomasha readily agreed. Palita went inside and slept in the lap of Lomasha. Everyone was surprised because of this strange friendship. Palita justified the alliance saying that it was forged in right time and it would be beneficial to both of them.[33] Both the enemies of Palita realized that due to this alliance, their victim could not be caught; hence, they decided to leave the place. Lomasha requested Palita to free it by cutting the net. However, Palita told Lomasha that it would do so in right time and asked it not to be in a hurry. It told Lomasha:

> I would definitely free you when the hunter comes to catch you. I would free you at that moment of time when you would have enough time to go to your home and I would go to mine because at that time both of us would care for our own life only.[34]

Lomasha again argued and requested Palita to free it. Palita, relying on the ancient wisdom of the Arthashastra, pointed out that when a person entered into an alliance with a powerful ally, he should be very careful about his personal safety because it was something like putting one's hand in the mouth of a snake. There was no permanent friend or enemy in the world, and friendship and enmity were decided on the basis of self-interest. As an elephant was caught with the help of an elephant, a man was used as a means to secure the goals. Lomasha was scared and waited

[33] Ibid., 12.136.44-56.
[34] Ibid., 12.136.74-93.

for the hunter. In the early morning, the hunter came to collect the victim. As soon as the hunter came near the trap, Palita cut the last thread of the net and ran fast to his pit and the cat also climbed the tree up in no time to save its life.

After the hunter left the place in disappointment, Lomasha came near the pit and requested Palita to come out of the pit so that both of them could live in friendship because its life was saved by Palita. But Palita refused to come out and told Lomasha that everybody should know who was his enemy and who was his friend. It held that the friendship with Lomasha was temporary, and since the cause of the friendship was over, now they were natural enemies. Mouse was food for cat. It was the principle of politics that due to change in the interest, enemies became friends and the vice versa. People who aim to succeed in life should not trust anyone because trusting the untrustworthy person would cause disaster. Palita pointed out that in this world, self-interest was a very powerful motive, only because of which sons, daughters, brothers, sisters and other relatives loved each other. Sons abandoned their parents if the latter caused harm to them. The people did not love each other without some reason. Palita told Lomash:

> You are expressing love and affection because you want to eat me. Now you are strong and I am weak, hence, there cannot be a contract between you and me. At that time, we became friends because I had ability to save you but now the situation is changed. There is no mutual interest that can bind us together. I can give you everything except my life because one should protect his self even at the cost of his family, village or state, because if we could survive the calamity, we could secure these things! Even a weak person could survive in this world, if he is alert, vigilant and cautious.[35]

While summarizing the argument, Bhishma told Yudhishthira that he had shown him the path of *Kshatriya dharma*. Its essence was constant alertness about friends and enemies, because these

---

[35] Ibid., 12.136.129.173.

change according to their interests. One should not commit grave errors, and even an intelligent man is destroyed if he had committed mistakes. One should always take into consideration all possibilities because one had to always think about dangers and devise ways and means to meet them. A reckless man can face many problems if he is not cautious about the dangers. Hence, he should correctly understand the meaning of war and peace and their appropriate application depending on time and place. Hence, he said, 'कालेन रिपुणा संधि: काले मित्रेण निग्रह :। कार्यइत्येव तत्वज्ञा: प्राहुर्नित्यं युधिष्ठिर:'.[36] It is the time and interest that forced us to have peace with enemies and war with friends. The king should understand this principle and act accordingly was the advice of Bhishma.

In the second animal fable, some key principles of political theory were discussed as the king raised some important points and Pujani, the bird, tried to respond to them.

In this dialogue, which took place between the king of Kampilya Brahma Datta and a bird called Pujani, Bhishma again pointed out the ruthless nature of politics. Bhishma narrated this fable in response to a question posed by Yudhishthira. Yudhishthira said that it would be difficult to survive in the world if everybody followed the advice of Palita. In the worldly course of action, one had to trust a large number of people. How could a king defeat his enemy if he does not trust anyone? Bhishma told him the story of Brahmadatta and Pujani.

In the Kampilya city, there lived a king called Brahmadatta. In his palace lived a bird called Pujani. She was a very intelligent bird, as she knew the languages of many birds and animals. Both king and the bird begot the sons at the same time. Pujani loved the young prince like her own son and always used to bring two fruits from outside. One fruit was meant for her son and the other for the young prince. Because of eating of the fruits, the prince became strong. One day, Pujani went away to bring fruits. The

[36] Ibid., 12.136.198.

prince, in his prank, caught hold of the young bird and killed it. When Pujani came back, she saw her son murdered. She was grief stricken and to avenge the death of her son, she attacked the prince with her claws and blinded him. She blamed Kshatriyas for their cruelty and decided to leave the place. Brahmadatta came there and requested Pujani not to leave the palace. She told the king that she had taken revenge by making his son blind because everyone in this life had to pay for his crime and the prince had paid it with his eyes! She told the king that everybody had to suffer for his offence, and even if he did not suffer in the life, his relatives, sons and the grandsons had to pay for it later on because enmity continued to remain alive through generations.[37]

Brahmadatta told Pujani that she should not to leave the palace because she had already punished the prince for his offence. Pujani told him that it would be wrong on her part to live in the same house where she had committed an offence. Now the enmity had begun between the king and the bird; a wise person would never trust anyone. Self-interest was the basis of relationship. Therefore, there was no permanent friendship in this world. On Brahmadatta's request to stay back, she told him that because of her action she had become his enemy, and whenever the king saw the blind eyes of his prince, he would resolve to kill the person who was responsible for it. This type of enmity would never end.

But the king persisted and told the bird that he did not believe in the principle of permanent enmity as he believed that with the help of love and association, one could overcome the enmity.

Pujani did not agree with the king and told him that there existed five types of enemies in the world. The first type of enmity was caused because of woman as Shri Krishna and Shishupala became enemies because of Rukmini. The second type of enmity took place because of kingship. The enmity between the Kauravas and the Pandavas illustrated this. The third type of enmity was caused due to use of harsh words and insults. The example was

[37] Ibid., 12.137.21-30.

that of Drona and Drupada. There was natural enmity between the mouse and the cat. Enmity between the king and Pujani was caused because of the offence committed by the prince. Pujani told the king that since they were enemies of each other, there could be no basis for friendship between them. Brahmadatta reasoned with the bird that the time was a great healer and, in due course of time, enmity would die down. Time was responsible for everything and he had pardoned Pujani for the offence.

Pujani told the king that if his argument about the time was accepted, there would be no cause for enmity because then every offence could be attributed to time. But this was not true. If everything was caused by time, the people would not have approached doctors to take medicine. If time was the dispenser of everything, there would not be any merit or sin in the world. Hence, the argument was absurd. She pointed out that men were interested in birds for two reasons: they wanted to either eat them or imprison them for entertainment. Killing or the imprisonment was the result of relationship between man and bird. Time would not heal the wound because both the prince and the bird had caused offence to each other. The grief caused by this injury would continue to haunt them throughout their life. This offence could not be forgotten even for 100 years. She said, 'I shall constantly remember my son and his memories would intensify grief and enmity. Blindness of your son would create similar feelings in your mind. Therefore, there cannot be any friendship between us'.[38]

Brahmadatta did not accept the argument of Pujani and told her that if her advice was followed, the lack of trust and the fears of reprisals would turn human beings into living dead. It would be impossible to organize society on the basis of this advice.

Pujani told him that in difficult situations, men had to act with the help of intelligence; otherwise, they would suffer. She gave an example of a man who, despite his injured feet, had tried

[38] Ibid., 12.137.68.70.

to walk through the road, got them further wounded. Hence, a person who knew his job well would use intelligence to go through the worldly course of life. Human efforts were more important than the fortune because a lazy person, who inherited a good amount of wealth, would lose it in due course of time if he did not exert. She maintained, 'That indeed is one's country where he earns his livelihood. Man could not earn his livelihood in the wicked country. Hence, one should shun a wicked king, wicked wife, wicked son and wicked country'.[39] She advised Brahmadatta to follow his *rajdharma* and protect the people. People had agreed to pay him taxes because of promise of their protection. Therefore, the king who did not protect the people was a thief. The king should see to it that both the people living in the towns and rural areas prospered due to his government. He should remember that enmity with the stronger king would not bring about happiness.[40]

Though Pujani did not answer the basic question raised by Brahmadatta, her emphasis on the concept to *rajdharma*, which was the result of social contract, clearly showed that, though the basic nature of politics could not be changed, the king could ensure the organization and working of political community by following the contractual agreement between the two. She had asked the king to distinguish between his enemies and the people and maintained that the king should ensure welfare of the latter.

In this chapter, we have discussed the problem of relationship between the concepts of *Vijnyana bala* and *Appadharma*. The concept of *Vijnyana bala* frees the actor of any bond of religious sanctions or moral consideration. There is emphasis on freedom of will of the individual to act in the difficult and confusing circumstances as the traditional norms of behaviour would scarcely help him. This strength to act independently is derived from the practical wisdom that he has gathered from a variety of experiences. Thus, the concept of *Vijnyana bala* can be compared with

[39] Ibid., 12.137.89-92.
[40] Ibid., 12.137.97-107.

Aristotle's concept of *phrenesis*, which is also based on the practical wisdom gleaned from one's experience.[41]

The Arthashastra content in the *Appadharma* section primarily belonged to the pre-Kautilyan stage, as most of the ideas propounded there are closer to the ideas expounded by these thinkers. Hence, there are frequent quotations from Ushanasa and Brihaspati to drive home the point. Also included in this section is a discourse by Bharadvaja, who was a prominent pre-Kautilyan Arthashastra thinker. The following are important principles of old Arthashastra tradition, which were approvingly quoted in the Apaddharma Parva.

1. Self-preservation is the fundamental duty of an individual. He has to save his self at all cost and by all means at his disposal.
2. In politics, self-interest is the most important factor, and interest of the state is sovereign. Friends and enemies are not permanent, and they change as the interests change.
3. There are no set moral rules in politics as the character of a particular thing changes on the basis of time and place, which are essentially dynamic. The current understanding of the given situation and the judgement of future course are the important factors for wise men.
4. The king should not follow one-sided morality and, in the ultimate analysis, human reason is important and the appeal is to the conscience of the individual.
5. The purpose of political activity is to ensure *Yoga-kshema* of the people, providing them protection from the powerful people bent upon anarchy and protection of their own interests.
6. It is desirable to further consummation of *artha* and *Kama Purushsarthas* with the help of *Varta* and *Dandaniti*.

It is to the credit of the redactors of the great epic that they have preserved the valuable Arthashastra material in the *Apaddharma*

[41] Chousalkar, *Rebellion and State*, 26.

section of the Mahabharata. The Apaddharma Parva begins with Chapter 129 and its political content is confined to Chapters 129–140. A preface to it was provided in Chapter 128 of Rajdharma Parva.

Bibliography

Agrawala, V. S. *Bharat-Savitri*. Vol. III. New Delhi: Sasta Sahitya Mandal, 1968.
Bowls, A. *Dharma, Disorder and Political in India*. Leiden: EJ Brill, 2007.
Chousalkar, A. 'Contemporary Relevance of Kautilya's Theory of Rebellion'. *Indian Journal of Political Science* 45 (1985): 29–41.
———. *Rebellion and State*. Ambala: Associated Publications, 2009.
Ghoshal, U. N. *A History of Indian Political Ideas*. Delhi: Oxford University Press, 1966.
Muller, Max. *Sacred Laws of the Aryas, as Taught by Apastamba, Gautama, Vashishta and Baudhayana*. Part I, Vol. 2. Delhi: Motilal Banarsidass, 2007.
———. *The Upanishads*. In *The Sacred Books of the East*, Vol. I, Part I. Delhi: Motilal Banarsidass, 2009.
Pant, A. D. *Introduction to Beniprasad's Theory of Government in Ancient India*. Allahabad: Central Book Depot, 1968.
Zimmer, H. *Philosophies of India*. London: Routledge and Kegan Paul, 1953.

9

Ethics and Politics in the Arthashastra Tradition

Arthashastra tradition formed the core of the ancient Indian *Niti* literature, which was subsequently developed by Kamandaka, Kshemendra, Somadeo Suri, Chandeshvara and Shukra. It is rightly pointed out by Dr Beni Prasad that the later *Niti* literature is not as original as the Kautilya's Arthashastra or the *Shantiparva*. One could see intermingling of the Arthashastra and the *Dharmashastra* traditions in the later *Niti* literature.[1] Thus, the originality of political speculation and preponderance of rationalism were two important characteristics of the early Arthashastra thought.

We have seen that the early Arthashastra thought originated during the 6th century BC as the Buddhist sources referred to the existence of *kshatra vidya* or *Lokayata* ideology. However, the full-fledged development of the science had taken place in the age of the Shishunagas and the Nandas when two important monarchies of Kosala and Magadha emerged. Some of the ministers of these kings, such as Dirgha Charayana, Katyayana and Vassakara, were experts in the art of politics, and they demonstrated it in their behaviour. Kautilya said that he had before him the texts of the great masters of the science of politics on the

---

[1] Prasad, *Theory of Government*, 243.

basis of which he composed his book. He mentions a long list of Arthashastra teachers and had quoted ideas of a number of them.

In ancient India, the concept of *trivarga*, or three goals of life, namely dharma, *artha* and *kama*, was expounded, which became a key concept in the development of positive sciences at the time. Around the concept of dharma was developed an enormous body of *Dharmashastra* literature, which sought to protect the validity of the three Vedas. Both the Arthashastra literature and the *Kamashastra* literature were developed based on the concepts of *artha* and *kama*, respectively. Kautilya and Vatsyayana—two of the greatest exponents of *artha* and *kama*—supported the Vedas and the *Varna* order, but as far as Arthashastra and *Kamashastra* traditions were concerned, they scarcely paid respect to the Vedic authority as their main purpose was secular activities of human beings. Hence, for them, *Varta*, or economics, and *Dandaniti*, or political science, were more important. Shukra, Brihaspati and Bharadvaja did not show respect to the Vedas and pleaded for the application of intelligence. In the Mahabharata, Bhimasena is the supporter of *kama Purushartha*, and in his various speeches in the *Aranayaka* and the *Shanti*, which reflect *kama* perspective, scarcely shows any respect for the Vedic dogma and, at times, criticizes Vedic scholars.

Although all the Arthashastra and *Kamashastra* teachers stated that all the three *Purusharthas* should be simultaneously and discriminately pursued and excessive pursuit of a single *Purushartha* is harmful to the king as well as to two other *Purusharthas*, still *artha* or *kama* is important for them as other two *Purusharthas* are dependent on it.[2] That means the *trivarga* ideal should be pursued keeping in view the importance of *artha*.

The *trivarga* ideal is closely related to four sciences—philosophy, theology, economics and politics—as three Vedas are concerned with dharma, *Varta* with *artha* and *kama*, and *Dandaniti* with *artha* or politics. Shukra stated that all three sciences are a part of *Dandaniti*. Here, he is trying to develop a

[2] *The* Arthashastra, 1.7.4.7.

Dandaniti-centred theory of social sciences. He is not eliminating philosophy, three Vedas or *Varta* but is making them a part of *Dandaniti*. Bharadvaja pleaded for the pursuit of *artha* and *kama Purusharthas* and stated that *kama* stood for pleasure, but its excessive pursuit would result in pain.

There was a close relationship between *Lokayata* philosophy and the Arthashastra politics, because both of them believed in the direct evidence of senses and held that benefits of the science could be enjoyed in this world only as the science had nothing to do with the other world. Second, there is always criticism of *Lokayata* philosophy as well as *kshatra vidya* that it is the science of low quality and believed in the theory of the end-justified means. Dandin parodied the Arthashastra teaching in his book *Dash Kumar Charitam* because he thought that the royal science taught king not to believe in any one. The *Lokayata* philosophy was also criticized for its doubtful commitment to morality as it pointed out that one should borrow to enjoy things in life because there was no rebirth of the human body. They held that material pleasures were important. Bharadvaja also said that all human beings seek to enjoy pleasures and avoid pains. *Lokayata* philosophers believed that worldly pleasures could only be enjoyed with the help of *artha* and *kama Purusharthas*. This could be done by developing sources of *Varta* such as agriculture, trade and cattle breeding. These professions could be developed only with the help of human endeavour. Everything in the world is achieved with the help of human action, and nothing is achieved with the help of fate. Thus, *Lokayata* ethic was not amoral as it is pointed out by its opponents, but it was strongly positivist as it envisaged development of sources of *Varta* to ensure proper *Yoga-kshema* of the people. The basic purpose of *Dandaniti* was proper management of human affairs to ensure right organization of the state for the happiness of the people. The philosophy that considers *Dandaniti* as its supporting science cannot claim that individual hedonism was its goal.

Lokayatas believed in the validity of direct evidence of senses, special inherent properties of atom that gave birth to consciousness and nonexistence of the supreme being. Thus, the *Lokayata* gave importance to the worldly or earthly goods and decried other-worldly philosophies. Political science kept this practice alive and Somadeo Suri, who wrote *Nitivakyamrita* in the 11th century AD, while opening the book says, 'अथ धर्मार्थ फलाय राज्याय' He salutes the state for delivering fruits in the form of dharma and *artha*. He saluted the state instead of *Teerthankaras*, because the *Barhaspatya* and the *Aushanasa shastras* were the main authorities of Somadeva, and Brihaspati had saluted the sage *Angirasa* and Shukra had saluted the state.[3]

The *Lokayata* had a strong moral commitment. They opposed Vedic dogma because it was against reason as it relied on textual authority. The sacrifices were costly, wasteful and obscene and superstitious. They destroyed trees and caused great sufferings for *dasas* and *karmakaras* (slaves and workers). Many of its rituals such as *Ashvamedha* sacrifice were obscene. It allowed the priests to preach fraudulent practices to subserve their selfish interests. The *Lokayata* criticism of Vedic dogma was reasonable and morally correct.

Some of the Charvakas were opposed to violent wars to win kingdoms. Yudhishthira was criticized by a *Charvaka* Brahmin for killing his own kinsmen for the sake of kingdom. This view might not be shared by other *Lokayata* thinkers or the Arthashastra teachers, but his moral commitment is noteworthy. The *Lokayata* held that there was no external agency that gave consciousness as it was generated through the combination of multiple factors as human being is born out of *shukra* (semen) of his father and *shonit* (blood) of his mother. All material elements consisted of atoms, and the combination of these atoms gives birth to new material elements. Hence, men need not believe in some external agency like god for consciousness as it is *Swabhava* of every material object to produce consciousness. Thus, *Lokayata* philosophy believes that ultimate moral decisions

[3] Jayaswal, *The Hindu Polity*, 10.

Ethics and Politics in the Arthashastra Tradition / 157

have to be taken keeping in view its rationality and the dictates of our conscience. This *Charvaka* position cannot be called immoral.

The time and place factors decide the outcome of every case. For example, the *Panchatantra* says:

> *A crocodile at home*
> *Can beat an elephant*
> *But if he goes abroad*
> *A dog can make him pant.*[4]

Regarding the time factor, it says:

> *Remember Rama,*
> *wandering far,*
> *Remember Nala's sinking star,*
> *with Bali's bonds the Vrishni's tomb*
> *And Lanka's monster monarch's doom.*
> *The Pandu's forest disaster,*
> *And knightly Arjun dancing-master!*
> *Time brings us woe in countless shape,*
> *what savior is there, who escapes.*[5]

The *Lokayata* teachers held that the sources of *Varta* such as trade, cattle breeding and agriculture should be developed. *Dandaniti* is needed to acquire things not possessed, preservation of things possessed, the augmentation of things preserved and bestowal of things augmented on a worthy recipient. On it depended 'the orderly maintenance of the worldly life'.[6] Kautilya further stated that *Danda* used with full consideration endowed

---
[4] Ryder, *The Panchatantra*, 239.
[5] Ibid., 300.
[6] The Arthashastra, 1-4, 3-4.

the subjects with dharma, *artha* and *kama*. If it is used in anger or passion, it enraged even forest anchorites and wandering teachers and, of course, householders. If it were not used at all, anarchy, logic of fish, would prevail. Hence, it should be used justifiably.[7] Emphasizing, ultimately, the importance of *Dandaniti*, Kautilya stated that three ends had their roots in *Dandaniti*. Administration of the science of politics, when rooted in self-discipline, brings security and well-being to living beings.[8]

It is true that the Vedic scholars, supporters of the *Dharmashastra* school and the Buddhist thinkers condemned *kshatra vidya* as science that taught kings to perform all sorts of cruel and criminal acts to safeguard or to subserve their interests. Dandin, in his *Dash Kumar Charitam*, parodied the *shastra* saying 'For the shastra is concerned with others, unless all are read, nothing is thoroughly known, let its principles be grasped after a short or a long times, when the shastra is learnt, the first lesson taught is 'not to trust one's wife or child'.[9] He said that the teachers of the *shastra* asked the king to study only *Dandaniti* and no other three sciences as studying these bore the fruits slowly.[10] Now, it is true that some of the teachings of the teachers of politics were immoral as far as the normal moral standards were concerned, but that was not the whole story. The entire thrust of the Arthashastra tradition was this-worldly, and it sought to make human life on this earth as happy as possible. Therefore, Kautilya specifically stated that proper application of *Dandaniti* by self-disciplined ruler ensured *Yoga-kshema* of the people. *Yoga* stood for acquisition of the sources of livelihood and *kshema* stood for 'peaceful' enjoyment of what was acquired through hard labour. Peaceful enjoyment of the object was possible only in the state which was properly governed. What is immoral in this teaching? Does *Dandaniti* ask the king to strive

[7] Ibid., 1-4, 11-14.
[8] Ibid., 1.5.3.
[9] Saletore, *Ancient Indian Political*, 498.
[10] Ibid., 497–98.

for self-aggrandizement at the cost of the welfare of the people? Kautilya said that in the absence of the king who held *Danda* or royal authority, the weak was devoured by the strong but if the weak were protected by the king, he gained influence.[11] Therefore, he stated that the king should acquire complete control over the senses so that he could effectively work for the welfare of the people and not for self-aggrandizement.[12]

If this is the case, why do Arthashastra teachers suggest use of immoral means in pursuit of a particular policy? This problem is related to the specific nature of politics. Manu, one of the important pre-Kautilyan Arthashastra thinkers, had said that due to peculiar nature of politics, the ordinary moral laws could not be applied to the royal behaviour. The same opinion was expressed by Bhishma in his discourses on *Rajdharma Anushasana*.[13]

The essence of politics is *Anushasana*. This is a technical word used by ancient Indian thinkers. The concept of *Anushasana* consists of five elements:

1. The king should be well trained in all four sciences.
2. He should have imbibed basic principles of self-discipline as well as control over the senses.
3. A well-educated and self-disciplined king will administer the kingdom for the sake of welfare of the people.
4. The king has promised the people that he would protect them in lieu of the taxes paid by them. He will compensate the amount to the person whose house is robbed by thieves and if the amount burgled is not recovered.
5. He has to protect his kingdom from the internal and external enemies and he has to constantly remain alert against different conspiracies of the enemy. Hence, protection of

---

[11] The Arthashastra, 1.4.14-15.
[12] Ibid., 1-7-1-2.
[13] Ibid., 12-16.

the kingdom is a part of *Anushasana*. Thus, *Anushasana* stands for good governance, which is not possible if the king is not well educated in philosophy.

When the king is entrusted with the security of state, he has to face all sorts of dangers from internal and external enemies who could be using all means fair and foul at their disposal to secure the state. While defending his control over the state, the incumbent king cannot be expected to use only fair means when his enemies are bent upon taking recourse to foul means. Hence, the Arthashastra teachers like Shukra, Brihaspati and Bharadvaja advised that the interest of the state and its seven constituent elements are of the supreme importance and whosoever including his own close relatives work against the interest of the state, he or she should be punished. Love for close kins cannot come in the way of interest of the state, and if a compromise is made on this issue, the king is likely lose his kingdom as well as his and his own family's life.

Thus, for the Arthashastra teachers interest of the state was important, and for that purpose they wanted the king to use all means fair and foul at his disposal to foil the attempt of the enemy. It is up to the king to decide when the security of the state is endangered and when the use of unfair means was absolutely necessary as there are no set rules. It is to the credit of the Arthashastra teachers in the Mahabharata that they had expounded the concept of *Apaddharma* or the duties of the king at the time of distress. They specifically stated that at the time of distress, the king could use both fair and foul means to defeat the designs of the enemy. He should rely upon the concept of *Vijnyanabala* to overcome the emergency. When the king is using *Vijnyana bala,* for him dharma and *artha* are outright issues, and he has to take decisions on the basis of the current understanding of the situation, relying on a variety of experiences as there are no set patterns to go by. It has to be altogether a fresh formulation. Time and place factors played a key role in this. Thus, the defining principle is self-preservation as well as protection and preservation of his kingdom. Therefore, the most extreme of the Arthashastra teachers, Bharadvaja, in both of his discourses had stated that these methods (at times evil) should be employed when the king is in distress, and once he overcomes the distress and gains strength, he should practice dharma. Governing the state is a difficult task. The *Panchatantra* graphically describes the merciless world of politics.

> *Through trust, the root of happy power,*
>
> *A creature wins kingship's flower;*
>
> *When lions, born to kingship, must,*
>
> *As tyrants govern, lacking trust.*[14]
>
> When kings are merciless as death,
>
> All foes are quick to knuckle under;
>
> Quick, too, to kill the king,
>
> Who fall into compassion's fatal blunder.[15]

Keeping this fact in view, Professor Kangle has pointed out that there are echoes of Bharadvaja's extreme ideas in all the books on political science, including such respectable books as the *Manusmriti*, because for both Manu and Bharadvaja, the interest of the state was important. At times, this position of Kautilya is compared with Machiavelli's concept of reason of state, where he points out that the state has both demonic and angelic forms and, as a progressive force of history, the state has to assert its existence by destroying the anarchic forces that sought to overwhelm the state.[16]

The preceding discussion will make it clear that the criticism of *Dandaniti* or Arthashastra was one sided as the critics like Dandin have taken out of context one part of the teaching of

---

[14] Ryder, *The Panchatantra*, 175.
[15] Ibid., 237.
[16] Rawat, 'Reason of State'.

the *Shastra* to criticize it. It is made specifically clear that these unfair means should only be used at the time of distress to save one's own self and not universally.

The pre-Kautilyan Arthashastra tradition was not an ideologically homogeneous thought, though it shared its salient features. There were three ideological currents—the first was the school of Manu, which was closer to then dominant *Dharmashastra* tradition. Manu held that philosophy was a part of *trayi* or three Vedas; hence, it did not exist as an independent science. He supported non-violence as a creed and steered middle course on many important issues. Comparatively, his attitude was liberal as far as awarding punishments to various offences was concerned. However, while dealing with enemies, he recommended harsh measures against them.

The second school of thought was that of Shukra and Brihaspati, which formed the mainstream, and Brihaspati believed in rationalism and realism. For them, interest of the state was important and they advocated the use of all means for the protection of the same. But Brihaspati held that unfair and violent means should not be used against general population because it would earn bad name for the king. They sought to separate politics from theology.

Bharadvaja represented the third school of thought which was extreme in nature. He stated that a minister was the most important constituent of the state, and during the succession crisis, he should seize power and assume sovereignty because the fate smiled on brave. In both the discourses in the epic, he suggested extreme measures to conquer the enemy, including bribery and deception. If we did not use these measures, the enemy would take recourse to these measures. He had used the animal similes of crow, snake, lion and wolf to tell the king how to behave with the enemy. In both the discourses of Bharadvaja, there is a little difference between the king and state as he held that their interests were identical.[17] He made a qualification that the most dreadful

---

[17] Kangle, 'Bharadvaja: An Ancient Teacher', 333–38.

advice is to be applied at the time of adversity, not in normal circumstances. However, the advice itself was so dreadful that even a blind crook like Dhritarashtra was stunned for a while but, nevertheless, he implemented his advice by sending the Pandavas to firehouse of Waranavat where he conspired to burn them to death. Bharadvaja said that the pursuit of three goals of life invites pleasures as well as pains. Hence, the king should secure pleasures and avoid pain. Excessive pursuit of dharma results in loss of *artha* and *kama* and, consequently, loss of pleasures of life. If *artha* or *kama Purushartha* is pursued in excess, the other two suffer. Thus, three goals should be pursued in such a manner that they do not harm each other, and we are able to enjoy pleasures flowing therefrom and avoid pain.[18]

Bharadvaja is a thinker who has close affinity with *Lokayata* philosophy as he pointed out that man wants to avoid pain and enjoy pleasure.[19] He did not believe in the sanctity of Vedas. The essence of teaching, as we learnt from the animal fable of the clever fox, is that one must always be alert and intelligent to serve one's own interests. Thus, Bharadvaja represents an extremely radical school of Arthashastra tradition.

The early Arthashastra thinkers developed the science of politics in ancient India by carrying out inductive investigation in the phenomenon of state. They have developed their own methodology, which could be seen in the last chapter of the Kautilya's Arthashastra. We know that there existed Arthashastras of Manu, Ushanasa, Brihaspati, Bharadvaja and Vishalkasha, and several *gathas* from their books are cited by the Mahabharata. However, unfortunately, these Arthashastras are lost forever. Kautilya claimed that he had written the Arthashastra on the basis of the texts of the science written by earlier masters. We do not know the nature of these texts, but if we go by Kautilya's text or the text of divine *Dandaniti* we find in the Mahabharata[20], we can

---

[18] The Mahabharata, 1-140-65-69.
[19] Ibid., 1-140-63.
[20] Ibid., 12.59.

safely argue that much speculation, efforts and research had gone into the subject.

Three important concepts of ancient Indian political thought are the theory of seven constituent elements of the state, the theory of *Mandala* (inter-state relations) and theory of social contract of origin of state and diplomacy, and it is possible that the seeds of these theories might be sown by the early Arthashastra teachers.

The greatest contribution of these thinkers is this worldly attitude and their advocacy of *artha* and *kama Purusharthas*. They asserted that with the help of human endeavour, great changes have been ushered into, such as the establishment of cities and settlement of villages, and efforts were made to scale the great mountains and to cross oceans. It is indomitable courage and spirit of the man that had changed the world; hence, it is through the manly action that rewards were won and the fruits of exertion enjoyed.

In the '*Kootdanta Sutra*', the priest of the king showed an alternative path of development because he realized that the sacrifices were violent, costly, oppressive and destructive to the nature. However, they were performed with blind belief that they ensured material progress. In fact, due to constant performance of these sacrifices, the king neglected his duties, and his kingdom was infested with robbers and thieves. The *purohita* told him that if he wanted to end the robbery and brigandage, he should give means of subsistence to the people so that they would get involved in productive activities, and as a result stop getting involved in robbery and brigandage. Advice of the wise *purohita* was followed with good results. This was a new path of development that encouraged people to develop the sources of *artha* such as cattle breeding, trade and agriculture. This was the most progressive message that was given by the Arthashastra teachers to the people.

Jabala told Rama that he should not accept wrong advice of his father or priests but consider the future consequences of his action.

It is wrong to say that Indian tradition was overwhelmingly spiritual, otherworldly and ascetic. The *Lokayata* philosophy and Arthashastra politics clearly showed that this impression was not correct, and they have provided a positive alternative during the 6th century BC.

Though Arthashastra and the Buddhist traditions adopted antagonistic positions and Buddha advised his followers not to listen to *Lokayata* doctrines but they shared some ideas as both of them were opposed to Vedic dogma, Vedic rituals and performance of sacrifices. They were against Varna distinctions; they also agreed that for the welfare of the people, institution of the state was needed. They differed on other philosophical issues as Buddha preached asceticism and renunciation and set up Bhikshu Samghas. The Arthashastra teachers opposed life renunciation as well as ascetic Sanghas of Bhikshus. Kautilya was hostile to them. It was *Lokayata purohita* of Mahavijita who suggested positive path of economic development by combining the Buddhist and Arthashastra insights.

There were two traditions, the Arthashastra and *Dharmashastra* traditions; the first followed *artha* and the second dharma ideals, and there was hostility between the two, which could be seen in Chapter 140 of the *Shantiparva*. It seems that in the later period, especially at the time of composition of didactic portion of the *Shantiparva*, there was a compromise between the two and before that Kautilya had accepted the efficacy of Vedas, importance of Varnashrama dharma and duty of the king to protect the Varna order. In the later period, *Rajdharma* became the part of *Dharmashastra* as there was a synthesis of Arthashastra and *Smriti* traditions. The compromise took place because the society of the 1st century AD did not require the Arthashastra prescriptions of the 4th century BC as stability was achieved through village economy, feudal and caste oppression.

Therefore, the *Smriti* ideology became more influential and political thought in ancient India increasingly became subservient to it.

Bibliography

Jayaswal, K. P. *The Hindu Polity*. Bangalore: Central Book Depot, 1955.
Kangle, R. P. 'Bharadvaja: An Ancient Teacher of Political Science'. *Bharatiya Vidya* 21–22 (1961): 34–45.
Prasad, Beni. *Theory of Government in Ancient India*. Allahabad: Central Book Depot, 1968.
Rawat, B. S. 'Reason of State in Kautilya's Arthashastra'. Paper presented at *All India Political Science Conference* held at Jodhpur, 1976.
Ryder, A. *The Panchatantra*. Mumbai: Jaico Publications, 2010.
Saletore, B. A. *Ancient Indian Political Ideas and Institutions*. Bombay: Asia Publishing House, 1971.

10

Supremacy of Politics

In the present book, we tried to revisit political thought of ancient India in the light of political thought of pre-Kautilyan Arthashastra tradition. It is rightly pointed out by Dr U. N. Ghoshal that the Indians belonged to that category of people who had left their impression upon the pages of history as the founders of original system of political thought.[1] The roots of ancient Indian political ideas could be traced back to the Vedic *Smhitas*, and its last major work was written in the 11th century AD. With the decline of Hindu India, the political thought also declined, though there was resurgence of these ideas during the Maratha period.

As far as the nature of historiography of ancient Indian political thought was concerned, we could discern three trends. The first was developed by Professor Beni Prasad who studied political thought in ancient India through the liberal democratic perspective and held that political science could never make itself completely independent of religion and ethics.[2] He also pointed out that the institution of caste and the pretentions of Brahminical supremacy dominated the ancient Hindu thought. The second viewpoint was represented by Professor Pratap Giri who held that the Hindu theory of government was based on the unequal caste system, and it was essentially authoritarian in nature

---

[1] Ghoshal, *A History of Indian Political Ideas*, 2.
[2] Prasad, *Theory of Government in Ancient India*, 3.

because the king enjoyed absolute power.[3] The third perspective was developed by Sri Aurobindo and Dr K. P. Mookerjee[4] who held that the Indian system of government was dominated by spirituality, which was master key of its mind. It was the opinion of Sri Aurobindo that Indian system was a complex system of communal freedom and self-government with each group of community having its own natural existence. It was flexible and the organically self-determining communal life. Dharma was a principle that provided link between different units. The state was an organic whole.[5] Thus, we have three different perspectives which dominated our understanding of political thought in modern India.

While describing salient features of ancient Indian political thought, Professor Beni Prasad had put forward the following features:

1. The Indian approach was a synthetic approach and politics was viewed as a part of religion and ethics.
2. Impact of Vedic dogma and divine hand is visible in the formation of the society and state.
3. The idealistic and imaginative bent of Hindu mind.
4. Impact of caste and the supremacy of Brahmins.
5. Influence of the concept of dharma and its metaphysics.[6]

In this book, we are revisiting ancient Indian political thought to correct the impression that Indian political thought was profoundly influenced by religion and metaphysics. It is our contention that political ideas of pre-Kautilyan Arthashastra tradition were radically different from the dominant version of ancient Indian political thought which was dominated by Arthashastra-*Smriti* tradition.

---

[3] Giri, *The Problem of the Indian Polity*, 93.
[4] Mookerjee, *The State*.
[5] Aurobindo. *The Spirit and Form of Indian Polity*, 1.
[6] Prasad, *Theory of Government in Ancient India*, 1–19.

It is true that normally the Indian thinkers followed the synthetic method and sought to synthesize two differing viewpoints. In the Christian era, there was an attempt to synthesize the Arthashastra ideas with that of the *Dharmashastra*, but the early Arthashastra thinkers did not follow this method as Shukra, Brihaspati and Bharadvaja considered the three Vedas or the *trayi* as *Samvaram* or a cloak or a cover. It is a cover to hoodwink the people. These thinkers, especially Shukra, held that politics was a separate science and it was not a part of religion and metaphysics.

The Arthashastra thinkers did not believe in the Vedic dogma and held that human reason was more important than the Vedic injunctions. They held that all social and political institutions were not created by God and they had human origin. It is with the help of human efforts and the hard work only that cities and villages were established houses were built and the land was brought under cultivation. Kautilya had pointed out that social contract was the basis of state. The teachers were opposed to performance of sacrifices which were costly and useless.

The Arthashastra teachers were not influenced by idealism and metaphysics, and they were not attracted by spiritualism. They supported human reason and held that sense perception was the true source of knowledge. They held that every principle should be tested on the crucible of reason. Teachers such as Jabala did not believe in existence of God, soul, hell and heaven, and argued that every action should be judged on the basis of self-interest and its future consequences. For him and for Brihaspati, independence of human will was important. The teachers gave more importance to the principles of *artha* and *kama*, as they helped people to secure pleasure and to avoid pain. In the *Apaddharma* section of the *Shantiparva*, the concept of dharma was interpreted in such a manner that it was purged of its metaphysical meanings. Chapter 140 of the Shantiparva clearly indicated the change.

It was argued by the teachers that the exact nature of dharma could only be understood with reference to time, place and the purpose for which it was performed. They held that factors, time and place, determined the nature of dharma. Thus, no universals were accepted. Relativism was preferred to idealism. They accepted direct evidence of senses, inference, analogies and the examples from the history as the valid sources but held that inference should not be used to advocate existence of God.

The *Lokayata* teachers rejected the validity of caste system and the supremacy of Brahmins. We do not have credible evidence to show that all the Arthashastra teachers did the same thing, but Jabala in the Ramayana and the royal priest in the *Kootdanta Sutra* rejected caste and Varna system. Both Shukra and Brihaspati said that a Brahmin could not be condoned, if he tried to harm seven constituent elements of the state.

The Arthashastra teachers were influenced by rationalism and relativism, and they were accused that they did not support the cause of morality. The Arthashastra teachers were of the view that political actions of the rulers should not be judged on the universal moral considerations because for politics, the laws of morality were different. It was the contention of these thinkers that the duties of the king were the most important for the survival of the civilized society. It was due to the intervention of the state that the weak people in the society were protected and the logic of fish did not prevail. In the Mahabharata, Brihaspati specifically maintained that in the absence of the state, the anarchy would prevail and the human life would be in danger. Thus, survival and the proper functioning of the state had moral purpose. This moral purpose and not self-aggrandizement of the king was the goal of state.

One of the important contributions of the Arthashastra teachers was the concept of *Vijnyana bala* which was expounded in the *Apaddarma* section of the *Shantiparva*. One can say that in this section, Bhishma talked about two types of intelligence of the intelligent person. The first type of intelligent person understood the danger in advance and took the appropriate steps to meet the situation. The second type of person had innate capacity to respond to the situation after apprehending the danger. He was of the opinion that the intelligent person had to study variety of situations and human experiences to arrive at conclusion. They cannot rely upon the stale formulation but they have to appeal to their conscience. Wisdom had many sidewise facets: it is like a river with many devious flowing currents. One-sided understanding of the situation would not help. Appeal is not to brute majority or sheer prosperity but current understanding of the situation. Hence, he asked the king to live by *Vijnyana bala,* the strength derived from practical experience. It was honey gleaned from different sources. He declared that a final authority of dharma was what was approved by one's own conscience.[7] The concept of *Vijnyana bala* could very well be compared with Aristotle's concept of *Phronesis,* explaining its meaning, Morall wrote:

> It rests on the application of central standard of sanity in a million varied and unpredictable circumstances. No cast iron rules can be given but the way to salvation lies through the training of political intellect through acquired experience of habit to choose the right cause of action in each particular case which may come up.[8]

Morall has correctly explained the meaning of *Vijnyana bala* also. It is argued by Professor Pratap Giri that the Hindu state was authoritarian, and all powers were concentrated in the hands of the king. There is no doubt that early Arthashastra teachers supported monarchy and pursuit of unfair means to safeguard the kingdom. But due to the Buddhist influence, the priest of king Mahavijita of *Kootdanta Sutra* is of the view that the king should take the consent of the *Paura* and *Janapada* as well as *dasa* and *karmakaras* before resuming the practice of performance of sacrifice. Thus, there are strands of democratic ideas in the tradition.

Another important aspect of the Arthashastra tradition was that it sought to free politics from influence of religion. It discounted the influence of the Vedas as well as Brahmins and held that politics or *rajdharma* had its own standards of functioning and religion should not intervene in the functioning of the state. Arthashastra teacher Jabala asked Rama not to follow the advice of Brahmins and take decision on the basis of his self-interest as

---

[7] Ghoshal, *A History of Indian,* 230.
[8] Morall, *Aristotle George,* 60.

well as interest of the state. In the *Kootdanta Sutra*, the royal priest advised to develop the sources of *artha* such as agriculture, trade and cattle breeding. He could develop his kingdom by providing the means of livelihood to the people who ensured progress and development of the state. Brihaspati also said that human efforts and exertion were more important and with the help of human exertion, only great cities and buildings were built, and vast tracks of land were brought under cultivation. Thus, the Arthashastra *school* gave positive message of development of material resources to the people.

It is pertinent to note here that the insights of the Arthashastra tradition could be creatively applied to oppose religious obscurantism, fanaticism and violence. We can defend freedom of individual will and autonomy of conscience when the forces of authoritarianism are going strong all over the world.

Note. After the establishment of the Maratha state in the second half of the 17th century by Shivaji, a number of books on political science were written. These books were written in Sanskrit and Marathi and prominent among them are the *Budhbhooshan* by Sambhaji, *Dandaniti* by Keshava, *Rajaniti* by Ramachandra and the *Rajaniti* by Malhar Ramrao Chitnis. The *Rajaniti* or the *Ajnya Patre* by Ramachandra is a noteworthy text.

Bibliography

Aurobindo, Sri. *The Spirit and Form of Indian Polity*. Calcutta: Arya Publishing House, 1947.
Ghoshal, U. N. *A History of Indian Political Ideas*. Mumbai: Oxford University Press, 1966.
Giri, P. R. *The Problem of the Indian Polity*. London: Longman and Green, 1935.
Mookerjee, K. P. *The State*. Adyar: Theosophical Society, 1952.
Morall, I. *Aristotle George*. London: Allem and Unwin, 1977.
Prasad, Beni. *Theory of Government in Ancient India*. Allahabad: Central Book Depot, 1968.

Annexure: Methodology of Kautilya's Arthashastra*

The methodology of the Arthashastra was rooted in *Anvikshiki*, which was called *hetushastra* or the science of reasoning. Its knowledge was necessary to arrive at right conclusions in the confusing situations. It is the opinion of Dr Ghoshal that the method of the *Shastra* was empirical. The teachers of the *Shastra* in general applied methods of observation, analysis and deduction in respect of phenomenon of political life. In Kautilya's work, this empirical method is supplemented by some interesting application of what may be called the historical method. He occasionally drew from traditional history to justify his arguments. He carried out an inductive investigation in the phenomenon of state.[1] Agreeing with Dr Ghoshal, Dr Saletore argued that his method revolved less than two factors—reason as connoted by *Anvikshiki* and past experiences gathered from history. With the help of the first, he analysed principles of politics and drew conclusions with the help of the second. Thus, there was a combination of critical and historical methods.[2]

Sources of Knowledge

According to the ancient Indian thinkers, there were four sources of knowledge and they were as follows: (a) *Pratyaksha* or direct evidences of senses, (b) *Aptopadesh* or the knowledge gleaned from the experience of reliable persons, (c) *Anumana* or inference and (d) *yukti* or continuous reasoning that helped men arrive at

---

* First published in *The Indian Journal of Political Science* 65 (2004): 55–77.
[1] Ghoshal, *A History of Indian Political Ideas*, 82.
[2] Saletore, *Ancient Indian Political Ideas and Institutions*, 286.

right conclusion. While discussing the nature of first two sources, Dr Chatterjee pointed out that they stood for 'Drishtartha' knowledge, which included the trustworthy assertion of ordinary persons and saints, scriptures in so far as they bore on the perceptible objects of the world. Thus, the evidences given by witnesses in law courts, the knowledge about the plants that we got from reliable farmers, the scriptural injunctions about rites and ceremonies for rainfall were the examples of 'Drishtartha'. 'Eitihya' or tradition was considered as the important source of knowledge. The tradition meant the continuous communication of body of beliefs from generation to generation. It had its origin in no living human being, but it was enjoyed by all human beings as the common property of race.[3] Perception meant the valid and certain knowledge that arose as the result of relation of self, senses, and mind and sense objects. Inference should be based on perception by which the concomitance of reason (*Hetu*) could be first observed. There were three kinds of inferences: (a) inference from effect to cause-inference of cohabitation from pregnancy. (b) Inference from cause to effect, future production of fruit from a seed with other attendant causes. (c) Inference by associations other than that of cause and effect as the inference of fire from smoke.[4]

The medical sciences in ancient India considered 'Yukti' as the fourth source of knowledge. 'Yukti' stood for continuous reasoning. According to Dr Dasgupta, 'Yukti' was not considered as a separate 'Pramana' by any other system of Indian philosophy. He wrote,

> When our intelligence judges a fact by complex weighing in mind of a number of reasons, causes of consideration through which one practically attains all that is desirable in life such as virtue. As an example of 'Yukti', Charak mentions forecasting of good or bad harvest from the condition of ground, the estimated amount of rain, climatic conditions and the like. Chakrapani rightly says

---

[3] Chatterjee, *The Nyaya Theory of Knowledge*, 1.
[4] Dasgupta, *A History of Indian Philosophy*, 374–75.

that a case like this where a conclusion is reached as the combined application of a number of reasonings is properly called 'uha'.[5]

'Yukti' was a method of arriving at conclusion as a result of series of reasoning.

Kautilya in his Arthashastra did not discuss the problem of sources of knowledge and their comparative estimate, but he borrowed the ideas of 'tantra-yukti' and *Anvikshiki* from different schools of philosophy and gave them important place in his scheme of things. In the medical sciences of Charak and Susruta, there is a mention of 'tantra-yukti' as the method of science.[6] Kautilya also adopted it perhaps, along with its epistemology, because all four sources of knowledge were liberally used by Kautilya in his Arthashastra.

Kautilya was of the view that the study of 'tantra-yukti' would help a person to understand how to argue logically. In ancient India, the science of *Anvikshiki* taught people how to isolate lies from truth. According to Vidyabhushan, the science of reasoning studied the subject through the process of enunciation, definition and examination. Enunciation was mere mentioning of categories by name, definition consisted in setting forth the character of categories, which differentiated it from other categories, and examination was settlement by reasoning of the question whether definition of category was really applicable to it.[7]

Kautilya used all these methods that were given to him by tradition. He wrote his Arthashastra on the basis of the Arthashastras written by his predecessors. He wrote, 'This single treatise on "Arthashastra" has been prepared mostly by bringing together teachings of as many treatises on science of politics as has been prepared by the ancient teachers for acquisition and preservation of the earth.'[8] But it is rightly pointed out by Dr Ghoshal that 'the

---

[5] Ibid., 375.
[6] Ibid., 389–92.
[7] Vidyabhushan, *History of Indian Logic*, 52–53.
[8] The Arthashastra, 1.1.1.

Kautilya's "Arthashastra" was much more than the summary of earlier works. Kautilya has a stamp of superior political insight and practical wisdom. His treatment involves closer analysis and a sounder judgement on the points at issue—a virtual reconstruction of the science'.[9]

Kautilya sometimes followed the method of supplementing his viewpoint with examples from 'Itihasa-Purana' or the 'Eitihya'.[10] He gave examples from the tradition to show how six enemies of senses destroyed the kings. He cited examples of Bhoja king Dandkya, Karala, Duryodhana, Ravana and the Vrishnis.[11] He gave instances from the history to show that how kings like Vidurath, Karush, Bhadrasena and Kashi were murdered in their own palaces because of lack of caution.[12] He wrote that the great Arthashastra teachers like Katyayana, Dirgh Charayana and Ghotmukha left the royal palace after observing the change in the behaviour of birds and animals because they sensed danger.[13] Kautilya used the historical evidences to substantiate his point of view or sometimes he used them to derive certain conclusions.

Thirty-two Methods of Science or Tantra-Yukti

In the last book of Arthashastra, Kautilya referred to thirty-two devices of the textual interpretation which was called 'tantra-yukti' or devices of science. These devices were also mentioned by Charak in his 'Charaka Samhita' and Susrut in his 'Susrut Samhita'. The medical texts tried to give the meaning of 'tantra yukti'. The knowledge of these devices was necessary to refute the statements of hostile critics and to establish one's own viewpoint. The terms used by Kautilya were terms of scientific arguments.

[9] Ghoshal, *A History of Indian*, 111.
[10] The Arthashastra, 1.6.3.120 and 5.5.10.
[11] Ibid., 1.6.3.
[12] Ibid., 1.20.14–16.
[13] Ibid., 5.5.10.

The list was not prepared either by Kautilya or by Charak, but it was prepared by the persons who wanted to establish debate on the scientific basis. The terms were more widely used in the 'Nyaya' philosophy.[14] The devices were necessary to write technical works and interpret them. It was said that these maxims were like the sun to a group of lotuses or like a lamp to the house for illustration or expression of the subject of discourse.[15] According to Dr Heesterman, the text claimed that its composition was ruled by 32 devices of exposition and argumentation which were enumerated, defined and exemplified from the text. It was helpful to articulate the debates and helped in reaching appropriate decision.[16] Dasgupta held that the devices were maxims for interpretation of textual topics and they were not logical categories. The basic difference between 'Anvikshiki' and 'tantra-yukti' was that the former referred to laws of thought and the latter to the technical mode of expression.[17] They, therefore, referred to ways of deducing the inner meaning or intention of the text from their abbreviated form of expression.

The Arthashastra of Kautilya falls in the 'Mangala' tradition of scientific books which opened with salutes to great originators of science of politics—Shukra and Brihaspati. According to Dr Agrawala, 'a requisite of literary composition was proper planning and presentation of subject matter'. This plan was called 'tantra-yukti'.[18] The science of politics deals with attainment and protection of *artha*. The book was composed with the help of 32 devices and following is the description of these devices.

1. Adhikarana: It means treatment of matter with the purview of the scope of work. It deals with the topic of subject. Kautilya illustrates this with example. 'This science of politics is composed mostly by bringing together teachings of as

---

[14] Vidyabhushan, *History of Indian Logic*, 24–25.
[15] Ibid., 389–90.
[16] Heesterman, *Inner Conflict of Tradition*, 130–31.
[17] Dasgupta, *A History of Indian Philosophy*, 390.
[18] Agrawala, *India as Known to Panini*, 309.

many treatises as have been composed by ancient teachers for the acquisition and preservation of realm'.
2. Vidhana: Statement of content. It is a special enumeration of content. For example, 'Enumeration of science, association of elders, control over the senses, appointment of ministers and so on'.
3. Yoga: Arrangement of sentence by taking into consideration meaning and inter relationship between different words. It means that the verb at a distant part of the sentence may be joined with its relevant case in another part of sentence. For example, 'The people of four varnas and four ashramas'.
4. Padartha: The meaning of the word is called 'Padartha'. We have to give specific meaning to words. According to Dasgupta, 'when a word having two or more senses is used, that meaning alone has to be accepted which suits the previous and later context, Thus, when it is said in the medical text that now we shall describe the Veda then only 'Ayurveda' is meant and not 'Rigveda' or 'Yajurveda'.[19] Kautilya gives an example of word 'Mulahara'. 'He who consumes in unjust ways the property inherited from father and grandfather is called "Mulahara"'.
5. Hetvartha: A reason for proving a thing is reason for establishing a thing. Here, the purpose of reason is to prove an assertion. Many times, it illustrates the condition of visible things by invisible things. For example, '"Dharma" and "Kama" (for their successful consummation) depend on "Artha"'.
6. Uddesha: Mentioning a subject in brief. It stands for mentioning the subject without going into details. For example, 'control over senses is motivated by training in sciences'.
7. Nirdesha: A detailed statement is explanation. It is a method of describing the subject in detail. For example, Kautilya's description of the control over the senses.[20,21]

[19] Dasgupta, *A History of Indian Philosophy*, 390.
[20] The Arthashastra, 15.1.17018.
[21] Ibid., 1.6.2.

8. Upadesh: Means advice. One should behave in this manner is advice. It means giving general instruction which has exceptions. For example, 'he should enjoy "Kama" without contravening his "dharma" and "artha"; he should not deprive himself of pleasures'.
9. Apadesh: Giving reference to somebody else's viewpoint. For examples, Manu asks the King to appoint 12 ministers. Brihaspati asks the King to appoint 16, Ushanas 20, but Kautilya says that the number should be according to the need of the state.
10. Atidesha: It stands for application. It is the analogy by which a present difficulty is solved in the way in which the past difficulty was solved. Old rules are applied in new situations. For example, non-payment of gifts is explained by non-payment of debts. The rules that govern the regulations regarding non-payment of debts are also applied to the rules for non-payment of gifts that are agreed upon. Since a medicine has cured Devadatta, it would cure Yajnyadatta as well.
11. Pradesha: Means indication. Setting forth a thing with what is going to be said in future. It is anticipating future event from present indication. For example, 'the king should overcome it by means of "sama" "dana" and "danda", as we shall explain in the section on trouble'.
12. Upamana: Means analogy. Setting forth an unknown thing with a known thing. For example, he should, like a father, show favours to those whose exemptions have been ceased.
13. Arthapatti: Means implication. That, which though not stated, as a matter of course is implication. Thus, that which is understood by implication, though not mentioned is 'arthapatti'. When a man says, 'he shall eat rice', it is understood that he is hungry and not thirsty. For example, one conversant with the ways of the world should resort to a king endowed with personal excellences and excellences of material constraints through such men as are dear and beneficial to the King. Implication is that he should not

approach the King through men who are not dear and beneficial to the king. In 'Nyaya' philosophy, 'arthapatti' is considered as a source of knowledge. It is understood as a source of knowledge because it consists in the supposition of some unperceived fact in order to explain a given fact, when a given or unperceived fact cannot be explained without some other fact even though we do not perceive it.[22]

14. Samshaya: A thing with reasons on both sides is doubt. When the statement of a reason is equally applicable to two kinds of circumstances, it is called doubt. Doubt may be a case of logical investigation. For examples, 'should one march against a King with impoverished or greedy subjects or a King with rebellious subjects'?

15. Prasanga: A thing common to another subject is similar situation is called 'Prasanga'. By virtue of it, an allusion is made to things repeatedly described in another chapter. For example, 'in a place assigned to him for agricultural work and so or exactly as before'.

16. Viparyay: Contrary corollary. Setting forth a thing with the help of the opposite is contrary (corollary). The inference of a reverse statement from a positive statement is called corollary. Thus, from a negative or a positive statement, its contrary is asserted. For instance, 'the opposite, as that of one displeased'.

17. Vakya Shesha: That by which a sentence is completed is completion of statement. For instance, there is a loss of all activity on the part of the king, as of a bird with clipped wings. There, 'of the bird' is the completion of statement.

18. Anumati: It is agreement. The statement of another, not contradicted, is agreement. When the opinion of other is stated in approval and not refuted is agreement. For example, Kautilya quotes the opinion of Ushanasa.

19. Vyakhyan: The description of speciality is emphasizing. One important factor is emphasized by highlighting its important aspects. Kautilya gives example of 'ganasangh'

---

[22] Chatterjee, *The Nyaya Theory of Knowledge*, 361–62.

to emphasize the fact that gambling was the most destructive of vices.
20. Nirvachana: It is derivation. Deriving the meaning of a word through its components is derivation. For example, 'It throws person from his good hence it is called "Vyasana"'.
21. Nidarshana: Exemplifying by means of example is illustration. For example, when the King decides to go to war with the stronger king, he engages as it were a fight on foot with elephant. It shows fruitlessness of such a fight.
22. Apavarga: It is exception. Taking away from a rule of universal application is exception. It allows exceptions to general principles. For example, 'He should always station alien troops in close proximity to himself except in case of fear of rising in interior'.
23. Sva Samjnya: A word not agreed by others is one's own technical term. The technical words are used in a special way, not used by others. For example, 'The would be conqueror is its first constituent, one immediately next to his territory is second etc.'.
24. Purva Paksha: A 'prima facia' view. It is the statement to be refuted. For example, 'Of calamity befalling the King and the ministers, the calamity befalling the minister is more serious'.
25. Uttar Paksha: A statement giving a final view. It is expounded by refuting Purva Paksha. For example, 'Being a dependent on him, for the King is in the place of head'.
26. Ekant: What is applicable everywhere is universal and invariable rule. It is applicable in all circumstances. For example, 'therefore, he should himself, be energetically active'.
27. Anagata Vekshan: This will be stated afterwards is reference to future statement.
28. Atikranta Vekshana: This has been stated before is a reference to past statement.
29. Niyoga: This and no other way is restriction. Here, the advice is to be emphatically given. For example, he should

instruct him in what conduces to spiritual and material good not in what is spiritually and materially harmful.
30. Vikalpa: Means option. Either in this way or in that way is option. It is a method of giving alternative directions.
31. Samucchaya: Means combination. In this way or in that way is combination. An attempt is made here to bring together two or more things which are mutually beneficial as having equal value. 'Begotten by oneself, the son becomes heir to father and brothers'.
32. Uhya: The doing of what is not expressly stated is what is understood. The purpose of this device is to acquire right knowledge by the combined application of number of reasonings. It means the things apparent from the context should be understood. For example, 'the experts shall fix revocation in a way that neither donor nor the donee is injured'.

Kautilya wrote, 'Thus, this science, expounded with these devices of a science, has been composed for the acquisition and protection of this world and of the next. This science brings into and preserves "dharma" "artha" and "Kama" and destroys "adharma" "anartha" and "hatred"'.[23]

These devices were used to understand the subject. According to Professor Dasgupta 'It is easy to see that of these 32 maxims, some are ways of interpreting ideas. Others are ways of interpreting the arrangement and manner of textual words and their connections, while there are others which are but descriptions of specific peculiarities of style.[24] He is of the view that 'tantra-yukti' is different from '*Anvikshiki*' in the sense that the latter stands for laws of thought and the former for devices of science. But if we carefully go through the list of devices, we can say that they deal with how to acquire knowledge, how to interpret it and how to arrange it in a systematic and scientific manner. They are aids to Anvikshiki and many a times part of it. Professor Shaha divides

[23] 15.71–72.
[24] Dasgupta, *A History of Indian Philosophy*, 392.

32 devices used by Kautilya in threw groups: (a) devices which are used to establish point of view, (b) devices which are used to explain meanings of words and (c) devices which are methods of expounding subject.[25]

The purpose of these devices was to prepare the scientific work without defects. These devices talked about rules regarding the composition of text. Kautilya also discussed the type of language to be used for the scientific discussion and writings. He held that arrangement of subject matter, consistency, completeness, sweetness, exaltedness and lucidity constituted excellences of writing. He maintained,

> Arranging in a proper order, the statement first of principal matter is called arrangement of subject matter. A statement of subsequent matter without it being incompatible with the matter in hand right up to the end is consistency and connection. Absence of deficiency or excess of matter, words and letters, description in detail of the matter by means of reasons, citations and expressiveness of word is called completeness. The use of words with charming meaning easily conveyed is sweetness. The use of words that are not vulgar is exaltedness and the employment of words that are well known is lucidity.[26]

He is of the view that absence of charm, contradiction, repetition, incorrect use of words and confusion are defects of the writing, which should be avoided. Incompatibility of the later with the earlier is contradiction, a statement of second time if what is said earlier without any distinction is repetition, the wrong use of gender, number, tense and case is incorrect use of word, and the making of a group and not making a group whether there should be a group, this reversal of qualities is confusion.[27] After observing and studying all sciences and practices, Kautilya said that he had prepared the rules for correctly writing royal orders.[28]

---

[25] Shaha, 'Of Artha and Arthashastra', 160.
[26] The Arthashastra, 2.10-6-12.
[27] Ibid., 2.10.57–62.
[28] Ibid., 2-10-63.

The purpose of tantra-yukti was to develop universal rules regarding writing of the science and they were developed by different schools of Indian philosophy.

One does not know whether it would be correct to attribute the authorship of the concept of 'tantra-yukti' to early Arthashastra teachers but at the time of writing of the Arthashastra, there was mention of it in the 15th Adhikasana, and it could be ahistorical to attribute the authorship of 'Tantrayukti Prakaran' to Kautilya alone. These methods of research had been widely used by the students of the Ayurveda and poetics after the Christian era. Therefore, it is difficult to say that the concept of 'tantra-yukti' was developed by the early Arthashastra thinkers because the available sources of their ideas do not indicate that they have used the methods of tantra-yukti. It is true that available sources are meagre and no definite conclusions could be drawn, but it would be more appropriate to say that tantra-yukti was Kautilyan innovation in politics that he borrowed from other 'Drishtartha' sciences to make his work scientific and precise.

Bibliography

Agrawala, V. S. *India as Known to Panini*. Varanasi: Prithvi Publications, 1963.
Chatterjee, S. C. *The Nyaya Theory of Knowledge*. Calcutta: University of Calcutta, 1960.
Dasgupta, S. N. *A History of Indian Philosophy*. Vol. III. Delhi: Motilal Banarsidass, 1975.
Ghoshal, U. N. *A History of Indian Political Ideas*. Bombay: Oxford University Press, 1966.
Heesterman, J. C. *Inner Conflict of Tradition*. Delhi: Oxford University Press, 1985.
Saletore, B. A. *Ancient Indian Political Ideas and Institutions*. Bombay: Popular Publication, 1971.
Shaha, K. J. 'Of Artha and Arthashastra'. In *Comparative Political Philosophy*, edited by A. Parel and R. Keith. Delhi: SAGE.
Vidyabhushan, S. C. *History of Indian Logic*. Delhi: Motilal Banarsidass, 1978.

Bibliography

Primary Sources

Vedic Literature

Bhagvat, Hari Raghunath, eds. *The Sartha Upanishad Sangraha*. Part I (Marathi translation). Pune, 1914. Pune: Pandurang Patvardhan, Pune.
———. *The Brihadarankya Upanishad*, with commentary of Acharya Sharkar. Gorakhpur: The Geeta Press, 1967.
Bhanu, Chitaman Gangadhar, ed. (1912a). *The Chhandogya Upanishad*, with commentaries. Mumbai: Damodar Sawalaram and Co.
———. (1912b). *The Kathakopanishad*, with commentaries of the Acharyas. Mumbai: Damodar Savalaram and Co., 1921.
Chitrav, Siddheshvar Shastri, trans. *The Rigveda* (Marathi), 1938. Pune: Shankar Ramchandra Date, Vaidic Vangmay Prasarak Mandal.
Muller, Max, ed. *The Hymns of the Artharvaveda*. Translated by M. Bloomfield. In *The Sacred Books of the East*. Vol. 42. Delhi: Motilal Banarsidass, 2000.
———. *Sacred Laws of the Aryas*. Vols. I and II (Apastamba, Gautama, Vasistha, Baudhayana). Translated by George Buhler. Delhi: Motilal Banarsidass, 2007.
———. *The Shatapatha Brahmana*. Vols. 1–5. Translated by Julius Eggeling. In *The Sacred Books of the East*. Vols. 12, 26, 41, 43 and 44. Delhi: Motilal Banarsidass, 2007.
———. (1965). *The Upanishads*. Vols. I and II. Translated by G. Buhler. In *The Sacred Books of the East*. Delhi: Motilal Banarsidass.
Patvardhan, Ramchandra Vinayak., trans. *The Rigveda* (Marathi). Pune: Shrutibodh Publication, 1929.
Shastri, J. L., ed. *The Hymns of the Rigveda*. Translated by G. T. Griffith. Delhi: Motilal Banarsidass.

The Epics and Other Texts

Bhagvat, D., ed. *The Kathasaritsagara* (Marathi). 5 Vols. Pune: Varada Publications, 1999–2001.
Bhandarkar Oriental Research Institute. *The Mahabharata* (Text). 5 Vols. A critical edition by V. S. Sukhtankar. S. K. Belvalkar, S. K. De

and R. N. Dandekar. Pune: Bhandarkar Oriental Research Institute, 1990–94.

Buhler, G. *The Valmiki Ramayana*, with English translation. Delhi: Motilal Banarsidass, 2003.

———. *The Laws of Manu*. Vol. 25 SBE. Delhi: Motilal Banarsidass, 2006.

———. *The Kamasutra* of Vatyayana. Translated by R. Burton and F. F. Arbuthnot. Delhi: Rupa Publications, 2008.

Buitenin, Von. *The Mahabharata* (English translation). 2 Vols. Harvard University, 1970–76.

Chandra, Rajan. *The Complete Works of Kalidasa*. Vols. I and II. Delhi: Sahitya Akademi, 1997.

Doniger, W., and B. K. Smith. *Laws of Manu* (English Translation). Delhi: Penguin Books, 2010.

Ganapati, S. T. *The Kautilya* Arthashastra, with commentary. Parts I–III. Trivandrum: Government Press, 1924.

Hivargaonkar, B. R. The *Kautilya* Arthashastra (Marathi translation), edited by D. Bhagvat. Pune: Varada Publications, 1988.

Kangle, R. P., ed. and trans. *The* Arthashastra *of Kautilya*. 3 Vols. Bombay: University of Bombay, 1963.

———. *The Kautilya* Arthashastra (Marathi translation). Bombay: Maharashtra Sahitya and Sanskriti Mandal, 1989.

———, ed. and trans. *The Sarva Darshan Sangraha* (Marathi translation). Mumbai: Maharashtra Sahitya and Sanskriti Mandal, 1998.

Kelkar, B., ed. *The Valmiki Ramayana* (Marathi). Translated by Kashinathshastri Lele. Vols. I–III. Pune: Varada Publications, 1986.

———. *The Mahabharata*. Translated by Appashastri Rashivadekar, C. G. Bhanu, R. B. Datar, K. N. Athalay, et al. New ed. Vols. 1–9). Pune: Varada Publications, 1992, including Vaidya. C. V. *Mahabharatacha Upasamhar*. Vol. 9, Pune: Varada Publications, 1992.

Madhavacharya (1985), *The Sarvadarshan Sangraha*. Translated by R. P. Kangle. Mumbai: Maharashtra Sahitya ani Sanskriti Mandal, 1985.

Neelakantha. *The Mahabharata*, with commentary, *Bharata Bhava Deepa*, edited by Ramchandra Shastri Kinjavadekar. Pune: Chitrashala Press, 1925–32.

Pandit, R. R., ed. and trans. *The Mudra Rakshasa of Vishakhadatta*. Bombay: New Book Company, 1944.

———. *The Manusmriti*, with the commentary, *the Manvartha Muktavali*, of the Kulluka Bhatta. Bombay: Narayan Ram Acharya, Niranaya Sagar, 1946.

———, trans. *The Raj Tarangini*. New Delhi: Kalhana Sahitya Akademi, 1998.

———. *The Nitishataka of Bhartrihari*. Translated by M. R. Kale. Delhi: Motilal Banarsidass, 2004.

Roy, P. C. et al. *The Mahabharata* (English translation). Vol. 13. Calcutta: Oriental Publishing Company, 1952–63.
Ryder, A., trans. *The Panchatantra*. Delhi: Jaico Publications, 2010.
Shamshasri, R. trans. *The Kautilya* Arthashastra. 1928, translated by B. Shamshastri and M.S. Sriniwasa (1968), Mysore: M. S. Srinovasa.
Tipnis, G. G. *The Kautilya* Arthashastra. Bombay: Pradeepa, 1923.

The Buddhist Texts

Bhagvat, Durga, ed. and trans. *The Siddhartha Jataka*, with notes. Vols. 1–6. Pune: The Varada Books, 1980–82.
Cowell, E. B. *The Jatakas or Stories of Buddha's Former Birth*. Vols. 1–4. Delhi: Motilal Banarsidass, 2008.
Davids, C. A. F. Rhys, ed. and trans. *The Book of the Kindered Sayings*, The Samyutta Nikay. Vols. I–V. Delhi: Motilal Banarsidass, 2005.
Davids, T. W. Rhys, ed. and trans. *The Dialogues of Buddha*, Digha Nikay. Vols. I–III. Delhi: Motilal Banarsidass, 2005.
———. *Buddhist Suttas*. Vol. II. In *The Sacred Books of the East*. Delhi: Motilal Banarsidass, 2006.
Horner, I. B. *The Collection of Middle Length Sayings*. Vols. I–III. The Sutta Nipata and the Majjhima-Nikaya. Delhi: Motilal Banarsidass, 2003.
Joshi, S. D. and Roodbergen, J. A. F. *The Ashtadhyayi of Panini*. Delhi: Sahitya Akademi, 2008.
Kale, M. R. *The Mrichhakatika of Shudraka*. Delhi: Motilal Banarsidass, 2009.
Mullar, Max, ed. *Jaina Sutras Part I*. Translated by Hermann Jacobi. In *The Sacred Books of the East*. Part I Vol. 22, Part II Vol. 45. Delhi: Motilal Banarsidass, 2003.
———, ed. *The Buddhist Mahayana Texts*. Translated by F. B. Cowell, Max Mullar and J. Takakusu. In *The Sacred Books of the East*. Vol. 49. Delhi: Motilal Banarsidass, 2005.
———. *The Minor Law Books*. Vol. 33. In *The Sacred Books of the East*. Delhi: Motilal Banarsidass, 2005.
———, ed. *The Questions of the King Milinda*. Translated by T. W. Rhys Davids. Parts I and II. In *The Sacred Books of the East*. Vols. 35–36. Delhi: Motilal Banarsidass.
———, ed. *The Vinaya Texts*. Part I–III. Translated by T. W. Rhys Davids and H. Oldenberg. In *The Sacred Books of the East*. Vols. 16, 17 and 20. Delhi: Motilal Banarsidass, 2007.
Rajwade, C. V., ed. and trans. *The Deergha Nikay* (Marathi). Vols. I–III. Translated by C. V. Rajwade. 2nd reprint. Aurangabad: International Centre for Buddhist Studies, 1999.

Woodward, F. L. *The Book of the Gradual Sayings*, Anguttar Nikay. Vols. I–V. Delhi: Motilal Banarsidass, 2002.

Secondary Sources

Books in English

Agrawala, V. S. *India as Known to Panini*. Varanasi: Prithvi Prakashan, 1963.
Aiyangar, R. V. R. *Considerations on Some Aspects of Ancient Indian Polity*. Madras: Madras University, 1933.
———. *Rajdharma: Political Thought of the Smritis*. Adyar: Theosophical Society, 1941.
Altekar, A. S. *The State and Government in Ancient India*. Delhi: Motilal Banarsidass, 1977.
Anjaria, J. J. *Nature and Grounds of Political Obligation in Hindu State*. London: Longmans Green and Co., 1935.
Aurobindo Sri. *The Spirit and Form of Indian Polity*. Calcutta: Arya Publishing House, 1947.
Bandyopadhyay, N. C. *Development of Hindu Polity and Political Theory*. Vol. II. Calcutta: Cambrey R. and Co., 1927.
———. *Kautilya*. Calcutta: Cambrey R. and Co., 1927.
Banerjee, P. N. *Public Administration in Ancient India*. London: Macmillan, 1961.
Banerjee, S. C. Indian Society in the Mahabharata based on the Smriti Material in the Mahabharata. Varanasi: Manisha, 1976.
Barua, B. M. *History of Pre-Buddhistic Indian Philosophy*. Calcutta: University of Calcutta, 1918.
Bary, D., Hay, Stephan, Weiler, Royal and Yarrow, Andrew. eds. *Sources of Indian Tradition*. Delhi: Motilal Banarsidass, 1972.
Basham, A. L. *The Wonder That Was India*. Delhi: Rupa Publishers, 1975.
———. *History and Doctrines of the Ajivikas: A Vanished Indian Religion*. Delhi: Motilal Banarsidass, 2002.
Basu, J. *India at the Age of Brahmanas*. Calcutta: Sanskrit Pustak Bhandar, 1969.
Bhandarkar, D. R. *The Carmaechel Lectures on Ancient History of India*. Calcutta: University of Calcutta, 1918.
———. *Some Aspects of Ancient Indian Polity*. Benaras: Benaras Hindu University, 1929.
Bhattacharya, D. N. *Ancient Indian Rituals and Their Social Contents*. Delhi: Manohar Publication, 2005.

Bhattacharya, Sibesh. *Secular and Pluralistic Elements in the Idea of State in Early India*. Shimla: Indian Institute of Advanced Study, 2002.
Bongard Levin, G.M. *Studies in Ancient India and Central Asia*. Calcutta: Indian Studies Past and Present, 1973.
Bowles, Adam. *Dharma Disorder and Political in Ancient India: The Apaddharmaparvan of the Mahabharata*. Leiden: EG Brill and Co., 2007.
Brown, M., ed. *The While Umbrella: Indian Political Thought from Manu to Gandhi*. Bombay: Jaico, 1970.
Chattopadhyaya, D. *What Is Living and What Is Dead in Indian Philosophy?* Delhi: Peoples Publishing House, 1976.
———. *The Ways of Understanding Human Past*. Delhi: Centre for Studies in Civilization, 2001.
Choudhary, P. K. *Political Concepts in Ancient India*. Delhi: S. Chand and Co. 1976.
Choudhary, R. K. *Studies in Ancient Indian Law and Justice*. Banaras: Motilal Banarsidass, 1953.
Chousalkar, A. *Social and Political Implications of Concepts of Justice and Dharma*. Delhi: Mittal, 1986.
———. *Rebellion and State*. Ambala: Associated Publications, 2009.
Coomar Swami, A. *The Spiritual Authority and Temporal Power in Hindu Theory of Government*. Delhi: Munshiram Manoharlal, 1978.
Dange, S. A. *India from Primitive Communism to Slavery*. Delhi: Peoples Publishing House, 1953.
Dasgupta, S. N. *History of Indian Philosophy* in 5 Vols. Delhi: Motilal Banarsidass, 1975–76.
Davids, T. W. Rhys. *The Buddhist India*. Delhi: Motilal Banarsidass, 2008.
Dikshitrar, V. R. R. *Hindu Administrative Institutions*. Madras: Madras University, 1929.
Drekmeier, C. *Kingship and Community in Early India*. Mumbai: Oxford University Press, 1962.
Fick, R. C. *Social Organisation in North East India in Buddha's Time*. Calcutta: Calcutta University, 1920.
Frauwallner, E. *History of Indian Philosophy*. Vols. I and II. Delhi: Motilal Banarsidass, 2008.
Ganguli, N. C. *Indian Political Philosophy*. Calcutta: Kamala Book Depot, 1939.
Ghoshal, U. N. *A History of Indian Public Life* (1964–66). Vols. I and II. Bombay: Oxford University Press.
———. *A History of Indian Political Ideas*. Bombay: Oxford University Press, 1966.
Gokhle, B. G. *New Light on Early Buddhism*. Bombay: Popular Publications, 2009.

Gonda, J. *Ancient Indian Kingship from Religious Point of View*. Leiden: EJ Brill and Co. Leiden, 1966.

Gupta, S. P., and K. S. Ramchandran. *The Mahabharata: A Myth or Reality? Differing Views*. New Delhi: Oriental Publishers, 1977.

Heesterman, J. C. *The Inner Conflict of Tradition*. Delhi: Oxford University Press, 1985.

Held, G. J. *The Mahabharata: An Ethnological Study*. London: Kegan Paul Trench-Trubner, 1935.

Hopkins, E. W. *The Great Epic of India*. Calcutta: Punthi Pustak, 1969.

———. *Social and Political Condition of Ruling Caste in Ancient India*. Varanasi: Oriental Publishers, 1972.

Jauhari, M. *Ethics and Politics in Ancient India*. Varanasi: Bharatiya Vidya Publishers, 1965.

Jayaswal, K. P. *The Hindu Polity*. Bangalore: The Bangalore Printing and Publishing Co., 1955.

Jha, N. R., ed. *Kautilya's* Arthashastra *and Social Welfare*. Delhi: Sahitya Academy, 1993.

Jog, K. P., ed. *Perceptions on Kautilya's* Arthashastra, Kangle centenary Vol. Bombay: Popular Publications, 1999.

Kane, P. V. *A History of Dharmashastras*. Vol. III. Pune: Bhandarkar Oriental Research Institute, 1930–72.

Kapur, K., and A. Singh, eds. *Indian Knowledge System*. Vols. I and II. Shimla: Indian Institute of Advanced Study, 2005.

Karve, I. *Yaganta*. Pune: Deshmukh and Co., 1969.

Keith, A. B. *Philosophy of the Vedas and Upanishads*. Vols. I and II. Delhi: Motilal Banarsidass, 2007.

Konow, S. T. *Kautalya Studies*. Delhi: Oriental Publishers, 1975.

Kosambi, D. D. *The Culture and Civilization of Ancient India*. Bombay: Vikas Publishing House, 1975.

———. *An Introduction to Study of Ancient Indian History*. Bombay: Popular Publications, 1956.

———. *History and Society: Problems of Interpretation*. Bombay: University of Bombay, 1985.

———. 'The Line of Arthashastra Teachers'. In *Combined Methods in Indology and Other Writings*, edited by B. D. Chattopadhyay, 260–78. Delhi: Oxford University Press, 2007.

Krisha Rao, M. V. *Studies in Kautilya*. Delhi: Munshiram Manoharlal, 1958.

Law, B. C. *India as Described in Early Texts of Jainism and Buddhism*. Delhi: Bharatiya Publishing House, 1980.

Law, N. N. *Aspects of Ancient Indian Polity*. Bombay: Orient Longman, 1960.

Majumdar, R. C. *The Corporate Life in Ancient India*. Calcutta: K. L. Mukhapadhyay and Co., 1969.
Marathe, M. P., Kelkar, M.K. and Gokhale, P. P., eds. *Studies in Jainism*. Indian Philosophical Quarterly Publication. Pune: University of Pune, 1984.
Masson, Oursel, Williman Grabowska, Helena and Stern, Philipp. *Ancient India and Indian Civilisation*. London: Routledge and Kegan Paul, 1967.
Matilal, B. K. *Moral Dilemmas in the Mahabharata*. Shimla: Indian Institute of Advanced Study, 1989.
Mees, G. H. *Dharma and Society*. Delhi: Gian Publishing House, 1986.
Menon, Ramesh. *Krishna: Life and Song of the Blue God*. Delhi: Rupa Publications, 2009.
Mishra, S. *Janapada States in Ancient India*. Varanasi: Bhartiya Vidya Prakasahan, 1973.
Mittal, K. K. *Materialism in Indian Thought*. Delhi: Munshiram Manoharlal, 1974.
Mookerjee, K. P. *Ancient Political Experiences*. Colombo: M. S. Gunasena and Co., 1961.
More, S. S. *Krishna: The Man and His Mission*. Pune: Gaaj Publications, 1995.
Nagraj, Muni. *King Bimbisara and King Ajatshatru in the Age of Mahavira and Buddha*. Ladaun: Jain Vishva Bharati, 1974.
Naik, B. B. *Ideals of Ancient Indian kingship and* Arthashastra *of Kautilya*. Dharwar: Author, 1932.
Oldenberg, H. *Buddha: His life, His Doctrine, His Order*. Delhi: Motilal Banarsidass, 2006.
Olivelle, P., ed. *Dharma-Studies in Semantic, Cultural and Religious History*. Delhi: Motilal Banarsidass, 2009.
Prasad, Beni. *Theory of Government in Ancient India with the Introduction*. Allahabad: Dr A. D. Pant Central Book Depot, 1968.
Pratap Giri, R. C. *The Problem of the Indian Polity*. Bombay: Longmans Geen and Co., 1935.
Radha Krishnan, S. *Indian Philosophy*. 2 Vols. London: Allen and Unwin, 1958.
Rai, Jaimal, *Rural–Urban Economy and Social Change in Ancient India*. Varanasi: Bharatiya Vidya, 1974.
Rapson, E. J. *Cambridge History of India*. Vols. I and II. New Delhi: S. Chand and Co., 1958.
Reimann, L. G. *The Mahabharata and the Yugas, India's Great Epic Poem and the Hindu System of World Ages*. Delhi: Motilal Banarsidass, 2010.
Riepe, Dale. *The Naturalistic Tradition in Indian Thought*. Delhi: Motilal Banarsidass, 1961.

Roy Choudhuri, H. C. *Political History of Ancient India*. Calcutta: University of Calcutta, 1950.
Roy, B. P. *Political Ideas and Institutions in the Mahabharata*. Calcutta: Punthi Pustak, 1975.
Ruben, W. C. *Studies in Ancient Indian Thought*. Calcutta: Indian Studies, 1966.
Saletore, B. A. *Ancient Indian Political Thought and Institutions*. Bombay: Asia Publishing House, 1971.
Sarkar, B. K. *The Positive Background of Hindu Sociology*. Delhi: Motilal Banarsidass, 1985.
Sarmah, Thaneshvar. *The Bharadvajas in Ancient India*. Delhi: Motilal Banarsidass, 1991.
Sen, A. K. *Studies in Ancient Indian Political Thought*. Calcutta: Chakravarti Chatterjee and Co., 1926.
Shah, K. J. 'Of Artha and Arthashastra'. In *Comparative Political Philosophy*, edited by A. Parel and R. Keith, 160–75. Delhi: SAGE, 1992.
Sharma, R. S., ed. *Indian Society: Historical Probings–Peoples*. Delhi: Publishing House, 1975.
———. *Origin of State in Ancient India*. Bombay: University of Bombay, 1990.
———. *Indian Feudalism*. Delhi: Munshiram Manoharlal, 2004.
———. *Aspects of Political Ideas and Institutions in Ancient India*. 5th ed. Delhi: Motilal Banarsidass, 2005.
Singh, B. P. *Readings in Kautilya's* Arthashastra. Delhi: Agam Publications, 1976.
Singh, H. N. *Sovereignty in Indian Polity*. London: Luzac and Co., 1968.
Singh, N. P. *Political Ideas and Ideals in the Mahabharata*. Delhi: Oriental Publishers, 1976.
Spellman, J. W. *Political Theory in Ancient India*. Oxford: Clarendon Press, 1964.
Sukthankar, V. S. *The Epic Studies*. Pune: V. S. Sukthankar Memorial Committee, 1944.
Thapar, R. *Essays on Ancient Indian Social History*. Delhi: Orient Longman, 1978.
———. *From Lineage to State*. Delhi: Oxford University Press, 1991.
———. *The Cultural Pasts*. Delhi: Oxford University Press, 2008.
Tiwari, K. N. *Classical Indian Ethical Thought*. Delhi: Motilal Banarsidass, 2007.
Vaidya C. V. *The Epic India Geekwad's Oriental Series*. Baroda, 1932.
Verma, V. P. *Studies in Hindu Political Thought and Its Metaphysical Foundations*. Delhi: Motilal Banarsidass, 1981.

Wilhem, F. *Politische Polemiker in staatslehrhuch de Kautalya* [Political polemics in the text on statecraft of Kautilya. Wiesbaden, 1960.
Winternitz, I. M. 'Dharmashastra and Arthashastra'. In *Sir Ashutosh Memorial Volume*. Part I, edited by J. N. Samaddar, 25–48. Patna: Sir Ashutosh Mukherjee Memorial Committee, 1926-28.
Winternitz, M. C. *History of Indian literature*. Vols. I and II. Delhi: Motilal Banarsidass, 1966-77.
Zimmer, H. *Philosophies of India*. New York, NY: Meridian Books, 1957.

Books in Marathi and Hindi

Agrawala, V. S. *Bharat-Savitri*. 3 Vols. New Delhi: Sasta Sahitya Mandal, 1962, 77.
Athavale, S. *Charvaka: History and Philosophy*. 3rd ed. Wai: The Prajnya Pathshala, 1990.
Bhagvat, D. *Vyasa Parva*. Mumbai: Mauj Publication, 1969.
———. *Collected Works of Rajaram Shastri Bhagvat*. Vol. I. Pune: Varada Publications, 1979.
———. *Sanskriti Sanchit*. Mumbai: Shabda Publications, 2015.
Chapekar, N. G. *Vedic Nibandha*. Badalpur, 1939.
Garde, D. K. *Ancient Indian Political Thought*. Pune: Vidyapeeth Grantha Nirmiti Manda, 1981.
Jha, Anand. *Charvaka-Darshan*. Lucknow: Hindi Samiti Information Department, 1969.
Joshi, Laxmanshstri. *Development of the Vedic Civilization*. Wai: The Prajnya Pathshala, 1995.
Kangle, R. P. *Ancient Indian Polity*. Bombay: Popular Publications, 1969.
Kantak, Prema. *The Mahabharata Reflections*. Kolhapur: Maharashtra Publishing House, 1970.
Karve, I. *Dharma*. Pune: Deshmukh and Co., 1969.
Kosambi, Dharmanand. *Buddha Leela*. Mumbai: Maharashtra Sahitya and Sanskrit Mandal, 2007.
Kumathekar, U., ed. *The Charvaka-Manthan*. Pune: University of Pune, 2001.
Mehendale, M. A. *Ancient India-Society and Culture-Select Articles*. Wai: Prajnya Pathshala, 2001.
Mirashi, V. V. *Bhavabhuti*. Bombay: Popular, 1971.
———. *Kalidasa*. Mumbai: Maharashtra Sahitya and Sanskiti Mandal, 1992.
Patil, Sharad. *Ideological Conflicts in Indian Philosophy*. Kolhapur: Shivaji University, 1980.

Pendse-Naik, Vasundhara. *Introduction to the Kautilya Arthashastra*. Delhi: National Book Trust, 2009.
Salunkhe, A. H. *The Charvak-Darshan*. Mumbai: Keshav Gore Trust, 2008.
Vaidya, P. L. *The Origin and Spread of Buddhism*. Wai: Prajnya Pathshala, 1980.

Articles

Brown, M. 'Indian and Western Realism'. *Indian Journal of Political Science* 15 (1954): 265–675.
Burrow, T. 'Chanakya and Kautilya'. *Annals of Bhandarkar Oriental Research Institute* 48 and 49 (1968): 17–31.
Chakravarti, N. 'Ghotamukha: A Predecessor of Kautilya and Katyayana'. *Journal of Royal Asiatic Society of Bengal* (1930), 75: 275–80.
Chousalkar, A. S. 'Development and Political Thought of Early Arthashastra Tradition'. *Journal of University of Bombay* 45–46 (1976–77): 32–44.
———. 'Political Philosophy of Arthashastra Tradition'. *Indian Journal of Political Science* 41 (1981): 51–66.
———. 'Contemporary Relevance of Kautilya's Theory of Rebellion'. *Indian Journal of Political Science* 45 (1985): 1–13.
———. 'Methodology of Kautilya's Arthashastra'. *Indian Journal of Political Science* 65 (2004): 55–77.
———. 'The Concept of Apaddharma and Moral Dilemma of Politics'. *Indian Literature*, Sahitya Akademi's bi-monthly magazine 25 (2004): 115–27.
———. 'The Concept of Dharma in Mahabharata'. *Journal of Shivaji University* 40 (2005): 1–11.
Dikshitar, V. R. R. 'Tantra-Yukti'. *Indian Historical Quarterly* 11 (1935): 313–16.
Joshi Rasik, Vihar, '*Lokayata* in Ancient India and China'. *Annals of Bhandarkar Oriental Research Institute* 70 (1988): 393–405.
Kane, P. V. 'The Arthashastra of Kautilya'. *Annals of Bhandarkar Oriental Research Institute* 6–7 (1924–26): 85–100.
———. 'Rajshastras of Brihaspati, Ushanasa, Bharadvaja and Vishalaksha'. *Journal of University of Bombay* 2 (New Seies) (1942): 79–80.
———. 'The Meaning of the Acharyah'. *Annals of Bhandarkar Oriental Research Institute* 23 (1942): 207–13.
Kangle, R. P. 'Bharadvaja: An Ancient Teacher of Political Science'. *Bharatiya Vidya* 3 (1960–61): 333–39.
———. 'Manu and Kautilya'. *Indian Antiquary* (New Series) 1 (1964): 48–54.
———. 'The Succession Crisis in the Arthashastra of Kautilya'. *Vishveshvaranand Indological Journal* 2 (1964): 298–303.

Kapadia, B. H. 'Predecessors of Kautilya'. *Journal of Indian History* 39 (1961): 355–58.
Law, B. C. 'A Short Account of the Wandering Teachers at the Time of Buddha'. *Journal of Asiatic Society of Bengal* (1918): 399–400.
Majumdar, B. K. 'How Kautilya's Arthashastra Influenced Hinduised Kingdoms of South East Asia'. *Proceedings of All India Oriental Conference*, 23rd session held at Aligarh. 1960.
Rawat, B. S. 'Reason of State in Kautilya's Arthashastra' A paper presented at All India Political Science Conference held at Jodhapur, 1976.
Ruben, W. 'The Beginning of the Epic Samkhyas'. *Annals of Bhandarkar Oriental Research Institute* (1956), 37: 174–89.
———. 'The Minister Jabala in Valmiki's Ramayana: A Portrait of One of Indian's Materialist'. *Indian Studies-Past and Present* 6 (October–December 1964): 445–65.
———. 'Fighting Against the Despots in the Old Indian Literature'. *Annals of Bhandarkar Oriental Research Institute* 50 (1968): 111–18.
Saletore, B. A. 'Some Historical and Quasi-Historical Incidents in Kautilya's Arthashastra'. *The Poona Orientalist* 1 (1935): 18–24.
Schetelich Eva Ritschi, Maria. 'Studies in Kautilya Arthashastra'. *Indian Studies Past and Present* 3 (1961): 407–17.

Index

Abhyudaya, 18
Adi Parva, 93, 111
Aditya, 45
Aitereya Brahmana, 22
Akhyan, 23
Anagata buddhi, 138
Anagata-Vidhata buddhi, 138
ancient dialogue, 106
Andhaka-Vrishni Samgha, 88
Anushasana meaning, 159
Apaddharma, 135
Apaddharma parva, 6, 137, 142, 151
  Shantiparva, 115
Apastamba Dharmasutra, 45, 136
Aranyaka Parva, 93
Artha, 69, 117, 129
Arthashastra, 1–3, 44, 102, 145
  ideas, 133
  Kautilya, 5–6, 9
  methodology, 173
  sources of knowledge, 173–76
  thirty-two method of science or tantra-yukti, 183–184
  passages, 108–110
Smriti, 136
  teachers, 76, 170
    Bahudantiputra, 87
    Bharadvaja, 81
    Brihaspati and Ushanasa, 86
    Dirgha Charayan, 82
    Digha Nikaya, 88
    Erotics and Vatsyayana, 83
    Ghotaka Mukha, 83
    Jabala, 88
    Kanika—Niti, 81

Katyayana, 79–80
Kautilya, 85
kshatravidya Vadi, 89
Manu, 84
Nandas, 80
originators of science of politics, 78
parivrajakas, 77
Rig Veda, 86
Sabhaparva, 88
Ushanasa and Brihaspati, 141
Vatavyadhi's views, 88
tradition, 4, 48, 108
Aditya, 46
advocacy, 164
ancient India, 163
Anushasana, 159
Apaddharma or duties of king, 160
Bharadvaja, 162
Briaharanyaka Upanishad, 44
Charvaka, 157
Danda, 44
Dandaniti, 50, 158
Dandin, 155
Digha Nikaya, 55
divine, 48
divine signs, 53
ethics and politics, 154
Kamasutra of Vatsyayana, 47
Kootdanta Sutra, 164
kshema stood for peaceful enjoyment, 159
Lokayata philosophers, 155
Lokayata Purohit of Mahavijita, 165
Mudra-Rakshasa, 57

Index / 197

Panchatantra, 161
parivrajakas, 54, 56
pre-Kautilyan period, 162
Shantiparva, 49
Shukra and Brihaspati, 53
Sinhanad Sutra, 55
Smriti ideology, 165
trayi, 44
Trivarga ideal, 155
vaktri and *prayoktri*, 52
Vedic scholars, 158
virgin territories, land and colonization, 51
Waranavat, 163
Atharva Veda, 14, 16, 19, 25, 37–38
Atharva Veda Arthashastra, 22
Atharvan, 17, 52
Atharvan Abhichara, 22
rites, 17
Atmarakshitam, 143
Aushanasa shastras, 99

Barhaspatya Sutra, 7
Barhaspatya, 99, 128
Barhaspatya phase, 67
Baudhayana Dharmasutra, 37
Bhagavad Geeta, 97
Bharadvaja, 110
Gaurishiras, 49
Bhishma, 144
Bhooridatta Jataka, 89
Brahmana Parimara, 20
Brahmanas, 14, 25
role, 34
Brahmins, 15
Brihadaranyaka Upanishad, 23, 26, 39–40
Brihaspati, 49, 86
Angirasa, 22
Buddhist literature, 35
kutuhalshalas, 36
Samyutta Nikaya, 36

Chandraka, 145
Chhandogya, 39
Chhandogya Upanishad, 40, 43, 135
curse of death, 21

Danda, 106
Dandaniti, 2, 68, 99
Dash kumar charitam, 155
Dasyus, 14
Dharmashastra tradition, 65, 78, 95, 158
Dharma, 127, 140
Dharmasutras, 41
Digha Nikaya, 55, 88, 130
divine signs
science, 53
Dying round the holy power, 21

early Arthashastra tradition, 60
Charvaka Philosophy, 63
Dandaniti, 68
Dharmashastras, 65
Digha Nikaya, Brahmajal Sutra, 64
Haitukas, 72
Hetuvadins, 67
Kama Purushartha, 62–63
Khabbagiya Bhikkhus, 64
Kshatravidya, 60
Lokayata Philosophy, opponents, 69
Matsya-Nyaya, 70
Samkhya philosophy, 72
Shantiparva *Charvaka* Brahmin, 65
Trivarga, 61
Vaisheshika, 72
varta, 62

Gana-Samghas, 32, 34
gatha, 23
Gautama Dharmasutra, 136
Ghotamukha, 83

gradual development of kingship, 16
grihapatis, 34

Harin, 145

Ibhyas, 14
intelligence and reason
   use of, 141
Itihasa, 23
   Gopatha Brahmana, 23
   Veda, 24
Itihasa-Puranas, 24–25, 37

Jabala, 88, 125
Janapada, 16, 30, 32
   states, 25
Janeshvara, 15

Kama Purusharatha, 62, 69, 117
Kamasutra of Vatsyayana, 7, 47, 83
Kampilya Brahma Datta
   king of, 147
Kangle, Bahudanti, 124
Kaninka-Shatruntapa Samvad, 111
Katha Sarit Sagar of Somadev, 7, 80
Kaunapadanta
   political ideas, 121–122
Kautilya, 85, 103
   Acharyas, 125
   ideas, 118–120
   views issues, 120–121
Kautilya's Arthashastra, 116
Keakatas, 14
Khabbagiya Bhikkhus, 64
Kootdanta Sutra, 130, 133, 164, 172
kshatravidya Vadi, 89
Kshatriya dharma, 146
Kshatriyas and Brahmans, 16
Kshatrvidya, 43

Kshudraka-Malava, 30
Kutuhalshalas, 54

Licchavi Samgha, 38
Lokayata ethic, 133
Lokayata philosophy, 3, 60
   Barhaspatya phase, 67
   Charvaka Philosophy, 63
   Dandaniti, 68
   Dharmashastras, 65
   Digha Nikaya, Brahmajal Sutra, 64
   epistemological and ethical position, 12
   Haitukas, 72
   Hetuvadins, 67
   Kama Purushartha, 62–63
   Khabbagiya Bhikkhus, 64
   Kshatravidya, 60
   Matsya-Nyaya, 70
   opponents, 69
   Samkhya, 72
   Shantiparva Charvaka Brahmin, 65
   Trivarga, 61
   Vaisheshikas, 72
   varta, 62
Lomasha, 144–145
Loukayatikas, 69

Mahabharata, 6, 103
   Aranyaka Parva, 127
   discourses of Bharadvaja, 108
   political theory, 117
   quotations of Brihaspati, 103–105
   Rajshastra of Shukra, 97
Mahajanapadas, 31–33
Mahavijita, 131
Mahendra, 49
Maitrayana Kausharva, 21
Manu, 49
Manu and Kautilya, 11

Manvantar, 84
Matsya-Nyaya, 70
MudraRakshasa, 7, 57

Narada Kautilya
  views of Pishuna, 123–124
Niti Literature, 153
Nitisara, 2, 7
Nitishastra, 2
Nitivakyamrita, 99

Palita, 146
  animal fable of, 144
Panis, 14
parivrajakas, 4, 5, 52, 54, 56, 77
Paura, 32
philosophies of India, 143
post-Vedic period, 16, 29
  territorial state in Ancient India
    emergence, 41
  post-Vedic Society, 38
Pratyutpanna buddhi, 138
Pratyutpanna mati, 138, 142
pre-Kautilyan
  Arthashastra
    political ideas of, 8, 144
    tradition, principles of, 142
  political thinkers
    political ideas, 4
  prevail logic of fish, 106
Pujani, 147
Purana, 23
Purohit
  conditions, 132
Purusharathas, 129

Raj Karmani, 38
Rajanyas or Kshatriyas, 15
Rajashastra of Brihaspati, 105
Rajashastras of Ushanasa, 10
Rajdharmanushasan Parva, 6
rajkartarahas, 15
Rajshastra of Manu, 93, 95

Rajshastra-Rajaniti, 2
Rajatarangini, 22
Ramayana, 125
Rig Veda, 14, 15
  hymns in, 86
  rituals and sacrifices
    Kanika, 113

Sabha, 15
Sabha Parva, 88
sacrifices
  Ashvamedha, 27
  Rajasuya, 27
  Vajpeya, 27
Samiti, 15
Sarva darshan Sangraha, 7
school of Parashara, 100
science of politics, 2
  India, 4
Shankha-Likhita Nyaya, 93
Shantiparva, 2, 102, 137, 141
  Mahabharata, 71, 136
Shatapatha Brahmana, 18, 20, 22,
    26, 33, 39
Shatrumtapa, 115
Shudras, 15
Shukra, 53, 99
Shukra Nitisara, 7
supremacy of politics, 168
  Arthashastra School, 172
  Arthashastra-
    Smriti tradition, 168
  chapter 140 of Shanti Parva,
    169
  Kautilya, 169
  Lokayata teachers, 170
  Prof Prasad, 168
  Vijnyana bala, concept, 171
Sutra, 132
Swabhav vada, 69

Tanunapatra, 26
taxes

pay by people, 150
The Hindu beast, 143
Trivarga, 47, 61
   concept, 154

Upanishads, 14, 135
Upaveda of Atharva Veda, 22
Ushanasa, 86

Vaisheshikas, 72
varnas, 32
   order, 32
varta and *dandaniti*
   growth of, 132

Vatavayadhi, 120
Vedic and post-Vedic period, 5
Vedic dogma
   influence of, 27
Vedic period, 14, 26
Vedic sacrifices and rituals, 126
Vijnyana bala, 139
Vish, 15
Vishalaksha, 49, 118, 120
Vishvamitra in *Mahabharata*, 136
Vyasanas, 138

Yoga-kshema of people, 158

About the Author

Ashok S. Chousalkar is a former Professor and Head, Department of Political Science, Shivaji University, Kolhapur, Maharashtra. He is the Editor of the Marathi quarterly journal *Samaj Prabodhan Patrika*. He is the author of multiple books in English and Marathi. He has received a number of literary awards for his contribution to Marathi language, including Maharashtra Foundation Award in 2000, Yashwantrao Chavan Award by the Government of Maharashtra in 2004, the M. P. Goenka Award of Maharashtra Tatvadnyan Parishad in 2010, the Bhauji Huddar Award of Vidarbha Sanshodhan Mandal Nagpur in 2012, and so on.

Dr Chousalkar earned his doctorate in Political Science from the University of Mumbai, Maharashtra. Later, he joined the Department of Politics at Shivaji University, Kolhapur, Maharashtra, as a lecturer and retired as a professor of politics. During this period, he carried out a number of research projects and guided many PhD scholars as a supervisor. He is a part of the various scholarly committees of the UGC, UPSC, NCERT, NACC, Indira Gandhi National Open University and the Government of Maharashtra. His main research interests include ancient Indian political thought, comparative political theory, modern Indian political thought and politics in Maharashtra.